D1484198

ACCIDENTALLY
LIKE A MARTYR

ACCIDENTALLY LIKE A MARTYR

The Tortured Art of
WARREN ZEVON

James Campion

Backbeat
Books

An Imprint of Hal Leonard LLC

Published in 2018 by Backbeat Books
An Imprint of Hal Leonard LLC
7777 West Bluemound Road
Milwaukee, WI 53213

Trade Book Division Editorial Offices
33 Plymouth St., Montclair, NJ 07042

Printed in the United States of America

Book design by M Kellner

Library of Congress Cataloging-in-Publication Data
Names: Campion, James, 1962- author.
Title: Accidentally like a martyr : the tortured art of Warren Zevon / James
  Campion.
Description: Montclair, NJ : Backbeat Books, 2018. | Includes bibliographical
  references and index.
Identifiers: LCCN 2018010849 | ISBN 9781617136726
Subjects: LCSH: Zevon, Warren. | Rock musicians--United States--Biography.
Classification: LCC ML420.Z475 C36 2018 | DDC 782.42166092 [B] --dc23
LC record available at https://lccn.loc.gov/2018010849

www.backbeatbooks.com

For Mary Lou Moore,
artist

CONTENTS

I'm having a good time, but I sense it's not permanent.

—WARREN ZEVON

The Restless and Literate Troubadour: Warren Zevon in his hotel room, Tokyo, Japan, 1977.
© *Joel Bernstein, 1977. All Rights Reserved. (joelbernstein.com)*

INTRODUCTION

Hell lies at the bottom of the human heart, and you find it by expressing your personality.
—Ross Macdonald

I think of Warren Zevon songs as chapters in the great American novel. Its story lies at the heart of his and our psyche. The lines are blurred. We never seem to know if we're looking in a mirror or peering through a window; we only know that when we listen, we *see* something. The music, a plaintive mixture of balladry and raunch, sets the scene—his voice a striking baritone, our guide through a labyrinth of harrowing narratives. The plot unfolds without subtlety; each lyrical arc awakens imagination. The songs are confessionals—unrepentantly raw—as well as testimonials to the entangled tragicomedy of the human experience. They speak of extremes, revel in contradiction, and parry with irony, taking random and often comedic stabs at calamity while seducing conflict. These are the sounds of both dread and hope, and very often they arrive at once.

"In the songwriting field, there isn't a section for fiction and a section for nonfiction; they're all mixed together," Zevon once mused to Jody Denberg of Austin's KGSR. And perhaps no songwriter balanced this more effectively. Zevon's friend and producer, Jackson Browne, told David Fricke of *Rolling Stone*, "He fully volunteered to undergo whatever trial by fire was necessary to get at the truth." Danny Goldberg, whose Artemis Records was the final spin on Zevon's record label roulette wheel, described it to me as "a psychological truth no one else could quite identify."

There is a special corner of our tickled soul that gets Warren Zevon that is not available to other artists. For nearly three decades, Zevon managed to fit a great deal into that corner. Until now, I am not sure anyone has dared divulge its contents.

I now humbly take on the challenge.

Welcome to the Zevon Corner.

It comes with a warning: No one emerges unscathed. The darkness must be embraced so that the light can be better appreciated, as street poet laureate Charles

Bukowski once imagined. And, as in Bukowski, the characters found between the light and dark, no matter how bizarre and disturbing, appear eerily familiar.

Zevon's creative alchemy can transform perspective with a single verse. His son, Jordan, expressed to me one day: "I can only speak through my bloodline experience, but there's a dramatic duality in my father's songs: 'The world is really fucked up, but look at that lily growing out of a crack in the sidewalk.'"

Zevon exploited touchstones in provocative literature and film and blended them with his everyday experience to achieve what eighteenth-century French novelist Victor Hugo describes in Maurice Shroder's *Icarus: The Image of the Artist in French Romanticism* as "[the transformation of] the banality of the human experience to a heightened level of knowledge about our existence through self-expression." Hugo expounds, "Every man who writes, writes a book; this book is himself. Whether he knows it or not, whether he wishes it or not, it is true. From every body of work, whatever it may be, wretched or illustrious, there emerges a persona, that of the writer. It is his punishment, if he is petty; it is his reward, if he is great."

Zevon's ex-wife, Crystal Zevon, left me with this nugget: "If you're looking at the themes through his songs and what influenced them, at the heart of everything is that Warren was an artist . . . first."

The music of Warren Zevon resonates today because he visited the places we fear to tread and returned with some of the most challenging, engaging, beautifully disturbing songs known to the craft, while never ignoring humor. "In Kurt Vonnegut's *Slapstick* every chapter ends with 'I had to laugh,' which is sort of an attitude I subscribe to," he shared with Rob Patterson of *Creem* magazine the month "Werewolves of London," his biggest and most memorable song, hit the charts. And we chuckled along with him, because if there is one thing lovers of Warren Zevon's music can attest to, it's that we are hooked. There are hardly any casual Zevon fans. We are lifers. I know, for I am one.

So is Taylor Goldsmith, front man and songwriter for the folk-rock band Dawes, who has chosen to cover several Zevon songs and basks in their fusing of humorous profundity. "Warren had his antenna up on the evocative and ridiculous," exclaimed Goldsmith when I first asked him about Zevon. "Not only does he give you something that would never occur to you, he follows through into something worthwhile that can speak to all sorts of aspects of our strange contemporary lives in a way that songwriters struggle with getting to because they're all so . . . damn . . . serious."

"His mind was busy exploding out of his head when he was writing," another charter member of the Zevon Corner, Adam Duritz, front man and songwriter for

Counting Crows, told me when I was finishing this book. "It wasn't enough to just write characters into his songs: They had to be larger than life and not fit for proper society; werewolves and gorillas, which are both funny *and* scary, like him. Their appetites are massive, like his. The scope of his work, the sweeping, almost cartoonish character portrayals against the intimate love songs forced you to look at all of it."

Master guitarist and Zevon's onetime bandleader David Landau concurred when I pressed him about the unique quality of Zevon's work. "Warren Zevon had a *voice*. Maybe you understand it, maybe you don't, but there's no other voice like that voice. To his credit, and a testimony to the fact that he really was an artist, he kept putting that voice out there regardless of whether anyone was listening or not."

Listening for that voice allows a light to go on somewhere, which illuminates the Zevon Corner and gives you a special pass inside that invites you to fully explore. And trust me, you never stop exploring. This is the musical and lyrical equivalent of a scar. You carry his music with you and you cannot understand how someone wouldn't want to bear the mark. You will quote it. You will hum it. You will revel in it.

As much as it is almost sacrilege to allow a glimpse into the Zevon Corner, I nevertheless shall forge ahead with the kind of relentlessly bold fervor with which Zevon penned his songs. He wrote, recorded, and performed dozens of these chapters to his novel and thus provided a road map of the Zevon Corner that I shall use to try and guide us through.

Now, this is not a complete deconstruction of the entire Zevon songbook. I have randomly chosen ten songs and three albums that I believe provide listeners insight into what best exemplify Zevon's life and art. I did not seek direction or curry favor in regard to these selections. I merely dove into the heart of the matter through the music that best reflects it.

"He had this incredible grasp of music," his good friend and prime musical instigator Waddy Wachtel made sure I understood. The great studio and performing guitarist, who worked feverishly with Zevon during several periods of Wachtel's peripatetic career, is just one of the many who cannot help but tout Zevon's skill as a composer and a musician, a distinctively evolved and passionate faculty that cannot be lost in all this fiddling with themes and subtext. Influenced heavily by classical, jazz, blues, folk, and of course rock 'n' roll, he explored all kinds of music, enriching his songs beyond the scope of many of his contemporaries.

One of those contemporaries, J. D. Souther agrees: "Frankly, I think it is time Warren gets his due as one of the most overlooked musicians of my lifetime."

Also, not all the works dissected here are quintessential Zevon "classics," if there is such a category, and I fully expect the obligatory "How is *fill-in-the-blank* not here?" Rest assured, somewhere in these essays you will likely find mentioned a snippet of almost everything Warren Zevon put down on tape and its connection to some other form of his expression.

This is also not a biography or some first-or-last statement on the man, although his life intuitively comes into focus through the songs. Much of what Zevon wrote was autobiographical, including his fantastical swipes at whimsy. The songs—and there are many he cowrote with colleagues—provide insight into the poignant parts of a whole: the manic, the troubled, the witty, the ridiculous, the vicious, the romantic, the vulnerable, the idiosyncratic, the endearing, the prophetic. It's all in there.

What is also in there is alcoholism. It is not possible to understand Zevon's music or the themes in it or really any step of his journey without confronting it, which he did with sometimes heroic, sometimes less so, vehemence. To call his alcoholism the elephant in the Zevon Corner would be to dramatically understate the issue. More apt would be to describe it as the blue whale that casts an oppressive shadow over the Zevon Corner. Its influence envelops his art, as it did his youth, his relationships, his performance, and the battles he waged with his demons. You will read in these pages observations of a complicated personality who was at once the consummate gentleman and a raging monster; a tender composer and growling rocker; an impeccably dressed, well-read, witty conversationalist who could fly into unwarranted rages and disappear for days on wildly absurd benders. He is the paranoid countenance of fear erupting from a generous, humorous soul. Or, as his daughter, Ariel, framed it for me more than once, "My father's heart and mind were *very* complex." It is this paradoxical figure that penetrates his songs like a virus and provides them a distinctively tortured depth.

To wit: His friend Bruce Springsteen told Luke Torn in a 2003 *Wall Street Journal* tribute that Zevon was "a moralist in cynic's clothing," while Burt Stein, Zevon's dear friend and traveling companion in the mid-'70s, imparted to me, "I sure hope you get in there that Warren Zevon was a total gentleman." His early-'80s confidant and aide-de-camp George Gruel whispered during our lengthy conversation, "Warren *loved* drama."

"I've always been strongly in favor of art as the expression of conflict," Zevon concluded to journalist John Soeder in 1990.

He wrote about death . . . a lot. He wrote about fear and confusion and what his friend author Hunter S. Thompson described as "bad craziness" . . . a lot. He wrote about guilt and atonement . . . a lot. He wrote about recidivism and redemption and revenge . . . a lot. He wrote about the ferocious, dizzying, combustible lascivious insecurity of love . . . a lot. The Zevon Corner is a place where poetic justice and poetic license converge to create something new. All of it is worth rummaging through, so I thought I'd give it a go.

Mostly, this book is my sonnet to the great Warren Zevon, who has been kicking my ass since that sweltering day in the summer of 1978 when I languished in summer school and some ingenious underachiever deigned to place *Excitable Boy* on the spindle of a dusty record player and alter my DNA. Some of the thoughts proffered before you have been popping in and out of my head for decades. The inspiration I received from being in the thrall of the Zevon Corner can finally be collected into one volume.

Inspired by Warren Zevon's insatiable desire to explore in his songwriting, each of these essays moves beyond the music and lyrics to expound on his themes, his times, the books he read, the films he enjoyed, and the music he absorbed, as well as the personal influences in his life. The songs took me places I hadn't considered when I began each one, and I had fun following where they led.

Alas, the first words I ever put to paper about Warren Zevon in the early 1980s while in college appear in a series of one-line aphorisms called "Chaos in Motion" that I cobbled together for a creative-writing assignment, but mostly to impress girls: "More people should listen to Warren Zevon." This edict still holds true today.

I am probably not going out on a limb here in predicting that you will echo some of the sentiments before you as readily as you reject others, but I believe without a doubt you will relate to my passion in all of it. You have the same. I know it, because if you have enjoyed just one Warren Zevon song you cannot deny it. And for those of you who may be discovering W.Z. for the first time, I am envious. It is all before you. And perhaps this volume of essays will spark something in you that may move you in our direction. But I think it best that before reading another word you delve into the Zevon catalog and start your own journey. There is no substitute for the songs. My endeavor here is merely a distilled version of the unabridged beauty of them, those fervidly personal and concussive chapters in his grand novel. I suggest you go in full blast with a hale and hearty heart and a spine of steel and listen.

To get beyond the songs to the man who lived and penned them, I've included my personal discussions with some of the key players in the Warren Zevon story. They provide rare insights into the artist as man, the performer as tormented soul, and the icon as living, breathing entity. These are the people who knew him best, who called him family, friend, and colleague, and those who call him simply an inspiration.

The true joy of this venture was meeting these people, especially his son, Jordan, whom I am now proud to call a friend. Jordan was truly a godsend throughout my journey to complete this work, and along with those of Zevon's ex-wife, Crystal, and their daughter, Ariel, his blessing was all I needed to forge ahead undaunted. I feel closer to Warren Zevon than I ever thought possible through them and so many others, now that he is no longer with us. Of course, much of what I have written here is speculation—speculation informed by reams of research, but nonetheless speculation. We no longer have the original source.

When I was informed by Warren Zevon's label that he would not be making our scheduled interview in the late summer of 2002 due to "personal reasons," I did not suspect that he was dying. Fully aware of Zevon's mercurial history with not just journalists but everyone who had come in contact with him, I assumed things had simply gone sideways in that charmingly bizarre Warren Zevon way. It was certainly bizarre, but hardly charming. Indeed, Zevon was dying of inoperable lung cancer—more candidly, peritoneal mesothelioma, a disease that attacks the lining of the abdomen. It was terminal. The clock was ticking.

Weeks later, the world would learn about Zevon's ticking clock. On All Hallows' Eve of that year, I would pen "Angry Ode to the Captain," which would become one of the more beloved pieces of my own canon. My dear wife, Erin, read it aloud on the occasion of its publishing in a compendium of my work and there was not a dry eye in the house. Mere weeks after her father's passing, we had trudged through a snowstorm in the winter to see Zevon play at some bar in Rochester, New York. It was early March 2000, and Zevon was so good that night it changed his music once again for me, and moved Erin so much it made her another comfortable resident of the Zevon Corner. And so she read, "This is a colder, blander, less fiery world without demented souls like Zevon."

And so it is.

With a mischievous gleam in his eye, Pulitzer Prize–winning Irish poet Paul Muldoon surmised to me, "You can't write a song called 'Excitable Boy' and not have a slightly weird view of the world, right?"

"*Vanity Fair* used to do this bit about what famous people are reading, so Warren found the most esoteric book on the planet," Jimmy Wachtel, a longtime friend and photographer for the covers of seven of Zevon's records, told me as he held back a snicker. "I can't even remember the name of it. It was an incomprehensible title and not only did he use that but he forced himself to read it! *That's* Warren."

Warren Zevon died at the age of fifty-six on September 7, 2003, two days before my forty-first birthday. His novel was complete, only because he was no longer around to add to it. But it will always be a damn good read and listen for those who wish to absorb it. Admittedly, to try and capture its subtext and characterization, its many dimensions, its exposition, its rising action, climax, falling action, denouement, and resolution is a dangerous game. To be blunt, this entire exercise is madness. However, I boldly choose to believe that he would have loved it.

"I think that writing songs is an act of love," Zevon told VH1 as the channel documented the final months of his life. "You write songs because you love the subject and you want to pass that feeling on."

This book is kind of like that, for him.

It begins with a city and ends with a declaration. In between are heartache, mischief, mayhem, villains and heroes, sin and reconciliation—a growling, prowling thrill ride.

Let the madness flow. . . .

Gower Avenue, April 23, 2017. *Photo by Suzan Alparslan*

"Desperados Under the Eaves"

Then he picked the glass up and tasted it and sighed again and shook his head sideways with a half smile; the way a man does when you give him a drink and he needs it very badly and it is just right and the first swallow is like a peek into a cleaner, sunnier, brighter world.

— RAYMOND CHANDLER, *The High Window*

The vast spring of disparate neighborhoods that make up Los Angeles is split down the middle by a long, winding thoroughfare named Gower Street. Its origin is the numerically self-evident corner of First Street in what is known as the Hancock Park district: an affluent, mostly Caucasian stretch developed at the dawn of the Jazz Age, whose genesis even today is blatantly reflected in its ubiquitously atavistic 1920s architecture. Gower perpetually moves across the economic and geographical spectrum, bringing to mind the players of and refugees from the American Dream while traversing centuries of every conceivable cultural shift—industrial, commercial, religious, racial—until finally terminating at the cross street of Beachwood Drive below the historic if not ragged HOLLYWOOD sign.

Like F. Scott Fitzgerald's *The Great Gatsby*, that sordid fairy tale of the author's "Lost Generation," Gower begins in fanciful prosperity, reinventing itself over the miles before ignominiously expiring as it becomes the western boundary of the Hollywood Forever Cemetery jutting just south of the more renowned Santa Monica Boulevard. Forever marking time, Gower beckons as brightly as Jay Gatsby's seductive "green light," reflecting Hollywood's symbols of dashed hopes and insatiable glitterati: a schizophrenic asphalt stream—the alpha, illusion, its omega, darkness.

Gower is also notable for housing Nestor Studios, Hollywood's first motion picture complex, built there in 1911. Fitzgerald would travel west to find a grander fortune than could be made by writing the Great American Novel, bankrolling his already legendary drinking habit with checks from the bevy of studios that would soon dominate the area. The novelist was an early-twentieth-century rock star at the dawn of Hollywood's stranglehold on the American psyche, its hypnotizing effects of shadow and light distracting those with an insatiable need to flout convention and ignore the absurdity of the Volstead Act. The far-reaching moral construct of Prohibition proved the American spirit would be relentlessly furtive in its pursuit of feeding its collective head. Thus began the drug wars for the pre–World War II generation, a series of politically untenable exercises that served only to reveal a nation's worst intentions.

By the boom of the 1960s, most of Hollywood's myths had been stripped bare. The speakeasies had been replaced by folk-rock clubs, and the celebrity mill now included musicians, who were fast replacing authors and movie stars as American deities. They would transform the burgeoning counterculture into big business, the color-saturated sounds of youth drowning out the black-and-white of the past. Attached like moorings to the vessel of this new star trip were what would come to be known as singer-songwriters who would descend upon Hollywood en masse.

The Beach Boys proved that the Beatles, a fully realized, self-made pop act that obliterated everything that had gone before it, were not a singularly British phenomenon but one that could be co-opted in a sun-drenched hymn to hedonism. For what made the alien comforts of the Fab Four so appealing would transform California into a paradise of string bikinis and tanned surfer dudes twisting their youth away to souped-up car elegies and odes to the everlasting wave. The Byrds would soon take the solemnity of Greenwich Village folk art that was pulling in cash for the former East Coast Brill Building crowd and turn it into Top 40 gold. Taking Bob Dylan's iconicity and electrifying his haunting "Mr. Tambourine Man," the band would ironically mirror Dylan himself plugging in and causing a stir. But it was the Mamas and Papas' call to action "California Dreamin'" that sent tremors through the counterculture and sparked a pilgrimage to the shores of Monterey.

They migrated to the sea as lemmings, the names that would encompass a vast swath of America's 1970s musical landscape: Stephen Stills, Graham Nash, David Crosby, Neil Young, Joni Mitchell, Linda Ronstadt, James Taylor, Jackson Browne, Carole King, Don Henley, Glenn Frey, J. D. Souther, Tom Waits, and dozens more.

"On and around Sunset, west of old Hollywood before one reached the manicured pomp of Beverly Hills, clubs and coffeehouses began to proliferate," writes British rock journalist Barney Hoskyns in his brilliantly researched history of the L.A. rock scene, *Hotel California*. "The Strip now became a living neighborhood—and a mecca for dissident youth."

Among the growing throng, perhaps more at its fringe, was a twenty-four-year-old pianist and budding songwriter named Warren Zevon, a bespectacled, quick-witted longhair whose disjointed efforts inside the music business were beginning to pay off. His serpentine professional journey had already included many arcs: He'd been one half of a teenage folk duo called lyme & cybelle, which made a minor blip on the 1966 charts with his whimsical "Follow Me"; had fortuitously composed a song that ended up as the flip side of the Turtles' number one 1967 hit "Happy Together," called "Like the Season"; and had written and recorded radio jingles for Boone's Farm, Gallo wine, and the Chevy Camaro, among others. A version of his song "He Quit Me" appeared on the 1969 movie sound track for *Midnight Cowboy*, and he released a totally forgotten debut album the same year titled *Wanted Dead or Alive*. He would become the bandleader for the legendary Everly Brothers and musical director for their short-lived television variety show, *Johnny Cash Presents the Everly Brothers*, which would air on ABC between July and September of 1970.

Recounting these times in a 1978 *Circus* magazine interview with Fred Schruers, Zevon said he always knew his goal was to remain true to his art. "The most important thing was to continue being a musician. In other words, not work in a bookstore, not sell dope, not do anything but be a musician."

Using the Tropicana Motel, a colorfully decadent artists' flophouse, as a safe haven from the rigors of his idiosyncratic lifestyle, he was nearly broke, mostly drunk, and in a perpetual feud with the mother of his son, Jordan, a beautiful but struggling would-be actress named Marilyn Livingston, whom he called Tule (rhymes with Julie). More than four decades hence, a forty-seven-year-old Jordan Zevon wistfully recounted the hazy memories of his impossibly young and volatile parents to me: "They started as teenagers and went through this journey together deeply in love." During the first of our many extended phone conversations bounding from one coast to the other, he described his parents as "modern hippies" who grew a few ears of corn in the backyard. "I have these pictures that show all sweetness and happiness, but then Dad got caught up in the drinking lifestyle and my mom was a no-tolerance person and said, 'I'm not going to raise a baby around a drunk,' and that was the end of it."

Not far from the maddening din of Sunset and Hollywood Boulevards, Zevon spent long nights binging in L.A.'s most notorious haunts—the Rainbow Bar and Grill, McCabe's or the Troubadour—seeking refuge among the denizens of the night drowning their troubles amid the hoots and hollers of revelry. The Tropicana provided the suddenly displaced Zevon with refuge to read, drink, and write, but due to a tragic lack of funds, even that would soon be over, and he would eventually end up in the stagnant squalor of the Hollywood Hawaiian Hotel. Faced with the underbelly of L.A.—homeless junkies and jabbering winos strewn along its corridors, then spilling out onto the expanse of Gower—he began to contemplate his role among them.

Look away down Gower Avenue, look away.

The song Zevon would write about Los Angeles, his adopted city, where he lived most of his life and perpetuated a schizophrenic love affair with its darkness and light, its promise and harrows, would be called "Desperados Under the Eaves," a folk ballad played so softly on piano it unfurls as less tune than tale but for one opening chord laid bare by wistful-sounding strings. The solemn baritone of the protagonist leans in to abruptly recite his lament of a solitary low-rent existence dependent on the whims of fate:

I was sitting in the Hollywood Hawaiian Hotel
I was staring in my empty coffee cup

The opening stanza provides little ambiguity. No man with solid roots or free of sorrow sits in a cheap hotel room peering deeply into the emptiness of anything. He is the drifter, a wanton wanderer having given up the search for place and purpose. This is the sound and meaning of desperation.

The song concludes the eponymously titled *Warren Zevon*, an album recorded between October 1975 and February of the following year and released in May of 1976 for the talent-friendly Asylum Records, a label rock critic Greil Marcus mischievously dubbed "a famous home for self-pitying narcissists." It was founded by young record mogul David Geffen, who hoped to provide a "creative asylum" and make a shitload of cash for burgeoning songwriters like the record's eventual producer, Jackson Browne. "I've always understood there was a certain thing that Warren was able to do which somehow was not in me, was not part of my nature, but which totally communicated with me," Browne shared with music journalist Paul Nelson in 1976. "It's that dark humor, man, that bo-wammo! He's so kinetic and free, so naturally meaningful; I'm more consciously symbolic, trying to be meaningful. Warren's rather raw, uncompromising in his language. I mean, I've never written about the things Warren has written about—but I've lived them. So why aren't they in my songs?"

The two songsmiths met in 1968 at music entrepreneur Frazier Mohawk's eclectic Laurel Canyon residence. A whimsical Hollywood character who could have been conjured by F. Scott Fitzgerald's booze-addled imagination, the former circus owner, aka Barry Friedman, hosted a repertory company of singer-songwriters that went by various names, such as the Elektra Recording Ranch and the Feather River Orchestra. It was there Browne first heard Zevon play his tender ballad of romantic remorse, "Hasten Down the Wind," and was blown away by its perfectly formed beauty. According to Zevon's account of the evening, the feeling was mutual. "It was like two gunslingers on Main Street at high noon," he told *Phonograph Record* in 1976. "Jackson played a song, then I played one . . . we squared off. Then we both decided that we respected each other, and it wasn't worth seeing who was best."

It would be the more marketable Browne who was signed by Elektra to front an ill-fated project called Baby Browning before he ventured out on his own solo career. In the early '70s, the two young songwriters would run into each other by happenstance and retire to Browne's home to imbibe a concoction forever known as the Waco Bloody Mary. Once sufficiently fueled, Zevon began playing a stunned Browne one amazing song after the other, "The French Inhaler," "Studebaker," and eventually "Desperados Under the Eaves"—the makings, Browne surmised, of a debut album.

Buoyed by Browne's enthusiasm, Zevon cut demos of his songs with Robert "Waddy" Wachtel, a master studio and performing guitarist from Jackson Heights, Queens, whom he'd hired to play in the Everly Brothers band in 1970. The moment Zevon and Wachtel met at the audition, the two volatile personalities clashed, Zevon challenging the razor-thin, wild-haired Wachtel to shave his beard and play what he was told, and the guitarist vehemently declining to do so while correcting his arrangements. "This guy really didn't like me," Wachtel remembered when we spoke in late February 2017. "Warren says, 'All right, wise guy, since you know every song, what's this one?' And he proceeds to play the *only* classical piece that I know. He could have picked any from the catalog of classical etudes he knew, but he happened to choose the *only* one I know. So I just looked at him and said, 'That's Beethoven's Fourth in G. See ya later, asshole.'"

The conflict-driven Zevon knew a musical kindred spirit when he saw one. He and Wachtel shared a love of Merle Haggard, the Rolling Stones, and composing. "The great thing about that tour was, almost from night one me, Warren, and Bob Knigge, the Everlys' longtime bass player, would get together and play music," Wachtel continues. "That was how we took care of our differences. We'd just play all night long, and Donald and Phil got wind of this and the next thing you know every night these guys that everyone told me had this great animosity toward each other were hanging with us drinking and smoking and playing music. It was phenomenal to hear the Everlys in a hotel room singing: the most incredible sound you will ever hear."

Wachtel would go on to dramatically alter both Zevon's creative life and his personal life, more pointedly introducing him to Crystal Brelsford, the woman who would become Zevon's wife and mother to his only daughter.

Crystal, who had followed Wachtel from Vermont, shared with me the story of the day she met the mercurial young songwriter in 1971: "I knew about Warren because Waddy had called me from the road and said, 'This guy is crazy but an amazing songwriter!'" After the tour, while retrieving Waddy from the airport, she ended up chauffeuring Zevon to the Tropicana. "He got into the back seat of my Chevy Super Sport, and it sounds corny, but our eyes literally met in the rearview mirror and there was some kind of spark. Waddy rolled a joint and was passing it around, and when Warren passed it to me our fingers touched a little *too* long."

After years of romance and turmoil, the couple married during a wild desert ride fueled by LSD and vodka, at the Chapel of the Bells in Las Vegas on May 25, 1974. They spent the ensuing years moving around Hollywood's less inviting neighborhoods and surviving on Crystal's income from her job at a photo lab, and Zevon's from any gig he could book. Eventfully they bunked in Phil Everly's tiny guesthouse, where they shared Kentucky Fried chicken and champagne in the local Laundromat with the rock 'n' roll icon. In her oral biography *I'll Sleep When I'm Dead: The Dirty Life and Times of Warren Zevon*, Crystal recounts Zevon's drinking episodes and their inevitable mishaps culminating in a drunk-driving charge that forced the couple to gather "$480, a beat-up Martin acoustic guitar, a Swiss Army knife, a Sony cassette recorder, and four hits of LSD smuggled between the pages of a diary" and escape to a tiny fishing village near Barcelona called Sitges, where Zevon would play country and western songs in an Irish pub.

"Our time in Spain freed him from the bondage of not having the melodious voice that kept him from getting record contracts and watching people he'd been playing music with become famous while he was left behind," Crystal recalls with a nostalgic tone. "We'd finish at the Dubliner at about two and go out to these discos dancing all night or sit on the beach until sunrise."

During his absence, Jackson Browne played Zevon's episodic songs of alcoholic visions, drug addiction, predatory women, and infamous outlaws around L.A., unsuc-cessfully pitching them to his friends in the Byrds and a band made up of veteran road cats beginning to make a name for themselves called the Eagles. Eventually, he used the influence he'd gained from his own highly acclaimed solo albums to convince David Geffen to purchase Zevon's publishing contract from producer Bones Howe with the promise to corral Zevon's best work into a debut. Soon after, Browne sent an excited note to Zevon imploring him to return to the states to record an album.

"We found an apartment and decided we would have babies, but then we got this postcard from Jackson saying, 'You can't give up. Come back,'" adds Crystal. "It was an agonizing decision because we were happy. But I said, 'You're always going to wonder if you could have made it,' so we went back home, and up to his dying days Warren always told me, 'We should have stayed in Spain.'"

Browne would devotedly assist the now twenty-eight-year-old Zevon in molding his emotionally tortured tales into a remarkable opening statement. *Warren Zevon* is the work of an uncompromising artist conjuring his salutations to the shadowy reflection of violence, regret, and noble redemption that closes dramatically with "Desperados Under the Eaves." Its sparse open is touched by a string quartet intuiting the tormented melody, like an overture, giving way to an inviting guitar lick reminiscent of the countrified "L.A. Sound" that drew a generation of musicians to the City of Angels.

Despite his harder edge and an acerbic wit, Zevon's odd place within the so-called L.A. Sound is mostly due to the indigenous musicians who would lend their talents to the backing tracks—Don Henley and Glenn Frey of the Eagles; J. D. Souther, who was often referred to as "the sixth Eagle"; Jackson Browne, who cowrote the Eagles' first hit, "Take It Easy"; Stevie Nicks and Lindsey Buckingham from the reborn West Coast incarnation of Fleetwood Mac; and the Beach Boys' Carl Wilson. A wonderful twist of dark humor resonates the very first time you hear these voices sing a perfect harmony on the pertinent word "California" just before they converge for the harmonic swell of the line, "Don't the sun look angry through the trees." Souther, who Zevon considered one of the finest songwriters of the era, told me in late 2017 that the line is "possibly the best chorus I have ever heard. That's pretty powerful language for a pop song."

Perhaps the most compelling connection to the L.A. Sound was proffered by the dutiful Linda Ronstadt cover of the song that floored Jackson Browne years before, "Hasten Down the Wind," which also happens to share the title of an album she would release three months later to great acclaim.

Playing with the warm and fuzzy preconceptions of the patched-jeans-and-sandals set, Zevon in his stark literary musings expertly placed his disturbed subterranean characters against the backdrop of his city and its signature 1970s musical vibe, just as his favorite filmmaker, Martin Scorsese, set enigmatic madman Travis Bickle in the glamorous disco milieu of New York City in his 1976 film *Taxi Driver*. "It sounds as though Zevon is out to demolish every cliché in the Asylum bin," writes Janet Maslin in her *Newsweek* review of the album, in which she describes

Zevon telling her that what appears to be a satire on the Eagles' saccharine ballad "Desperado" is really an homage to Hungarian composer Béla Bartók.

"Warren was a bit of an unusual character coming out of California, because his tone was obviously not [that of] a typical Californian, unless you went back to Nathanael West or something," observed Bruce Springsteen in Crystal Zevon's wonderful oral biography *I'll Sleep When I'm Dead*. "He had the cynical edge, which was not a part of what was coming out of California at the time."

"I was a surfer in the '60s, I was all that California junk," Zevon dutifully explained to Michael Barackman in *Phonograph Record* the week the album was released. "It was emotionally important to me to make a statement about it. Sure, I'm competing with the Eagles, but I'm also competing with Joan Didion, Nathanael West, and Raymond Chandler."

It is the voice of L.A. noir author Raymond Chandler that echoes deeply in "Desperados Under the Eaves." The song's shadowy grit and poetic subtext of isolation can be found in books like *The Big Sleep*; *Farewell, My Lovely*; or *The Long Goodbye* as told in the obdurate detective-speak of Chandler's most famously unrepentant protagonist, Philip Marlowe.

In contrast to the tension of the song's opening meter and to its dusky theme, the narrator of "Desperados Under the Eaves" is unbowed, almost comically accepting of his fate—penniless, directionless, pathetic, with nothing left to lose. Just as the music pensively descends from its opening strains, laying the groundwork for the solitary figure in a hotel starting into emptiness, now the dramatic swell of the ensuing string accompaniment lifts Zevon's voice to ride the melody proudly:

I was thinking that the gypsy wasn't lying
All the salty margaritas in Los Angeles, I'm gonna drink 'em up

The arrogant intonation of the vocal belies a man who is lost in remorse. Instead he is emboldened to ride the crest of Gower's many twists and turns to find every bar in town with a salted glass and make his stand. His dreary fixation on the emptiness of despair bemoaning the dark premonitions of the gypsy's curse suddenly shifts to defiance, which acts as a prelude to what I would argue is the finest verse ever to grace a rock/folk song:

And if California slides into the ocean
As the mystics and statistics say it will
I predict this hotel will be standing until I pay my bill.

Following this brilliantly satirical line with its delicious inner rhyme of "mystics and statistics," the song strikes a new aural stance, one reflective in early-twentieth-century American composer Aaron Copland's most lauded odes to the common man. The music becomes symphonic, as the orchestral accompaniment takes center stage, touched by a hint of the opening guitar and a final "Huh!" from Zevon before a rousing choral.

A stripped-down band demo of the song released in 2007 on the posthumously compiled *Preludes: Rare and Unreleased Recordings* has Zevon blurting, "Ha!," as if discovering the cruelly absurd tragicomedy in which he finds himself. In the 1976 recording, Zevon uses the guttural exclamation to move from inner dialogue back into geographical description and with it a returning dread. This is where the song's central theme—the barren, soulless landscape of Gower Avenue piercing through the heart of Los Angeles—comes home, however transient and doom-struck.

Jackson Browne recalled to *Rolling Stone* this concussive vocal device heralding his friend's presence in the cloistered L.A. music community when Zevon, drunk at the piano and playing an impromptu version of "Desperados Under the Eaves," halted a party packed with the city's biggest musical stars and harshest critics: Joni Mitchell, Carole King, Neil Young, and the Eagles. "Of course everybody keeps on talking . . . he sings a line and goes: 'HUT!' And eighteen motherfuckers turn their heads so fast it makes a wind. It was his coming-out party."

By the time Zevon composed the song, the L.A. scene—the radical-chic uto-pian youth empire of creativity and bravado from the canyons of Laurel to Topanga laced with psychedelic drugs and Native American ideals—had eroded into an ego-mad, cocaine-fueled cesspool of backstabbing millionaire freaks. The "Me Decade" was going full tilt, and many of these waylaid artists were friends and colleagues. Zevon had watched the passionate ideologues of his generation break molds; upon his return to the States, he noted that they appeared paranoid and corrupted, their plight evocative of the opening lines of Beat poet Allen Ginsberg's opus "Howl" or of Fitzgerald's "Babylon Revisited." The purveyors of the exploited counterculture were coming unglued as the stench of failed opportunity and blatant hypocrisy filled the smog of Los Angeles, everyone seemingly swallowed up by the false prom-ise of the American dream.

"The '70s were in full swing," writes Barney Hoskyns in *Hotel California*. "This was where rock's new royalty dwelled, rubbing sandy shoulders with movie idols and moguls." Linda Ronstadt is telling reporters it is "groovy to look like you're winning, to look like you're very rich" and no one thinks the sentiment sardonic.

These are not desperados under the eaves, singular victims of circumstance, but desperados betrayed by their own excesses.

Zevon's earlier Hollywood elegies set against an alcoholic haze of despair also appear in *Preludes*, specifically the opening track, "Empty Hearted Town," in which the narrator finds himself wandering the sidewalks of L.A. (perhaps Gower, which "started out all right" [affluent] and "ended up all wrong" [graveyard]) and "wishing I had a warmer jacket." He finds himself "just another man with an empty-handed heart in an empty-hearted town." But Zevon is still "all dressed up for the masquerade" and contemplating the duality of the city's fantasy and desolation: "The lights of the city stretch as far as the eyes can see / Look what wonders man has made." And while "Empty Hearted Town" is a melancholy piano ballad, the lyrics remain committed to the romance of the city's restless illusions and therefore never bound into the obstinacy of "Desperados Under the Eaves."

In fact, the consistent undercurrent to the songs on *Warren Zevon*, an album that Zevon biographer George Plasketes cleverly terms a "geomusical neighborhood novella," scours the incredible depths of anguish that lead us to this stirring epilogue. It is the culmination of the Hollywood imagery found in the funky "Join Me in L.A.," a darkly seductive invitation to the sinners' town that fretfully recounts Zevon's time at the Tropicana with its telling refrain, "I found something that will never be nothing," as well as "The French Inhaler," a scathing reply to a broken heart with its narrator once again calling out from a Hollywood bar, surrounded by "phonies" and drinking up all of the promised money that was supposed to save a struggling couple from the demimonde. If only his woman had made it as an actress instead of becoming a failed dreamer with tender and frail fingers who will never make her way in the world. Her failure has doomed him. And then there is "Carmelita," with its luridly seductive Mexican accompaniment, presenting a woman as salvation. The final plea of a junkie for the gentle arms of his love, whose stream of welfare checks has run dry, is all he can hope for to ease the inevitable agony of smack withdrawal.

Here, Zevon takes us through the seedier parts of Los Angeles broached in "Desperados Under the Eaves":

I hear mariachi static on my radio
And the tubes they glow in the dark
And I'm there with her in Ensenada
And I'm here in Echo Park

Echo Park was a well-known drug trafficking area of Los Angeles in the early to mid-1970s, which lends credence to Zevon's tale of a character "strung out on heroin on the outskirts of town": His spirit is with Carmelita in Ensenada, a coastal Mexican town on the Californian Baja peninsula, while his weakened flesh drifts off to his street connection. It is a powerful image of the schizophrenic nature of the addict trapped within the duplicity of a city that indelicately balances its glamour with debauchery.

Well, I pawned my Smith-Corona
And I went to meet my man
He hangs out down on Alvarado Street
By the Pioneer Chicken stand

Like "Desperados Under the Eaves," with its hotel/prison and Gower/subculture symbolism, "Carmelita" also hints at the geographical: specifically, Carmelita Avenue, a major thoroughfare cutting through the swanky Beverly Hills section of West Hollywood. Carmelita's notorious rich, celebrity-studded environs expose the cultural and economic chasm Zevon reflects in the expanse of Gower Avenue. The location of the junkie's Pioneer Chicken stand, a popular local fast-food chain founded in 1961, which, at the time of this writing, only exists in three locations (although no longer on Alvarado near Echo Park), could mean an excruciating trek for a busted and luckless smack-head trembling from fierce withdrawals and baked by the California sun; hence the reference to "hold me tighter" and "sinking down" by the blessed trail that leads him to his fix. Either way, geography places the narrator's dilemma directly at the feet of the listener, who must both ask the glaring question, "Don't you feel like Desperados under the eaves?"

Ultimately, though, this is a song drenched in alcohol imagery. There is a long history here, as Zevon began drinking before his teen years. By this time he had dropped his share of acid, sampled a myriad of pills, and smoked copious amounts of marijuana, indulging in the mind-expanding drugs of the era, which were especially prevalent in the 1960s rock scene, but you write "Whiter Shade of Pale" on acid, you pen *Blonde on Blonde* on speed, and you compose "Desperados Under the Eaves" on the bottle. The bottle takes you there; the piano coddles the id as the voice breathes consolation.

Don't the sun look angry through the trees

One needn't wonder what kind of sun: a California sun, relentlessly oppressive unless one is lounging on a beach or hiking the mountains. For those hungover while stuck in low-rent hotels staring into emptiness and raging against unpaid bills its vehemence is palpable. The trees, too, are obvious: the palm trees seen lining many of the boulevards of Hollywood, pleasantly welcoming the hordes of tourists who conveniently pass by the destitute to get better glimpses of movie stars. But through the eyes of the poet, the trees are harbingers that cannot be ignored. Zevon sings:

Don't the trees look like crucified thieves

The line is a striking biblical reference to first-century Jerusalem, the original schizophrenic city, with its victims hanging from gnarled trees lining the main roads, a warning to potential dissenters against the Roman Empire, which would hardly tolerate any frantic attempts to skip out on the bill.

The rousing staccato instrumentation, hauntingly backed by harmonic voices beneath the imagery, breaks back into the tender piano lines, allowing the singular voice to once again finish his thought:

Don't you feel like desperados under the eaves

A slight ritardando provides the listener a chance to realize that this is an ode to an inescapable place to mourn. It is an acute observation, however subjective, to being trapped—in plight, in concept, in symbol . . . in anything that takes immeasurable grit to escape:

Heaven helps the one who leaves

The lush background vocals once again return to underscore the terrifying truth of the song: Leaving means awakening from the fantasy of Hollywood, as both a place and a dream—"Dreamland" stripped bare and given a new definition. Jackson Browne once effused to VH1 that Zevon had the uncanny ability to "mytholize and satirize" at once. Here, in the finest song he would produce of Zevon's, is a striking example.

The transformation from surrender to resurrection is evident in the song's de facto chorus, which cleverly matches "desperado" with the multilayered "eaves." Given the notion that the narrator is unable to pay for his lodging, whatever course of action he chooses—to flee or sit staring into oblivion—he already sees himself as a criminal. However, Zevon does not use that word. He is a "desperado" simply because the term evokes the word *desperate*, and desperation is the core of his lament.

This led many to believe the song was a cynical nod to the fame and fortune of his buddies in the Eagles, a band so beloved and reviled in their time it makes some sense, but the composer repeatedly denied this. The correlation, beyond the band's aforementioned signature ballad "Desperado," is dubious. However, more overlooked is Zevon's influence on the Eagles megahit single "Hotel California" (recorded three months after the release of *Warren Zevon*), which expanded on his theme of the hotel (taking as its subject a grander and more mysterious dwelling) as a metaphor for a spiritual and cultural purgatory: *You can check in, but you can never leave.* Henley, who cowrote the song, told ABC News four decades later, "It's a journey from innocence to experience. It's not really about California—it's about the dark underbelly of the American dream. It's about excess, it's about narcissism. It's about the music business. It can have a million interpretations." It's the ultimate Californian dirge for aging boomers who once swarmed to the coast in search of freedom, but ended up broken, drug-addled prisoners of a false dream, "desperados" peering from beneath the shadowy eaves.

Indeed, *eaves* is the second intriguing word used by Zevon that works on two levels: one being that it refers to the overhang of a Californian-style roof that casts a welcoming shade to protect the buildings from the unforgiving western sun, and the other being its lesser known use as a term for the brim of a hat. The latter is more apt for Zevon, who saw himself as a relic from another age, an anachronistic character out of a rough-and-tumble 1940s pulp novel by Nathanael West, whose 1939 novel *The Day of the Locust* reflects a condemned Hollywood inhabited by lost souls with "eyes filled with hatred," who "had come to California to die." Raymond Chandler's *The Big Sleep* arrived the same year and was set in the darker corners of sunny Los Angeles, where hard-bitten protagonist Philip Marlowe attempted to gain the favor of a femme fatale.

The invisible femme fatale of "Desperado Under the Eaves" is revealed in the song's second verse, wherein the narrator wakes up with "shaking hands" (a telltale sign of alcoholism) still looking for "a girl who understands me" (that is, who accepts his alcoholism), harkening back to another ominous figure from "Empty Hearted Town," who has "wrapped it all in darkness and I can't find my way." But once again Zevon immediately replaces the female specter, the ostensible scapegoat for his troubles, with the city built on illusions. He forlornly exhales:

But except in dreams you're never really free

This prompts him to return to the angry sun; however, this time it is not a sweeping condemnation of a ruined landscape, but of himself:

Don't the sun look angry at me

The line serves as the final indictment of the scoundrel before Zevon returns to the opening theme, a solitary man in a hotel, insulated in a prison of his own making:

I was sitting in the Hollywood Hawaiian Hotel
I was listening to the air conditioner hum

Crystal Zevon told me that Zevon indeed began penning the song at the Hollywood Hawaiian Hotel, as he sat silently listening to the air conditioner hum, finishing it later during a bout with the London flu at her North Poinsettia apartment. She also revealed that he would eventually escape his air-conditioned purgatory in the back of his friend David Marks's station wagon, after leaping out of his hotel room's bathroom window in true Philip Marlowe idiom. Even the getaway reeks of Californian symbolism, as Marks was a studio guitarist who had first made his bones as an original member of the Beach Boys. Both Crystal Zevon and Marks agree that years later the villain returned to the scene of the crime and attempted to pay his outstanding debt, but the owners of the Hollywood Hawaiian settled for an autographed copy of the album in which the offending confession appears.

Now halfway through his elegy, Zevon recalls the moment of truth, as he begins humming along with a new melody, introduced as if it were a rollicking tribute to the Henri René and Bob Russell instrumental theme to the classic television series *Wagon Train*. One can almost picture the open prairies and endless skyline unimpeded by the temptation of cruel cities and cheap hotels. The solitary humming is joined by a chorus of same, a symphony to the lost souls of Hollywood, as the orchestra takes up the refrain, giving it a majestic air. And then, as if to put an exclamation point on the wings of its musical ascent comes the telling line:

Look away down Gower Avenue, look away

Part church hymn, part chain-gang moan, the lyric echoes a city in turmoil forever embattled with its images of immense riches and broken hearts, imbued with the cries of the redemptive soul. The song forever entwines the man and his city: the inner conflict, the yin and yang, the goodness and evil transposed one upon the other, making it impossible to see the difference. The desperado finds his Taoist nature under the protective yet imprisoning eaves.

It is, in the end, according to Zevon himself, this redemptive spirit that inspired the work on *Warren Zevon* and specifically this song, so full of reflective contradiction. "I'm very much not a cynic. I think I'm quite idealistic," he argued to famed music critic Robert Hilburn of the *Los Angeles Times* when the album was released. "I think caring is, perhaps, the most positive force in life. I've always felt there is something redeeming about every experience, something affirmative, and it's that quality I hope people would see in my work; not that I'm an 'expert satirist' or a 'dissector of L.A. culture,' but someone who looks at life good-naturedly and has the ability to see the human side of things."

"I think that when anybody talks about L.A. songs, being a guy from L.A., there is just no competition," says Dawes's Taylor Goldsmith, just one of a new generation of California-inspired musicians who have found kinship with Warren Zevon. "'Desperados Under the Eaves' captures the weariness but also the beauty of L.A. in a way that I feel people have a hard time finding the balance of. There is a distinct 'we've seen too much' attitude in L.A. that a lot of people are unnerved by, whereas for those of us that are from there, there's a romance to it. And I feel like Warren Zevon is able to get that across better than anyone I have ever heard, *especially* in that song."

Counting Crows' Adam Duritz agreed when I told him about dedicating an essay to this song, "Having lived there, Zevon portrays the exhaustive beauty of life in Hollywood with more detail than almost anyone. You get where Zevon is at—the way sunshine is cleansing and purifying, yet unchanging and exhausting: this sense of beautiful exhaustion."

"Desperados Under the Eaves" is the final song on what would turn out, as Jackson Browne had hoped, to be the truest musical statement of Warren Zevon's career. Indeed, many of the songs on the album would become staples in Zevon's new career: the soul-searching "Carmelita," the unflinchingly scathing "The French Inhaler," the rousing "Poor Poor Pitiful Me," the image-driven "I'll Sleep When I'm Dead," and in the two gorgeous piano ballads "Hasten Down the Wind" and "Mohammed's Radio." Zevon believed and strongly argued that after his death the album's lesser-known "Back Turned Looking Down the Path" would be considered the finest song he would ever write, yet, a few months after its release in October of 1976, and before performing a heartfelt version of it solo, Zevon told Cleveland's WMMS radio that "Desperados Under the Eaves" was "an important song for me, it's one of my favorites." He maintained until his death in 2003 that it was his most personal song.

In 2002, David Letterman dedicated an entire *Late Show* to his dying friend, whom he had featured since 1982. When Zevon asked what songs the talk show legend wanted to hear, Letterman secretly hoped for "Desperados Under the Eaves" but felt it might be asking too much. More than a decade later, in one of the final shows of Letterman's thirty-three year career, he chose the aforementioned Dawes to finally play it. "It was really incredible watching Letterman hold onto his mic with his head down walking back and forth when we played that song," remembers Taylor Goldsmith, who sings it with the kind of reverence he exuded when we spoke about that performance one idle winter evening in 2017. "Just knowing that this was our own kind of trip into their deep and long-standing mythical relationship was a high honor. Zevon has always meant a lot to me, and to represent something to the relationship between him and David Letterman is beyond anything I could have imagined."

The noirish album cover of *Warren Zevon* completes the sympathetic villain of "Desperados Under the Eaves." The photograph was taken in the parking lot of the Hollywood Palladium (two blocks off Gower on Sunset Boulevard) on the evening of the 1976 Grammys by Jimmy Wachtel, who lived right down the block (on Gower, if you can believe it). When we spoke in the autumn of 2016, Wachtel, who besides being Waddy's brother is an accomplished photographer of rock's elite, told me he was prompted to try and crash the event by a warmly lubricated Warren Zevon.

Like the music it contains, the cover is the polar opposite of any gracing albums by Zevon's "L.A. Sound" brethren. Gone are the earthy tones and country and western attire connoting the back-to-nature mythos of Southern California reflected in feel-good harmonies and mellow flair. The photo—a barely focused, blue-hued shot of a long-haired, bespectacled Zevon nattily dressed against a blurry night sky that is eerily illuminated by an enormous floodlight normally used to herald blockbuster Hollywood openings or vacuous award shows— perfectly underlines the songwriter's nocturnal character. His right hand moves as if he is unaware he's being photographed or at least aware enough to begin his escape.

"I always felt like Warren and I were just a little bit weirder than our friends," concludes J. D. Souther, who, along with his lover Linda Ronstadt, would move into Zevon's Beachwood Canyon house, when the narrator finally escaped the bitter end of Gower Street. "We were always inveterate loners, just one step outside that Laurel Canyon group—not only stylistically, but personality-wise. Neither of us were really joiners."

It is hard to look at this photo and not see the man who composed and sang "Desperados Under the Eaves," an amazing piece of work for an artist in his mid-twenties discovering his voice. It is one part confession, one part defiance, and a generous helping of lean Los Angeles allegory, but it was only the beginning.

Three Generations of Zevon Men: Warren, Stumpy, and Jordan. *Courtesy of the Jordan Zevon Collection*

"Studebaker"

Because he had no place he could stay in without getting tired of it and because there was nowhere to go but everywhere, keep rolling under the stars. . . .

—Jack Kerouac, *On the Road*

It's difficult to say with any certainty that "Studebaker" stands up with much of Warren Zevon's best work. He apparently didn't think much of it. It's not on any of his albums and there is no evidence he ever performed it live. Maybe it struck me harder than most since I first heard it performed by his son, Jordan, on the posthumous tribute album *Enjoy Every Sandwich* when I was forty-four years old. I think it's a song that spoke to me in middle age the way side one of his second Asylum album, *Excitable Boy*, turned my head at fifteen and *Sentimental Hygiene*, his first for Virgin Records, kicked my butt at twenty-four. I heard it only a couple of years after Zevon's passing, and so starved was I for anything new I initially hit the replay button on the CD player at least four times. It is a wonderful performance, so full of ennui and a loving tribute. It makes perfect sense that Jordan would record it. After all, he found it.

The story goes that shortly after Zevon's death Jordan was rummaging through a daunting pile of unmarked boxes stacked away in his father's storage unit. Unsure what he might find, "a bunch of guitars or a human head," he stumbled on reels of early recordings and demos. "I remember sitting and basting in the evil sun of the San Fernando Valley and just winding all these tapes back up," recalls Jordan with a measure of his dad's sardonic humor. "I kept repeating to myself, 'It's all going to be worth it,' and at the end of the day we got some great stuff out of it, and it gave people a little glimpse into where these songs came from."

During this long afternoon, Jordan would unearth raw rehearsals and discarded takes of well-known material and reworks of lesser-known gems like "Empty Hearted Town," even those stuck in anonymity on the very-little-referenced (and I am apparently carrying on that tradition here) *Wanted Dead or Alive*, like the wistful "Tule's Blues."

And then there is "Studebaker."

"How I understand it, my maternal grandmother [Mary] kind of being who she was made my dad sit down and record a bunch of songs into her recorder," explains Jordan. "So I have 'Hasten Down the Wind' and a few other songs, but the only song that didn't really see the light of day was 'Studebaker.' Yet when I started going through the tapes what I discovered is that he recorded 'Studebaker' for almost every single album. He did a demo of it for *Excitable Boy*, *Bad Luck Streak in Dancing School*, and *The Envoy*."

There is something mysterious about the absence of "Studebaker" in the Zevon canon, despite it being every bit as solid as most of his ballads. Its opening piano sequence is exquisitely formed in a classical motif. The melody, both in the verses and into the sweeping chorus, is as gentle as it is unnerving. Lyrically, it is a time bomb. On the surface it's a song about a shitty car owned by a fraught loser who cannot get to where he is going, but its hidden qualities mirror its mysterious neglect in Zevon's recorded works. It gets fans wondering if there was something about it that may have been too close to the bone for him. This seems odd, as Zevon was unerringly comfortable digging up rawer emotions for a tune. Confronting demons and chasing ghosts was his raison d'être. Yet "Studebaker" remained unfinished.

A few years after his version on the tribute album, Jordan put together *Preludes: Rare and Unreleased Recordings*, which would include one of his father's many rough demos of "Studebaker." Although the track sounds professionally recorded, Zevon's subtle but noticeable musical hiccups on the piano and occasional stumbles over lyrics lend it a crudeness. The performance is anything but self-assured, yet its tentative nature heightens the emotion. Zevon is literally struggling to get through it. Then, as he begins to approach the chorus again, he abruptly halts. Maybe the tape ran out, since it ends right in the middle of his reciting the title. Maybe he felt he had enough to go on and didn't bother to complete the final word. Maybe he could not— as Jordan suggests—get it right, and just abandoned ship, forever holding his peace. No matter the reason, for Warren Zevon "Studebaker" would be no more. Buried away—not erased or destroyed or thrown out, mind you—only to be rediscovered and recorded in earnest by his only son after his death.

And with that forgotten recording comes the father-son connection. The fact that it is a song about a classic American car, notably a dated model that has the *distinction* of tradition set against its inevitable *extinction*, and that in this country the passing down of the car—especially a car that meant something to the father in his salad days, when a car means everything—is as significant as passing on a name. In this case, Jordan Zevon gives new life to a *song* about a *car*, thus uniting the symbols of cherished possessions being passed down from composer/father to composer/son. Indeed, Jordan is a singer-songwriter in his own right, with a self-titled EP and his 2008 full-length release titled *Inside Out*, which, along with a sequel to his father's epic "Desperados Under the Eaves" called "Too Late to Be Saved," includes his impassioned version of "Studebaker."

The lineage is there in the reading of the piece. Jordan does a fine job of expressing what his father intended to: unmitigated frustration. The rendition's further poignancy lies in the timing of both recordings. When Zevon wrote and recorded the demo for Tule's mother, he was still in his mid-twenties, singing in the first person about a "low prospect's man" running out of excuses to grow up. Here is Jordan Zevon, in his mid-thirties (he changed the age of the lyrics' protagonist from twenty-five to thirty-five, to match his own), who would only come to know his father much later in life, mourning his passing and offering up a solemn tribute by resurrecting his abandoned song.

The other noteworthy touchstone to the song is its allusion to Fresno, California, where Warren Zevon was raised after moving there from Chicago as a small boy. Fresno is where the young artist came of age and absorbed the habits and developed the talents he would take with him through life. It would be the only time the southern California town is mentioned in Zevon's work until his final album, *The Wind*, when he alludes to his youth and "a Fresno matinee" in "Disorder in the House."

Although Zevon was not averse to pilfering memories of his distant past for material, as many songwriters of the day did, his "Studebaker" is loaded with symbolism. And this is where the mystery gets deeper for me. I see it as an open window into Zevon's past: his childhood, his rearing, his need for closure from a mostly absent father and a doting mother. It is all there. Jordan, who had endured a similar pattern with his parents, knew where to look for it.

I'm up against it all like a leaf against the wind
And the Studebaker keeps on breakin' down again
This Studebaker keeps on breakin' down again

I thought I'd go to Fresno to see my friend
This damn Studebaker keeps on breaking down again

Warren Zevon was born to William Rubin Zivotofsky and Beverly Simmons on January 24, 1947. Zivotofsky, a forty-two year-old Russian-Jewish immigrant and former boxer, was already a notorious gangster and professional gambler when he met the sheltered twenty-one-year-old Simmons in her hometown of Fresno, California. Simmons was of Scottish-Welsh descent, born with a congenital heart condition, and so was kept under round-the-clock care throughout her youth, which took the form of a strict Mormon upbringing. In a tale reminiscent of countless Hollywood films, the innocent Simmons fell for the bad boy nicknamed Stumpy hook, line, and sinker, her story in this regard paralleling the one Warren Zevon would relive time and again in his romantic relationships throughout his entire adult life.

The couple married and had their only child, naming him Warren William. Within a year they'd settled in Chicago, which was still, in postwar America, the most corrupt city in the nation. Like his son, Zivotofsky would ignore the rigors of mature responsibility—wife, home, and child—to continue pursuing a rogue's life of constant turmoil. This led to several breakups and makeups, an on-again, off-again love/hate melodrama that was endured by the young Zevon until his ninth year, when Simmons finally left the unbridled Stumpy and headed back to Fresno and the welcoming arms of her Mormon family.

The seminal moment when all the stars align for the young Warren Zevon, recounted vividly in Crystal Zevon's *I'll Sleep When I'm Dead*, happens on Christmas Day 1956 in the living room of his new home in Fresno. Having returned from a successful gambling bender with a Chickering piano he'd won in a poker game, Stumpy proudly presents it to his son. Beverly, perhaps envisioning this as the tool of the devil being handed to her only child by what had become a bestial figure to her, demands it be removed at once. The young Zevon, craving the attention and love of his absentee father, clings to the piano as to a lifeline. Zivotofsky, having made a career of deducing which way the scales of fortune would lean, makes a dramatic play for the piano to stay in his son's possession, thus solidifying his place in the boy's heart. With desperation and rage in his eyes, Zivotofsky reaches for the carving knife meant for the holiday turkey. What happens next would forever burn an indelible mark on Zevon, as described by his ex-wife's passage in her 2007 account: "It was the chilling image of Stumpy's poker face as he hurled the knife at Beverly's head that made a lasting impression on Warren. Time stood still as he watched the lethal blade miss his mother's head by no more than an inch. Without a word, Beverly stalked out the door and went to her parents' house down the block." The scene ends with Zivotofsky sitting on the piano bench and telling his son that all the haughty Christian talk his mother had filled him with would never alter the truth. "You're a Jew, son," his father says. "Never forget that."

Whew.

Wherever you wish to begin deconstructing this drama, it does not simply end with “Studebaker.” However, the song may go a long way in describing why this eventful Christmas Day would *never* be over for Zevon, who would be haunted by it for the remaining forty-seven years of his life. In fact, nearly four decades hence, Zevon would pen a stirring review of his life as a musician going against the grain in “Piano Fighter” with its direct reference to his parents and the fateful Chickering piano: “I practiced hard; it was more than a whim / I played with grim determination, Jim.” The most telling lyric arrives in the song’s bridge with a not-so-subtle nod to what the piano would mean to Zevon as warrior companion and tender confidant—a suitable replacement for the human condition. “Ain’t going down that long, lonesome road,” Zevon sings with the bravado of an artist armed with his weapon of choice as family heirloom.

The never fully resolved aspect of Zevon’s nine-year-old experience is another reason why I may have been subconsciously attracted to “Studebaker.” For as long as I can remember, I have had a reoccurring dream wherein I cannot get to where I’m going. Doesn’t matter what setting: When I was in school, I could not get to the bus on time; when I was in college, to class on time; when I was in a rock ’n’ roll band, to the gig on time. As a writer, I could not make the looming deadline; and in almost every romantic relationship, I could not get the girl. To say the least, these dreams—or, more aptly, nightmares—are beyond frustrating, but it has gotten so comically relentless that over the past ten years or so I have had moments of déjà vu within the dream which prompt me to communicate to the conscious part of my brain that I am indeed dreaming: “Don’t you realize, you idiot, your subconscious is fucking with you again?”

I’m not sure when this dream cycle began for me or if similar nightmares were visited upon Warren Zevon. I had nothing like his traumatic childhood experience, although I had a few of my own not worth mentioning for the purposes of this volume, as had we all, the kind that shape our sense of self and place in the world. But suffice to say, the events depicted in “Studebaker” are a subconscious passion play of someone who has unresolved issues. The key to these issues for me is Zevon’s use of the actual Studebaker, a car: the American, masculine symbol of self-worth, ownership, freedom, and conveyance to another life and another identity. But perhaps more intriguing is the mention of Fresno as a destination, the place where a significant event has occurred that the narrator is trying to get back to but never will.

A couple of little tidbits from Zevon’s youth also need to be discussed here: His father was never far from his early life, while his mother was continuously there. It wasn’t as if the moment on the piano stool was the last Zevon would see of his father.

In fact, into his teen years Stumpy would lavish him with gifts, one of which was a 1962 Corvette—coincidental, when considering the song at hand—that Zevon drove around town with peacock pride. Stumpy frequently handed his son wads of cash, which Zevon used to buy fancier clothes than his teen pals could ever dream of, affording him the dashing reputation of being a gangster's son. "Warren bought lots and lots and lots and lots of clothes," recalls childhood friend Glenn Crocker in *I'll Sleep When I'm Dead*. "He was shopping all the time. He took me along everywhere to tell him how he looked."

Burt Stein, who as the head of the rock 'n' roll department radio promotion team at Elektra/Asylum, would accompany Zevon on his first two tours, made sure I understood this fascination with ornamental apparel: "Warren was always a clothes hound and a sharp dresser, and he was the first to compliment you on your attire, which I think he got from his dad, Stumpy. One of the things that he would do with me is if I showed up looking good with a nice sport coat on or something, he would take his thumb and his forefinger and kind of rub my lapel and he would say, 'Ahh, Burt . . . nice material.'"

George Gruel, Zevon's aide-de-camp for much of the late 1970s into the early '80s, concurs: "He spent a fortune on clothing and the guy was an impeccable dresser. He was trying to be the gentleman of rock 'n' roll. There was a store in Beverly Hills called Bijan. His name is chiseled in this crystal wall for being the customer of the month. And this is Beverly Hills! Of course, he'd slide across the stage and a one-thousand-dollar pair of Armani pants would be just *gone*."

Early in our discussions, Jordan shared with me his vivid memories of Stumpy through his visits with his dad: "We would go to the city of Commerce [near Los Angeles], where Grandpa was living, because you could gamble there, and my dad would say, 'Okay, here's what's going to happen. We're going to sit down. We're going to eat. He's going to give you a hundred-dollar bill. Just take it, don't argue, and move on.' And so I had that experience of sitting down at the casino, ordering a steak, and him handing me a crisp one-hundred-dollar bill. I'd say, 'Thank you,' and then we moved on. When I cleared out his apartment later on with dad it was a weird mix of *Ring* magazines and a bunch of really nice ties. I felt like I was in the middle of a Martin Scorsese film, which is probably why Martin has always been a fan of dad and vice versa."

Flush with winnings and the proceeds from other nefarious moneymaking schemes, Zivotofsky would later be instrumental in his son's career development, introducing him to music industry types as call-ins for favors or gambling debts, including one in San Francisco: a corpulent, cigar-smoking mover and shaker right out of central casting named Ben Shapiro, who also threw money at young Zevon's rough-and-tumble rock 'n' roll combo. Zevon told journalist Fred Schruers that later, when he followed "in the footsteps of Dylan" to Greenwich Village in pursuit of what he snidely described as "definitely a nonprofit enterprise" to play the folk houses like the famous Cafe Wha?, then nervously lost all of his fingerpicks in the hole of his cheap acoustic, he called Stumpy for the funds to keep going.

Zevon's mother would eventually accept her son's genuine love of the piano as a vehicle for expression. In fact, her marriage to Zivotofsky, which was never legally dissolved, had a second act, as her manipulative husband convinced his still impressionable young wife to leave her family once again and join him in his new home befitting a gangster, which overlooked the Pacific Ocean in San Pedro, California. It was there at Dana Junior High that Zevon honed his piano skills and musical chops enough to impress a teacher who got him an audience with the nearly eighty-year-old legendary Russian composer Igor Stravinsky. This is a story for another essay entirely, as it happened long after Mrs. Zivotofsky finally booted her criminal husband to the curb and started up with a roofer named Elmer, who would come between Zevon and his mother while challenging the boy incessantly throughout his teenage years. According to sources from the time, this second dysfunctional father figure would beat the young Zevon while inadvertently introducing his troubled stepson to alcohol through his well-stocked cabinet. "Elmer always hated Warren," Crystal Zevon shared with me. "He mercilessly teased him about being, you know, 'the kid with glasses who played the piano.'"

His piano-related battles with Elmer along with his lingering attachment to his father impelled Zevon to fully express his anti-establishment bent against his mother's patrician ways and the monster she was bedding. Eventually, after several runaway attempts, Elmer kicked the young rebel out of his house. Coincidentally, this is when Zevon began to dabble in local garage bands and warm to the idea that music could be not only a career but a way out of his disjointed childhood and an escape from what he learned from his peripatetic father were the chains of "normal life."

The image of the Studebaker as a symbol for Zevon's scandalous father, who gleefully flouted convention, has many interesting connections, not the least of which are the year of origin of the automotive brand's first electric vehicles (1902) and that of its gasoline models (1904). Smack in the middle of those two seminal years in American automotive history, 1903, William Zivotofsky is born. The manufacturer's heyday, however, came during the emergence of the most significant middle class ever formed by a republic in the 1950s when Studebaker merged with Packard to create an industry juggernaut, marking the period most associated with America's lasting fascination with the automobile and, along with it, rock 'n' roll. Significantly, this is the time when Warren Zevon witnessed his father heaving a knife at his mother's head over a piano he knew deep down he must own and conquer.

As it does in many Zevon songs of the period, "Desperados Under the Eaves," "Carmelita," "Empty Hearted Town," and "Join Me in L.A.," geography plays an important role in "Studebaker." The narrator's trek is due east from the scenic and artsy Pacific Coast town of Monterey, where years earlier, in June of 1967, the first of many counterculture musical festivals was held. Made famous by documentarian D. A. Pennebaker in his 1968 film *Monterey Pop*, the Monterey Pop Festival was the precursor to the mass hippie movement, heralding the overhyped Summer of Love that would bask in the California sunshine forevermore. He is driving to Fresno, back to his friends, his place of origin, his past, spurning the westward migration made by so many young people of the time looking to break free from the predetermined futures set forth by their parents. Our "low prospects man" is running counter to this movement. His is the voice emanating from the dreary 1970s, fraught with the heady notion that the revolution of love and peace has long been shattered by drug addictions, assassinations, the Manson murders, the tragedy at the Altamont festival, the Kent State killings, the unchecked escalation of the Vietnam War, and the Watergate scandal. By not having "traveled far," he is unaware of the extent of his scuttled future. He is a seeker, but instead of looking forward, looking out west to the frontier, he is in retreat.

> *I left my home in Monterey just another low prospects man*
> *I'd rather work in the foundry than put fishes in a can*
> *I'm twenty-five and I haven't traveled far*
> *And I've spent all my money on this misbegotten car*

The opening lines, as in any good short story, reveal the background of our protagonist: a wandering, unemployable man watching his prime slip away thanks to his having rejected a lower-middle-class existence to chase the dream of *anything* better. The narrator's choice of car, likely hoisted upon him by his lack of fortune (a prime Zevon theme), is an out-of-date model, a relic of a bygone American age. Of course the car breaks down, as all illusions eventually must: Here, the car functions as a symbol for virility and power, a strong resistance to maturity, and the futility of trying to refigure the past.

In this way the Studebaker, an anachronistic symbol of masculine invincibility, becomes the pathetic relic of yesteryear, not unlike Zevon's father, who with his gangster ways must have seemed to a teenage boy invincible but now only seems pathetic and sad. This also reflects Zevon's nomadic origins as a songwriter, moving stealthily through several incarnations: writing jingles and sound track one-offs, trying to be a pop star, a folkie, and then a bandleader, from there honing his craft through the haze of alcohol and finally abandoning his roots to live as an expat abroad in Spain before returning home to begin his career anew, rejuvenated and in many ways reinvented. Forever seeking a definition, Zevon tried on a myriad of new faces and personalities, shedding skins like a reptile.

This search for creative identity, reasons Crystal Zevon, was again rooted in Zevon's familial turmoil and his descent into the bottle. "I don't think you can separate those two," she insisted to me when I pressed her on the subject. "I think alcoholism is something he endured, but the emotions that would rise to the surface that would be unleashed when he drank had everything to do with trying to reconcile things with his parents and his past and, I think, yes, this macho image.

"When I first met him, he told me all about his father having been in jail and how he needed Warren to write a letter to the judge and go to court and testify what a good father he had been, and it was agonizing for Warren, because, of course, he wasn't *really* a good father. But, at the same time, Warren loved that image of the gangster. He very much glorified his father's exploits. Then when he'd be drunk he would often say, 'I think he killed people.' That was agonizing."

I was speeding south on ninety-nine when the manifold started smokin'
I ran her off the shoulder and now the axle's broken

As anyone with even a rudimentary understanding of the automobile knows, the axle is a crucial component to keeping the vehicle moving forward. Its demise forces the car to the shoulder as the verse describes. The car has abandoned him. He counted on its heritage and even, according to the choruses, invested all of his money in the damn thing, as Zevon had surely spent much emotion on his father. An impeccably literate man, Zevon chose his words very carefully, which is reflected in all of his work. The placement of the rarely used *misbegotten* instead of words like *contemptible* or *despicable, wretched*, or *miserable* provides further insight. Another meaning for *misbegotten* centers on a plan that has gone awry: The idea of even attempting to go home again, as author Thomas Wolfe once warned, is a dead end. (Interesting note: The book that features Wolfe's famous title *You Can't Go Home Again* was, like "Studebaker," posthumously published. In this case, the novel was taken from a larger, unfinished work). *Misbegotten* can also mean "ill-conceived" or "harebrained," all terms an acute observer might use to describe the attempt to retrospectively fix sins long since buried.

What follows then would be the sound of the crushing realization of the past, which is in the blood coursing through our veins; the instincts and genetic damage we receive from our parents; domestic violence, incorrigible behavior, a flat rejection of maturity, alcoholism, a fascination with the outlaw life at the peril of all who may love or count on us.

When the subject of Stumpy came up in our discussion, his friend and collaborator, Waddy Wachtel laughed nervously and said, "One day as we're getting to know each other Warren says, 'My father said to me, "If you had any guts at all you'd take a gun and shoot yourself."' I went, 'Excuse me? I'm sorry. What? Your father said that to you? Nice. Okay, what exactly did your father do? My father was in the shoe business.' He said, 'Yeah, my father was a gangster.' And I remember I said to him, 'Jesus fucking Christ, man. No wonder you're the way you are!'"

Indeed:

It made a sound that cracked my heart in half
and with only half a half pint of vodka left

Zevon did in fact finish a song more specifically about his parents' relationship and think enough of it to include on his first Asylum album. Unlike "Studebaker," it does not deal in an only child's loss or feelings of regret with passing time. It also dispenses with symbolism. The story, like the title, is so blatant it could be argued it is about as straightforward an autobiographical expression as Zevon ever conceived. This time, though, while he is more direct in the telling, the composer decides to sing "Mama Couldn't Be Persuaded" as a third-person narrative and concentrate on the more harrowing aspect of his parents' courtship.

"If my dad felt his mother kept my grandfather away, then at the same time, I can play devil's advocate and say, 'Well, that's not who you wanted as an influence,'" reasons Jordan. "But that was the thing, you know. Grandpa bought him a piano, so it's that kind of dynamic that really sucks for a mom, which is the dad can walk into the picture and say, 'Hey! We're going on this cool road trip and I'm going to let you take a hit off my cigarette,' which seems so attractive to a young man, but [is] not necessarily a good thing for him."

Like many of the songs on *Warren Zevon*, "Mama Couldn't Be Persuaded" finds humor in the combative dysfunction of an ill-suited couple while providing the characters a requiem for their confused lives together. Conversely, "Studebaker" is forlornly angry, its frustrated narrator unable to reach his destination, and instead of looking inward blaming the conveyance, the road, the trek. Here, Zevon confronts the destiny of an obviously ill-fated romance between a "gamblin' man" and the smitten woman who could not be persuaded to ignore his advances:

> And my mama couldn't be persuaded
> When they pleaded with their daughter
> Don't marry that gamblin' man
> When they pleaded with her
> No, no nevertheless
> I said my mama couldn't be persuaded
> when they pleaded with her,
> "Daughter, don't marry that gamblin' man."

"Mama Couldn't Be Persuaded" also differs starkly from "Studebaker" musically, in both tempo and melody, the former played with the aggressive force of a country-rock song taking the listener through the whirlwind courtship orchestrated by an obviously predatory male character (the narrator's father) with moral flaws who preys upon the innocence of a young girl (his mother). Within a year, Zevon would revisit this theme from a father's perspective ("Tenderness on the Block"), experiencing the birth of his only daughter before recording the follow-up to *Warren Zevon*, *Excitable Boy*. And while "Studebaker" is sung with sweet melancholia, even when the narrator is railing against his fate, the song Zevon decided to officially record and put on this amazingly honest and sometimes confessional album is not. The narrator of "Mama Couldn't Be Persuaded" is as matter-of-fact as the one describing the exploits of the murderous outlaw brothers Frank and Jesse James in the opening track that precedes it.

Here, as well as in "Frank and Jesse James" and, frankly, many of Zevon's most poignant songs, he is practicing what poet John Keats, a Romantic-period contemporary of one of Zevon's heavy influences, Lord Byron, called "negative capability." Originated in the works of William Shakespeare, "negative capability," the eschewing of a specific philosophy in order to present both sides of a conflict, which allows the writer to better sympathize with his characters, runs deep in Zevon's oeuvre. This is partly due to Zevon's belief that destiny dominates the human experience, holding us in its sway and therefore removing responsibilty and leaving fate to the spin of a wheel. We both shared a knowing chuckle when Crystal Zevon told me he loved to watch game shows when composing.

Zevon's mother, ever the true gambler, shows no signs of budging on her love for a man so clearly wrong for her or, really, for anyone ("Gambler tried to be a family man / Though it didn't suit his style"), forcing him to merely present her situation as devoid of a hero/villain. Zevon even ends one verse pushing through the dramatic "fourth wall" and playfully winking at the listener: "She was determined that she wanted Bill / They'd all be offended at the mention still / If they heard this song, which I doubt they will."

The final line of the last verse tells us all we need to know about the effect this mess has on the innocent bystander, our humble narrator—evoking Anthony Burgess's demented criminal protagonist, Alex, in *A Clockwork Orange*: "They all went to pieces when the bad luck hit / Stuck in the middle, I was the kid." Of course, unlike Alex, who is at first the novel's predator and then its prey, the young Zevon is plagued simply by having been born. These are real people, not characters, and he is not merely a songwriter working through this gnawing psychological conundrum, nor is his father literarily transformed as a classic American car nor his mother the elusive home to which there is no way to return. For being born *is* the grand crapshoot, foisted upon each and every person. Some are born with the proverbial "silver spoon" in their mouths and others in abject poverty. Some are born to privilege in love, comfort, and financial prosperity and some are born into pure chaos. In "Studebaker" Zevon chooses his conveyance, but in "Mama Couldn't Be Persuaded," he is thrust into a cauldron of his parents' making.

Jackson Browne, the song's producer, believed "Mama Couldn't Be Persuaded" opened a window into its author's makeup: "For lovers of Warren Zevon songs, there is always an insight about him in each one, and when you consider this song and who his father was and who his mother was, [it] might provide some clues on his psychological makeup and how he turned out to be who *he* was. His dad was a Russian Jew gambler and his mother a Mormon . . . gambler; if you listen to the song, it more or less implies that."

Like all great artists, Zevon works through the issue of his past, his lineage, his blood and tissue with meticulous calculation, perfecting his expression of everything from sheer disappointment in his own failed decisions to trust his vehicle as a means of salvation ("Studebaker") to a more direct approach of seeing it as dumb, young, lust/love gone awry that ultimately achieved his existence ("Mama Couldn't Be Persuaded").

The fate of these two songs—one eventually abandoned, the other finished and added to his first album—lies in a place Zevon always felt simultaneously at home with and at times weirdly lost in: his machismo. In much of his work it acts as a defense against the densest of subjects; love, life, death. For while it is sprinkled with several subtle and not so subtle references to Zevon's past and his persistently shifting moods, "Studebaker" also remains for me one of the single greatest expressions of male emotion set to music. This is a song from deep inside the heart of a tough guy whose otherwise outward appearance is cloaked in off-color humor or bedraggled by drink or violence.

It is a gray-Sunday-afternoon, hungover song of regret. It is also a song of surrender. There are so many punches you can take before you succumb. But the man is expected to suck it up, and within that chasm comes an echo so fierce it needs an outlet. There is a preponderance of Warren Zevon "guy" songs, but this is one that hits home, literally. The only thing that comes close is Kris Kristofferson's pitying "Sunday Morning Coming Down," a song so full of male regret it borders on complaint without becoming one. No one who sings it with a too-many-cigarettes growl should be asked to explain it.

Kristofferson's confession is as conciliatory as the tough-guy voice can be, unable to face retribution with being stoned, the narrator coming to the terrible realization by the light of day that none of the cussin', fightin', or boozin' has erased the haunting feeling of abandonment. "Studebaker" also is a song about regret, memory, unresolved father issues, fear of retribution, but mostly it is a song about abandonment, and not only abandonment, but repeated abandonment: "The damn Studebaker is breaking down *again*." It is a cyclical curse, a branding from childhood that will be played out again and again for Zevon with those he counts on and for those who count on him. It is the bane of the one who is trying to escape (and escape is a major theme in most of Zevon's work) that the vehicle for such a getaway—whether the piano, car, clothes, alcohol, drugs, women, stardom—will never suffice. It cannot salve the scars of youth. It cannot help the narrator return to the scene of the traumatic event and correct it.

"The song keeps on 'breaking down,'" Jordan surmises more than a decade after he discovered the demo. Nevertheless, he also shared with me the original version of "Studebaker" as it was initially recorded for his maternal grandmother, admitting he had listened to that version quite a bit as a kid, as it became the preferred song in his father's catalog. And so I pressed him as to why he thought it was lost to the ages. He took a moment and then exhaled. "My theory is that the version that he recorded for my grandmother, which is almost verbatim the one that I do, no matter how many times he would revisit it later on would be one of those things where he would forget to do *this* part or he'd forget to do *that* part, or he would forget even the tiniest little thing like the 'With only half a half pint of vodka left. . . . ' And once he was sober that line wasn't as fun to sing, so it didn't have the same kind of intensity to it. And he kept trying to find it and he would record it and say, 'Ugh. It's *not* happening.' I think that is what you hear on the demo that I found in his storage space. And so when I did it, I went back and got David Lindley and Jorge [Calderón] and Waddy [Wachtel] and all the original cats and just said, 'We're going to do it the way this demo is,' and that's why it came out the way it did, because that is 1972 Warren Zevon personified."

"Oh, I knew the song, because we played it for years," remembers Wachtel. "That was a sweet, emotional time doing the *Every Sandwich* record. I just played it the way I remember it, and it worked out. I didn't attach that much to it. If I was to stop and look at it emotionally, I'd never get through a lot of songs. You look at it as the musical work that it is and try to capture the best performance of it, and from then on then it takes on its own life. I was proud of Jordan. He did good."

It is the original demo recorded on Tule's mother's home tape recorder that would haunt Zevon for years. It had never been heard before outside of the family until after our long discussion one lazy August afternoon when Jordan sent it to me. Once opened, the now digitized piece of Zevon's personal history comes to life.

The opening piano chording is gorgeous, so delicately played, as it might be by a young man presenting his work to his only son's grandmother, who ironically may have still been wary of her daughter's choice of man. Perhaps given this rare opportunity at twenty-five to express through his tortured art a glimpse into what growing up in a broken home had done to him or *for* him, he lays it all out there.

His vocal is strong, without the hint of emotional detachment heard on the *Preludes* collection, Zevon telling the tale as if it is happening to him, not as if he's trying to recall it. When he croons, "I'm up against it all, like a leaf against the wind . . ." and leads into the chorus, he strikes the ascending notes with a passion heard on some of the best work that fills *Warren Zevon*, which proudly brims with a wonderfully dramatic naiveté. There is no hesitancy. The man playing this is assured that this is the song that rattled around in his psyche and came pouring out as natural as breathing. It is a remarkable performance that informs the listener of his fears, passions, and hopes, all out there in front of him.

It is this perfect moment in time that he could not dream of re-creating, no matter how many times over the years he tried. In other words, the song never gets there. It breaks down and disappoints the expectations of its author. And so Zevon made sure it was not completed or set in stone for posterity . . . yet. He abandons the song his son would eventually find decades later and record as a tribute to his late father, making sure the rest of the world would hear his lost cause.

Perhaps, in the end, Warren Zevon is the Studebaker.

Warren Zevon's passport, October 13, 1971. *Courtesy of the Crystal Zevon Collection, photo by Crystal Zevon*

"Poor Poor Pitiful Me"

You have been trapped in the inescapable net of ruin by your own want of sense.

—AESCHYLUS

Music critic turned Bruce Springsteen's manager Jon Landau said in Crystal Zevon's book that what he found unusual in Warren Zevon was "a high level of perseverance mixed with equal parts self-inflicted adversity." This is borne out beautifully in the opening lines of one of Zevon's more beloved songs, "Poor Poor Pitiful Me," a self-effacing serenade of paranoia and guilt masked by a preternatural fear of women.

It is first and foremost a rollicking thumper, so a mere review of its lyrics hardly does it justice. To hear Zevon bark out the words as if rough-riding his way up San Juan Hill, later accentuated in raucous live performances of the song, is quite extraordinary. He is rallied along by a musical hyperventilation that does not let up for three minutes and four seconds of *yahoo!* The best thing to do really is just put the damn record on and let it wash over you.

> *Well I lay my head on the railroad track*
> *Waiting on the Double E*
> *But the train don't run by here no more*
> *Poor poor pitiful me*

There are far more stellar compositions on Zevon's first Asylum record, but none may be more adored by fans. A close rival is "I'll Sleep When I'm Dead," which can be added to the exclusive list in which "Poor Poor Pitiful Me" resides. These two songs in particular fill in the colors of Zevon's growing paint-by-numbers image as a merrily twisted soul. Not many songwriters were mining this territory during his era—if Zevon indeed could be said to have belonged to an "era." Only Randy Newman comes close and in some ways surpasses this level of treachery. But Newman rarely placed himself in his songs, choosing instead to almost always use a character's voice to probe the darker corners of the human psyche—what Newman biographer Kevin Courrier calls the "untrustworthy narrator." Zevon unflinchingly put himself *inside* his own crafted dementia and serenaded it with impish delight.

"Poor Poor Pitiful Me" is replete with overtones of autobiographical confession— granted, it's masked in black humor and mock hillbilly hoots, but it's confessional nonetheless. It exults in victimhood, another primary color of the Zevon palette that he cultivated through his art and more so his lifestyle, which around Los Angeles from the late 1960s on became the stuff of legend. This is why, among other things, "Poor Poor Pitiful Me" is a snapshot of his hard-line position of how he viewed himself in the eyes of the women he loved and who loved him, the ones he fucked and who fucked him. It is a song of fear, and not the fear usually found in pop, folk, or rock songs—so chock-full as they are of trite worries about loneliness, rejection, loss, and the phone call that never comes.

Oh, the call comes, all right. Most importantly, it is answered.

This is righteous fear, well-earned and fraught with danger. Zevon's diaries, as presented in *I'll Sleep When I'm Dead*, reveal intellectual fisticuffs with his raging libido and the assertion that for him sexuality was a series of constant battles: existentially, morally, and, of course, physically. He claims with no sense of irony that he must have a daily sexual release to maintain his sanity, even going as far as once explaining to his then lover Julia Mueller that orgasm was akin to being "regular."

Crystal expounded on this key point when we spoke in early 2017: "I kind of knew for a long time, but . . . really confirmed when I was doing interviews for my book, that Warren was a sex addict and he needed that physical part, and when he didn't have a girlfriend per se he had women where, well, it was like going to the store to pick up a carton of milk. He had these relationships that were purely sexual, with no emotional attachment. I'm not saying that he didn't share insights with some of them, but that's what it was *really* about."

For an addictive personality, sex would fit the mold set by an already Herculean consumption of barbiturates and booze. This sentiment creeps into many of Zevon's songs dealing with intermittent, almost toxic relationships that, while providing a deviant sense of pleasure, would inevitably lead to the kind of burn that is not easily salved. The predatory women humorously (one would assume) described in "Poor Poor Pitiful Me" would be further deconstructed in Zevon's future work, as if he was trying to define the cause of a behavior that led him to grapple with a higher sense of self.

"When you were the woman he loved, he placed you on a pedestal," Crystal continues. "And they became somewhat of an extension of him. They were by and large exceptionally intelligent and they would also come from a normal background with more traditional morality codes."

I asked his daughter, Ariel, a young woman who grew up with a father whose romantic proclivities sometimes swerved into, to put it mildly, the idiosyncratic, to provide some insight. "You could write an entire book about that," she chuckled. "He was a passionate creative artist, so he felt things very much in extremes, *very* deeply, which can torment a person and can distort reality. So I do think he loved: In his passions, his feelings were true. His intense feelings for women were true in the *moments*. On the other hand, I saw him be very two-faced about women, but also with any relationship, really, whether friendships or romantic. He could be all-in, amazed with them, and completely in love, and then turn around and be a complete asshole and completely diminish the worth of the woman he was just adoring. So, needless to say, as his daughter, it has given me plenty to work with as a woman on my own and in relationships."

Zevon's last personal manager, Brigette Barr, was quite candid about her client's mercurial attitudes toward the women in his life when we spoke in February of 2017: "He could be hot and cold very fast. There was a period where he dated a lot of women, but there were certain women that he would hurt terribly, but they would be around. He was there and then suddenly he wasn't, and then there was a new one that would come in for a second and then in the dark times he'd have a certain girlfriend. I think he had a real love/hate thing with women. I really do."

Yet Barr made a point of telling me that Zevon had shown her nothing but the utmost respect in a business in which she had to work, in her estimation, "ten times as hard as a man" to compete. "He was always so supportive," she said with conviction. "Completely trusting of what I said and always took my business advice. There was never any second-guessing. Sometimes as a woman you get that. Not [with] Warren. He respected me equally. There was an open honesty right from the start."

Still, as she made perfectly clear, she never became romantically involved with Zevon in all the time she worked with him. "I would never have wanted to be in *that* kind of a relationship with him, because I knew what he would be."

"When I did interviews for my book, there were a lot of women who think 'Accidentally Like a Martyr' is about them," adds Crystal. "I can tell you when he wrote it, it was about us. I know this because he called me and played it. But that doesn't mean that he didn't let other people believe that it was about them as well, because that's what he did with women."

This propensity to love, to be hurt, and in turn to hurt, revealed itself in Zevon's use of sex, if perhaps not in life then in song, as a kind of experiment, not unlike novelist Aldous Huxley's ostensibly scientific dalliance with mescaline in 1954's *Doors of Perception*. Zevon was an avid reader of Huxley and mentions him in his diaries as an influence. This is not to say that experimentation for experimentation's sake with sex as a vehicle for his art was the songwriter's excuse for acting at times like an insatiable beast with women, but the results of the experiments found the subjects either at fault or at the core of his addiction. "Warren didn't really need to be with 'other' women," Crystal Zevon concludes with some humor. "But he needed to be with 'a' woman."

In "Genius," a song from his penultimate 2002 album, *My Ride's Here* (cowritten with many celebrated authors, this one with fellow songwriter, Larry Klein), Zevon captures this lifelong combativeness with the fairer sex in striking perspective. In a rare first-person/third-person romp through many paradigms of men and women who are intellectually and sexually disingenuous, he provides the poetic answer to life's query on his irascible heart:

> *I've got a bitter pot of je ne sais quoi*
> *Guess what—I'm stirring it with a monkey's paw*
> *Since I saw you coming out of my barber's shop*
> *In that skimpy little halter top*
>
> *Did you light the candles? Did you put on "Kind of Blue"?*
> *Did you use that Ivy League voodoo on him, too?*
> *He thinks he'll be all right but he doesn't know for sure*
> *Like every other unindicted coconspirator*

Clearly admitting his inability to escape trouble in a sexual construct, while first accusing the predatory female of using the old blues trope "voodoo" to seduce him into peril, Zevon then uses the end of the second verse to lay blame at his own doorstep, mischievously referring to what many in his surroundings saw as a flawed genius running amok through the playground of Hollywood while using rock stardom as an excuse for libertinism, going so far as to juxtapose the singularly brilliant Albert Einstein with the troubled womanizing drug fiend Charlie Sheen:

> *Albert Einstein was a ladies' man*
> *While he was working on his universal plan*
> *He was making out like Charlie Sheen*
> *He was a genius*

The last line in the song combines a mysterious if not somberly seductive resting of his case.

If I could only get my record clean
I'd be a genius

Zevon's unclean record begins with a declaration of despair twenty-six years prior, in "Poor Poor Pitiful Me":

These young girls won't let me be
Lord have mercy on me
Woe is me

But one would not have to wait a quarter century to feel Zevon's wrath. It is no coincidence that perhaps his meanest song, "The French Inhaler," follows "Poor Poor Pitiful Me" on *Warren Zevon*, effectively wiping the smirk from that song's coda. After hearing Zevon perform it solo over many years in the late 1980s throughout the '90s and beyond, I find that the studio version almost seems rushed, as if it's trying to bring the listener down from the galloping high of the previous track, or as if it can't bear to linger too long on its scathing commentary. Its composer never again made that mistake, and to be sure, he selected the live, piano-only, dirgelike version from 1994's *Learning to Flinch* for the 1996 Rhino retrospective *I'll Sleep When I'm Dead: An Anthology*: Every word—Zevon proclaimed it was one of the only times he wrote lyrics to a song before he had a melody—is clearly pronounced, as if sharp knives slashed at the ghosts of his past:

How're you going to make your way in the world
When you weren't cut out for working?
When your fingers are slender and frail
How're you going to get around in this sleazy bedroom town
If you don't put yourself up for sale?

Where will you go with your scarves and your miracles?
Who's gonna know who you are?
Drugs and wine and flattering light
You must try it again till you get it right
Maybe you'll end up with someone different every night

It is difficult to not interpret the lyrics to "The French Inhaler" as anything other than an attack. All of the angst presented as humor that spices "Poor Poor Pitiful Me" is ground into a fine dust and funneled into this musical diatribe. Set against a gorgeous melody (one of Zevon's most effective songwriting traits was to meld vitriol with warmth) the lyrics don't let up on their subject for a moment:

You said you were an actress
Yes, I believe you are
I thought you'd be a star
So I drank up all the money, yes I drank up all the money
With these phonies in this Hollywood bar
These friends of mine in this Hollywood bar

His theme of victimhood presented in the damaging sexual excursions of "Poor Poor Pitiful Me" is now put on trial in "The French Inhaler":

Loneliness and frustration
We both came down with an acute case
When the lights came up at two I caught a glimpse of you
And your face looked like something
Death brought with him in his suitcase

Your pretty face it looked so wasted
Another pretty face devastated

Whereas "Poor Poor Pitiful Me" was meant as a sweeping allegation regarding what Zevon is clearly describing as the predatory nature of women, "The French Inhaler" had one particular villain in mind: Marilyn "Tule" Livingston, Zevon's live-in love for much of the late '60s and the mother of his only son, Jordan. It was to be, as Jordan shared with me in 2016, "a fuck-you to my mother for cheating on him," but one that was never lost on its subject, who would often sip wine while marveling at its rebuke. "The story, as it was told to me, was that my dad was being a prick to the tenth degree," Jordan recalls. "So my mom said, 'Okay, well, you want to see what it feels like?' And that's where the song came from."

Jordan describes him and his mom listening to "The French Inhaler," as she would mouth the lyrics and cry. "At the same time, she'd say, 'Isn't that fucking brilliant? Listen to how good that is!,'" he told me. "Her own 'fuck you' song and she still recognized that my father was a genius. I would say, 'But this is a mean song about you!' But she could disassociate herself from the content and say, 'I know, but God, it's good.'"

Zevon's other battle with women centered on his chronic infidelities and a hypocritical possessive side that he grappled with his whole life. His early years were largely a series of rambling benders spent with mostly male friends, wherein women provided sexual or affectionate refuge, and the fights could be epic. "One of my first childhood memories is my parents screaming at each other," remembers Jordan.

However, these pale in comparison to Zevon's longer and highly combative romantic relationship with his wife, Crystal. Mrs. Zevon is quite descriptive in her book when exposing her husband's sudden bursts of unprovoked rage, during which he would become physically violent, at times brandishing guns or storming onto the bar circuit to cause mayhem. Much of the time, these mood swings would culminate in a self-loathing plea for forgiveness. Just the same, they were self-centered and inwardly hostile, providing fertile ground from which the songwriter could harvest not only some of his most deeply disturbing lyrics, but also his most heartfelt sentiments. "Warren was never violent with me except when he drank," explains Crystal. "We could argue, but he would never lash out physically or get really violent, and he could be very tender."

Zevon's greatest triumph may be that his affectionate, almost out-of-character ballad "Hasten Down the Wind" precedes the biting "Poor Poor Pitiful Me," which gives way to the spiteful "The French Inhaler." This pattern, established on his versatile first Asylum album, *Warren Zevon*, would endure throughout all of his work. That "Hasten Down the Wind" was the first of Zevon's songs the sweetly provocative Linda Ronstadt would choose to cover (she would famously sing four) is not a quirk of fate. The vulnerability completely absent in the ensuing songs, save the boozy mise-en-scène "Desperados Under the Eaves," overflows here. Featuring a stunningly beautiful harmony by Zevon's friend the legendary vocalist Phil Everly, the song is honey poured upon honey:

She tells him she thinks she needs to be free
He tells her he doesn't understand
She takes his hand
She tells him nothing's working out the way they planned
She's so many women
He can't find the one who was his friend
So he's hanging on to half her heart

He can't have the restless part
So he tells her to hasten down the wind

Zevon is still the victim, but there is an acceptance of shared guilt and undeniably a shared loneliness. Recalling Harold Arlen and Johnny Mercer's seminal torch song "One for My Baby (and One More for the Road)," which was given haunting resonance by Frank Sinatra, this is the softer side of the sinner serving penance for his inequities. Even Zevon's voicing takes you by surprise, as he hangs in a higher register than he does for the rest of the album, sounding as if he were on the verge of tears. The song preludes "Poor Poor Pitiful Me" in the prescient manner that "The French Inhaler" acts as the musical triad's malicious epilogue.

His baring of the darkened soul only to turn tail and run in the opposite direction into the demented protagonist of "Poor Poor Pitiful Me" reveals much of what made Warren Zevon's creative motor run. He returned to this theme again and again, as if trying to finally face the part of himself that accepted the role of victim and the other that lashed out to avoid being further humiliated by making victims of the women in his life.

In the opening track to 1991's *Mr. Bad Example*, "Finishing Touches," Zevon once again paints a portrait of a doomed romance, but this time he is careful to include the narrator's part in its ruination:

I'm getting tired of you
You're getting tired of me
And it's the final act
Of our little tragedy

So don't feign indignation, it's a fait accompli
You can screw everybody I've ever known
But I still won't talk to you on the phone

It's a hopeless cause, there's no use crying
And I can die, you can die, we can die trying
Thanks anyway, no use hangin' around
You try to put the finishing touches on me

The song's second verse offers a glimpse into what is initially described in "Poor Poor Pitiful Me"—the glutton for punishment whose repeated wounds are self-inflicted:

You say it's all my fault
Who's keeping score?
Some people like to be punished
They keep coming back for more

And Zevon would be back for more, with the passionate strains of "Accidentally Like a Martyr" (*Excitable Boy*, 1978); the murderous nymphet of "Jeannie Needs a Shooter" (*Bad Luck Streak in Dancing School*, 1980); the unfaithful minx in "The Hula Hula Boys" (*The Envoy*, 1982); and the parade of undesirables that inherit "Sentimental Hygiene" (*Sentimental Hygiene*, 1987). All these songs carry the mangled genes of "Poor Poor Pitiful Me."

Perhaps tellingly, a demo of "Poor Poor Pitiful Me" originally featured a different opening verse, which was scratched for the above reference to the ironic suicide-by-train image, which could easily mirror the gender reversal of the iconic damsel in distress from the silent-film era of a woman being tied to the rails by an ebony-clad villain. What was later resurrected for live performances and even slid into the second verse of a duet by Jackson Browne and Bonnie Raitt for the star-studded posthumous tribute *Enjoy Every Sandwich* blatantly reveals the length and breadth of the song's implications:

Well, I met a girl from the Vieux Carré
Down in Yokohama
She picked me up and she throwed me down
I said, "Please don't hurt me, mama"

Trying to ignore the clever use of a town square in New Orleans French Quarter set beside the second largest city in Japan is less vexing than discounting the fact that it describes a grown man begging for mercy as he is being violently heaved to the floor by a woman. We may assume Zevon's exclamatory use of *mama* is more in the blues sense of the word and less a Freudian connection to his own mother, who was a devout Mormon and therefore likely to find any of this behavior abhorrent. Yet Zevon would be quite forthcoming about how his father was perceived by his mother's family, which would inform a sense of victimization in his own roguish existence: "My mother's relationship with her parents, Elsworth and Helen, was a tremendously destructive factor in the lives of both my father and me," he told friend and rock critic Paul Nelson in 1982. "I was told my birth nearly killed my mother. They treated my father like a vagabond and roustabout. It must have been terribly uncomfortable for him, so he wasn't there a lot of the time. I wouldn't have been either, if I'd had a choice."

"Warren's mother abandoned him in such a different way than his father," says Crystal Zevon. "His father might kick him out when he was mad at him, but he always took him back and he was kind of there for him, while his mother, who by all superficial appearances was normal, divorced his father without telling him. She married Elmer, this macho guy who had come to fix their roof, and when [Warren] came home one day, there was his stepfather."

Nevertheless, it is a fantastically alliterative vehicle to illuminate a song about being harmed by women. This verse was replaced in the *Warren Zevon* version with one about a woman whose name he refuses to utter to protect either the guilty or the innocent. She meets the narrator in West Hollywood and works him over like the infamous outlaw Jesse James. The idea that Zevon would equate the subject of a presumably romantic tryst to a notorious nineteenth-century murderous criminal becomes more poignant when considering the song was also important to Zevon for another reason: Not unlike "Studebaker," it reflects the ghosts of his past, specifically that of his father.

He confessed as much to VH1 in 2002 mere months before he died: "Essentially, my father was a gangster in the 1950s in Los Angeles. I'm really not that comfortable talking about it in any more detail than that and never have been. But certainly, to use that term the critics always like to use, it 'informs' my work and my approach to it, and I guess, my identity. My friend Tom McGuane, the novelist, wrote a book called *Panama*, in which the protagonist is a rock musician who has the delusion that his father is Jesse James. And I said to him, 'Tom, this is about me, my father *was* Jesse James!' And he said, 'I know, you're the only one who gets it.'"

The tale of the outlaw brothers who keep on "riding, riding, riding" to clear their names reads as a poem of their exploits, neither forgiving nor condemning. Only four songs later, in "Poor Poor Pitiful Me," the composer would give due props to the female predator who has robbed him of his treasure, heart, and dignity: "She was a credit to her gender."

The roaring live version from 1980's *Stand in the Fire* picks up the tempo with shredding guitars and pounding drums and features a far more snarling vocal performance than the original. Playing off his airtight band, Zevon calls for his road manager George Gruel halfway through. Gruel, a heavily bearded mountain of a man, who would customarily wear an ALL HELL'S BREAKING LOOSE T-shirt, begins berating the audience, "Dance or I'll kill ya!" Gruel recalled the nightly ritual when I spoke to him in the spring of 2015: "Warren came up with the line 'Dance or I'll kill you, and I have the means!' It got people going. At the end of every show, the crew would carry him off on a stretcher!"

The song's placement on *Stand in the Fire* is notable, much like its spot on *Warren Zevon*. "Poor Poor Pitiful Me" rumbles in at the finish of "The Sin," which almost reads like a preface. Zevon screams the lyrics as a high priest of the Spanish Inquisition forcing a prisoner on the rack to spit out anything that resembles contrition. Although there is no gender here, there *is* a villain and the voice of the wronged.

> *It's none of my business but if I may*
> *Remind you of the time when you did something*
> *You knew was wrong, it wasn't called a crime*
> *And I'm not saying that you should give*
>
> *A sucker an even break, I'm talking about the time*
> *That you were cruel for cruelty's sake*
> *How you gonna pay for the sin?*

Musically, "Poor Poor Pitiful Me" is one of Zevon's sincerest nods to country music, specifically the country music being mined by his Californian brethren for the first half of the 1970s: the Appalachian/Bakersfield throwback sound that was co-opted by bands such as the Flying Burrito Brothers and a later incarnation of the Byrds (both pushed into the genre by the enigmatic Gram Parsons), and eventually the Eagles, among many others—all of them flying in the face of traditional Nashville country music that dominated the airwaves at the time.

Beginning with the return to roots prevalent on his 1968 album *John Wesley Harding* and his work with the Band on *The Basement Tapes* (not to diminish the seismic impact of the Band's *Music from Big Pink* that rose from those sessions), Bob Dylan would influence an entire movement away from the psychedelic sounds of the period to American backwoods melodies and traditional instrumentation. Suddenly, country and western music heretofore reviled as racist nonsense by the hippie set and folk enthusiasts began to take hold. And although Zevon's songs "Hasten Down the Wind" and even "Poor Poor Pitiful Me" were dutifully covered by Californian country darling Linda Ronstadt with great aplomb, their composer more than occasionally worked in this style.

There are flirtations with county music all over *Warren Zevon*, and when motivated, as in "A Bullet for Ramona" off his mostly unrecognized debut *Wanted Dead or Alive* and the *Mr. Bad Example* cut "Heartache Spoken Here," Zevon created truly formulaic country songs. Despite the western flourishes, specifically embodied by its infectiously derivative piano break, I don't consider the aforementioned "Frank and Jesse James" necessarily a country song, but more of a folk ballad with clear classical overtones, as noted above, additionally instantiated by the gentle ritard and ensuing reprise of the opening piano lines that preface the song's final verse. There is a distinct country flair to "Mama Couldn't Be Persuaded" on the same record—certainly Jackson Browne thought so, as he chose the song nearly forty years later to include in his set at the late, great Band alum Levon Helm's Midnight Ramble in Woodstock, New York, and still later toured it with country artists Larry Campbell and Teresa Williams in 2015. However, during a solo tour in 1993–'94, Zevon dropped all pretense and stripped "Poor Poor Pitiful Me" down to its bare essentials, picking away at the countermelody on acoustic guitar with effects that gave it the timbre of a banjo. At one point during the nearly ten-minute version he begins singing Silas S. Steele's Civil War–era standard "Rose of Alabama."

Returning our attention to Ronstadt, who was an early admirer and perhaps aside from Jackson Browne the leading advocate of Zevon's rare musical and lyrical talents, her performance of "Poor Poor Pitiful Me" may actually be more tongue-in-cheek than its author's original. "Linda had such a good ear for songs," recalls fellow songwriter J. D. Souther, whose career also greatly benefited from Ronstadt covering his work. "She not only knew which songs were good, she knew *why* they were good and *how* they were good, which are kind of two different things, too, and she also knew how to sing them. And I especially loved her recordings of Warren's songs. I always felt like she really ironed the kinks out of them and put them in a place where the average listener could hear them because they were delivered with this magnificent voice and power."

It is as if Ronstadt understood the song's overt misogyny as pure satire and not as cringing anecdote. This is true of many women who have interpreted Zevon's songs over the years to great effect: specifically, Stevie Nicks and Chrissie Hynde, both of whom cut representative versions of 1987's beseeching "Reconsider Me." There is also Jill Sobule's hauntingly beautiful "Don't Let Us Get Sick," Shawn Colvin's sweetly gospel-tinged rendition of "Tenderness on the Block," Rebecca Pidgeon's fragile interpretation of "Searching for a Heart," and the sexually charged reading of "Werewolves of London" by Latvian-born singer-songwriter Masha that not only appeared in a 2015 Three Olives vodka ad, but cleverly dissected the bestial/gigolo subtext of the song missed by every male artist who covers it.

Considering her larger fame at the time, Ronstadt brought "Poor Poor Pitiful Me" to a wider audience, added it to her live set, and, due to her naturally fetching looks and independently aloof demeanor in a male-dominated rock scene, turned it into an understandable sigh of relief. Listeners could sympathize with a beautiful and seemingly demure woman being manhandled by some goon when Ronstadt sang, "Why won't these boys let me be," changing the gender, and, by doing so, the song's pathos. When she sings about being worked over by Jesse James, who is a "credit to his gender," it's as if a feminist wrote the song as stinging critique. In 1996, Canadian country artist Terri Clark would use a similar "solitary gal against a torrent of insatiable men" angle in her amped-up version that catapulted the song to the top of her country's charts and No. 5 in the States.

Ronstadt's 1977 version appears on her vividly elastic *Simple Dreams*, in which she also takes a fine pass at Zevon's "Carmelita" and a host of songs by male artists from Buddy Holly to the Rolling Stones. Notorious for having broken hearts and taken names on her way to stardom, Ronstadt cleverly uses a collection of macho songs to channel an aggressiveness that some may have labeled threateningly masculine. She even reintroduces the discarded verse about Yokohama, but this time, while the offending man is picking her up and tossing her down, he's the one who cries, "Please don't hurt me, mama!"

Backed on the recording and later onstage by some of the musicians who played on the original track—most notably Waddy Wachtel, whom Zevon credits for turning him on to country music when the two toured with the Everly Brothers—Ronstadt delivers a unique rendition of his sardonic tale of woe while also embracing its country roots.

"When we met, Warren had already written songs with a country flavor, but we mutually developed a deep love for country music together," recalls Wachtel today. "We spent a lot of time singing a lot of country songs, especially Merle Haggard, whom we both loved."

Ronstadt's version is played in half-time with a concentration on acoustic guitar, giving her ample room to comfortably recite the snarky lyrics, reflecting the singer's aim to get into the headspace of the songwriter. Not coincidentally, her first impression of Zevon was that he was a psychopath, but she would nevertheless be back again for his headspace, ironically putting in perspective the cry for help in female recidivism echoed in the song.

To be sure, one need look no further than the mere fact that Ronstadt ignored the song's final and funniest verse:

I met a girl at the Rainbow bar
She asked me if I'd beat her
She took me back to the Hyatt House
I don't want to talk about it

While "Poor Poor Pitiful Me" appears on the surface to be a send-up in more ways than one, the exclamatory "Ha! Never mind!" that Zevon shouts in its coda pretty much puts everything before it to rest.

Unlike many of the songs on 1978's follow-up, *Excitable Boy*, that come across as a frat party gone sideways, the overall lone-voiced ambiance of *Warren Zevon* is abruptly jostled by "Poor Poor Pitiful Me" and to some extent "I'll Sleep When I'm Dead," although the latter is known to have been put together with almost no one playing on it in the same room at the same time. Traditional banjo and fiddle picking are lent by the versatile David Lindley, and an infectious boogie-woogie piano and sax are also added by Jai Winding and Bobby Keys respectively, while the choral harmonies feature Fleetwood Mac's Lindsey Buckingham (his ex-lover and bandmate Stevie Nicks sings backup on two other tracks on the album). The band cooks as if running down an alley just ahead of the marauding women thirsting for the kill.

Ultimately, there would be twenty-seven credited musicians on *Warren Zevon*, clearly illustrating that many talents in the Hollywood scene had great respect for him. "Los Angeles at that time was this amazingly shared musical place where everybody wanted to help everybody do whatever they were doing," explains Wachtel, who while sitting in on several tracks introduced Stevie Nicks and Lindsey Buckingham to Zevon and even talked the pair into joining Fleetwood Mac. "Don [Henley] and Glenn [Frey] would just be hanging out in the studio having a drink or a smoke: 'Oh, you need a hook? Sure, I'll sing that.'"

Throughout *Warren Zevon* significant artists subjugate their egos for the greater good, and ofttimes the record sounds as if a very expensive backing band is realizing these finely crafted tunes: The exception is "Poor Poor Pitiful Me," which comes off as unbridled fun. This vibe would frame Zevon's first tour supporting the release, which opened raucously at Greenwich Village's Bottom Line to great acclaim. It would also herald the record to follow that would not only continue to impress critics but put Warren Zevon on the pop culture map.

Original movie poster of the 1935 Universal horror classic that inspired Warren Zevon's biggest hit.
Alamy

Excitable Boy

Deep into that darkness peering, long I stood there wondering, fearing,
Doubting, dreaming dreams no mortal ever dared to dream before.
                                        —EDGAR ALLAN POE, *The Raven*

Songs did not come easily to Warren Zevon. He told VH1 in 2003, "Inspiration always came painfully, brutally, and rarely." He could spend weeks scrupulously mulling over a single line in a verse. Melodies would emerge and be held onto for dear life. He never abandoned a musical idea for experimentation or blithely discarded anything viable, as many of his peers ritually did. During his creative epoch in 1978, he told *Circus* magazine, "My job is to be miserable waiting for the next flash."

He preferred songs that evolved or matured, and, speaking in 2003 to Jon Pareles of the *New York Times*, likened the process of songwriting to that of creating charcoal sketches as preludes to a later final painting: "I always knew when something was going to be worth working on, however long it took. And then I'd work on it for a year, sometimes just waiting for the words to come, waiting for the third verse. Or the bridge—that can take fourteen years. Or else you rationalize that it doesn't need a bridge."

Those who knew music well said that when inspiration did come, his songs had a certain detailed quality. Their construction, which Zevon described to *Songwriter* magazine in 1981 as "a scary commitment," was hailed in Crystal Zevon's book as "magnificent" by his late friend and collaborator LeRoy Marinell. Session drummer Eddie Ponder said in the same volume that his songs "made my weenie hard." With less vulgarity, rock legend Roy Orbison told Zevon that he reminded him of the prolific Buddy Holly, a man he knew personally. Bruce Springsteen marveled at his arrangements. J. D. Souther told me, "Warren's songs were incredibly well-founded structurally, and of course lyrically he had his own style of combining images and his own set of metaphors."

But always, as Zevon would often say, the creative process was tough, with each song coming harder than its predecessor. "I write so few songs and I need them so desperately," he admitted in a 2000 radio interview with KGSR's Jody Denberg.

"Werewolves of London," though, came right away. Those who were there figure it took about ten minutes to compose. Marinell was there. So was Zevon's new bride, Crystal, as was Waddy Wachtel, whose close but rancorous relationship with Zevon turned into one of the latter's most professionally and personally cherished partnerships.

Zevon had been tasked by rock legend and former employer Phil Everly with producing a "dance craze" based on the 1935 horror classic *Werewolf of London*. After sharing some fine sinsemilla and listening to Zevon yammer on about werewolves, Marinell looked over at Wachtel, who had happened on the scene merely looking to pick up a guitar for a scheduled studio session. The guitarist shrugged his shoulders and shouted to Marinell to "play that fucking lick of yours!'"

Zevon leapt on the piano and began to hammer along with a bouncing, roll-out-the-barrel revelry. Wachtel started howling *a-woooo!* Zevon demanded an opening lyric. Wachtel found it hard to believe how easily the words tumbled from his brain: a verse filled with predatory notions of the beast wandering through Soho clutching a Chinese menu and desperately searching for beef chow mein. "I had just returned from a European tour with the singer of my old band, Judi Pulver," remembers Wachtel. "And I went to this little restaurant called Lee Ho Fook, and I just spit out the whole first verse."

Immediately inspired, Zevon added an alliterative verse about little old ladies getting "mutilated late last night," prompting Marinell to chip in parts of a third verse about the damn thing's hair being perfect. All of it was complemented by a chorus of Wachtel's impromptu *a-whooo!* For her part, the newly minted Mrs. Zevon scribbled the proceedings in a journal to present the next day to the hungover participants, none of whom remembered any of it. "I was sitting there with my steno pad that I carried everywhere because Warren didn't remember things," confirms Crystal today. "He would come off with these one-liners and I'd jot them down. The next day we were in the studio with Jackson and I said to Warren, 'Play him your new song.' And he said, 'What new song?' I pulled out the notebook and I said, 'Werewolves of London.' And he said, 'Oh, yeah!'"

This was the simple origin of Warren Zevon's only hit record, what he would later describe in *Entertainment Weekly* as "a stupid song for smart people," an albatross in miscasting him as some kind of failed one-hit wonder when he would chalk it up as a rare good fortune for a folk singer. "Werewolves of London," ending up tantalizingly just outside the *Billboard* Top 20, may have been quirky and somewhat bizarre, but it was nonetheless a hit. And while it would never slake Phil Everly's desire for a dance craze, the song would be the centerpiece of Zevon's best-selling and most celebrated album, *Excitable Boy*.

Ultimately, it would be what the greater public would know him for.

Warren Zevon? He's the guy who sang that werewolf song, right?

Yeah, that guy.

"Werewolves of London" is a microcosm of the unbridled excesses of *Excitable Boy*. Where his first Asylum album, *Warren Zevon*, sounds like the musings of a moody voyeur peering into a lavish Hollywood party, sneaking glimpses at how the other half lived before happily returning to his tragicomedy on the other side of the tracks, *Excitable Boy* reeks of the collective. It is a record of collaborations and jams, a party unto itself. "It's more wholesome than my last album, because of the spirit of fun," Zevon snickered to *Rolling Stone* while promoting it. "Fun is my idea of art—fundamentally, I mean."

This is manifest in the trajectory of "Werewolves of London," written in 1974 and demoed during *Warren Zevon* but shelved due to Jackson Browne deeming it unfit to stand beside more refined songs with introspective themes like "Frank and Jesse James," "The French Inhaler," and "Desperados Under the Eaves," all of which were a far cry from resembling songs about lycanthropy.

Part of the clubhouse enthusiasm of *Excitable Boy* begins with Zevon's trusted musical sparring partner, Waddy Wachtel, who was brought in by Browne both to coproduce and to keep his friend's kinetic alcohol spasms to a minimum. This allowed the veteran studio cat a rare opportunity to experiment with guitar sounds. "For example, on the album's first song, 'Johnny Strikes Up the Band', the solo that kicks it off is three different tracks," explains Wachtel. "It's a very subtle thing, but if you listen to it carefully you'll hear these notes ringing into other notes that you physically *can't* do on the guitar. Your fingers can't make these notes happen. It's just this little layering thing that I *always* wanted to try."

There is something seductive about the opening few seconds of the album's last track, "Lawyers, Guns and Money," a peak behind the curtain of what it could have been like in that studio at that time with those musicians. It doesn't quite sound ready, stumbling in before the tape is set to capture it. It suspends your belief in polish and rekindles your joy of the garage. It reminds the listener that those who had been in awe of Zevon's unwillingness to compromise his art were having a ball celebrating it.

Perhaps more than any of his other albums, *Excitable Boy* sounds as if Zevon's black-as-coal humor is being enthusiastically indulged in the most communal way, his storytelling distinct, his diverse mélange of danger and light coming through. It is right that this album defines him. It is right that it towers over the rest, and it is good that its legacy is a fine one.

Excitable Boy is where the queer nature of Warren Zevon, a man comfortable dissecting the hilarious horrors of the human condition with interesting chord patterns and memorable titles that offer a wink to the bleakest allusions, would assimilate into the vox populi, what stalwart rock critic Robert Christgau would call in his *Record Guide: Rock Albums of the '70s* the uncanny ability to "exorcise male psychoses by mock celebration."

It is when the stars aligned for a minstrel satirist. The late 1970s was the hoary period during which the veil had been lifted on the American dream. This was the indulgent, cynical, tongue-in-cheek, quasi era caught betwixt generations, sort of the end of one thing and not quite the beginning of something else, but certainly not the finish of another. It was cultural purgatory, a halfway house where the countercul-ture could commiserate with those who would make a fortune off its bones. It wasn't yet the 1980s, when the salesmen stopped pretending they were still radical hipsters and reveled in unfettered mendacity. People were still *pretending* in 1978 when *Excit-able Boy* hit the shelves. Filling up discos and worshipping the Fonz, reading up on CIA secrets and African murder kings, and fully embracing the free fall of heavy drugs, movie blockbusters, seemingly daily airplane hijackings, political criminals, antiheroes, ritual murders, Patty Hearst, Jim Jones, the New York Yankees beating the hell out of each other on national television, the death of fat bloated Elvis and the birth of punk, the warm blood of reckoning in the dreary wake of Vietnam, and a who-the-hell-is-Jimmy-Carter malaise.

It was also the first time I heard Warren Zevon. I was in summer school, having been remanded there for failing Mr. Bishoff's sophomore year biology class. Bishoff was a horrid albino, thin and sickly, who told my friend Mitchell with some measure of glee that he had passed his class by "a cunt's hair." Bishoff eschewed such pithy commentary in favor of merely shaking his head before failing me. He knew I already understood my fate. I sucked at biology. Actually, to be fair, I sucked at most subjects, and by *sucked*, I mean I did not give a flying fart and therefore zoned and in this case found myself stuck in the same miserable stale classroom rank with the odor of mid-October when the July sun was shining outside on all the non-failures who were running free. During our daily break, the inmates were allowed to play music. On that fateful day, I had brought my copy of Queen's *Jazz*, the wonderful seventh album by the eclectic British musicologists, whose "Bicycle Race" and "Fat Bottomed Girls" had rumbled across FM radio the past winter. Next, the class was presented with the crackling sounds of vinyl that had clearly not been tended to properly. Man, kids whose inability to keep their records clean tested my patience. But my angst was suddenly assuaged as the opening strains of brightly hypnotic guitar picking, almost country in style, wafted through the room, the band cheerily loping along. Then the snap of a snare drum and the baritone voice of an impish rogue:

Dry your eyes my little friend
Let me take you by the hand
Freddie get ready, Rock steady
When Johnny strikes up the band

And I was off to the races.

But I didn't give it up just yet. I waited to let the next song ease its way in. It didn't, though. It burst in, as if there was something that needed to be told . . . *now.* The piano line, not contrived and overwrought like the Elton John I had so loved but had abandoned with the fading of middle school innocence, and not the rollicking Broadway pap of Meatloaf, even though I liked the one with Phil Rizzuto describing two teens sex-wrestling in the back seat of a car, or even how Queen used it to better smear the camp onto the rock. This was a carefully fingered and bold statement. It forced you to listen to the lyric. Each note was evocative of something sinister, as the voice ever deeper sings:

Roland was a warrior from the Land of the Midnight Sun
With a Thompson gun for hire, fighting to be done
The deal was made in Denmark on a dark and stormy day
So he set out for Biafra to join the bloody fray

My closest friend in the summer of 1978 was named Roland. Before him (and really after him), I had known no one else by that name. Suddenly he was a mysterious Antarctic warrior joining bloody frays in a song on what I presumed was a pop/rock album. The figure of Roland emerges as if following in the footsteps of a calculated killing machine convinced of his righteous path, from the Nigerian Civil War to the post–Congo Crisis Kisangani Mutinies. It all sounded so Voyages of Sinbad to me: a relentless predator of the international/geographical chess game traipsing through the Cold War. It was a time we knew well, '70s kids having been born on the cusp of the Cuban Missile Crisis and the spy-versus-spy mentality of our hidden subterranean government from J. Edgar Hoover's invasive FBI to the shadowy CIA.

Of course, a fellow mercenary murders Roland, which is what mercenaries do. "The deal was made. . . ." However, the villain of the tale, Van Owen, would be hunted down by the ghostly apparition of a headless marauder and killed in a morality tale devoid of morals.

It is after all a ghost story, this Roland and his Thompson gun, running wild through the conflicts of our youth throughout Ireland, Lebanon, Palestine, and Berkeley, California. Shit, even Patty Hearst makes an appearance. Hearst was *our* ghost, one day a debutante, the next a machine-gun-toting revolutionary. We read the stories of how this could be *us*: It could be *your* children who could one day decide to alter the current state of things, to violently take up arms and blindly go forth from being brainwashed to bank robbing. She was the symbol of the terrible state of youth in America, who foolishly toyed with the status quo for a decade only to become zombie radicals. Ah, but waiting out there, like a right-wing horseman from Washington Irving's darkest imagination, is Roland, headless and out for blood.

The eternal Thompson gunner
still wandering through the night
Now it's ten years later but he still keeps up the fight
In Ireland, in Lebanon, in Palestine and Berkeley
Patty Hearst heard the burst of Roland's Thompson gun and bought it

It was maybe halfway into "Werewolves of London" when I rose slowly from the uncomfortable wooden desk chair and coolly made my way across the room. "What's this?" I asked, perusing the cover, which bore the face of a thirty-one-year-old Warren Zevon flush with a bemused smirk and a pirate gleam behind tinted granny glasses. I was strangely satisfied with the image, which perfectly matched all the *a-ooohs*. Oh, and the inside sleeve revealed a handgun sitting in the middle of a dinner plate adorned with broccoli and potatoes. Yeah, that's about right: a firearm with a serving of the basic food groups.

Zevon's palette for *Excitable Boy* was vast, and none of it approached the ordinary. Even for rock standards of the late 1970s, considering this was the landscape of Alice Cooper, David Bowie, Kiss, and a host of other shock-oriented static, the subjects covered and the language expressed in its songs are remarkably bizarre. The music also crosses several styles—there's even a stab at disco on it—lending melodic credence to the drama and humor. Even Zevon's baritone works to separate him from the pack. Absolutely no one sang like him, especially those played on rock stations at the time. Seemingly every voice soared into the higher register. The combination of caustic lyrics, eclectic musical choices, and Zevon's rumbling, subterranean growl burrowed deep into your psyche.

I am glad I heard this one first, before *Warren Zevon*, which in many ways over the years has surpassed it for me on repeated listens. Overall, I may like the totality of the songs on that one better, but there is something seminal about *Excitable Boy*, a frozen reflection of its time and place.

"I really can't tell you where my songs come from, but my interest in things and my writing come from the way things sound . . . the way they sing," Zevon told *Creem* magazine during the making of the record. "There are meanings that are sometimes consciously explored, and there are other things I explore the meaning of which are a total mystery to me."

In late 1977, Zevon entered the Sound Factory in downtown Los Angeles to record the best batch of songs that didn't make *Warren Zevon* and a few others he was paining to craft. Much of the material was written over the course of more than a year in several places with different collaborators. The earliest songs reach back to 1974: The weed-rich, vodka-soaked "Werewolves of London" was created around the time of the soulful "Mohammed's Radio," which ended up on *Warren Zevon*, as was the disturbingly jaunty title track. Despite keeping them off the debut album, Browne loved "Excitable Boy" and "Werewolves of London" and even began adding the latter to his own live set-list, where he immediately began getting compliments and suggestions that he might record it. However, such as sophomore efforts go, he was sure Zevon would need them to fill out his inevitable follow-up.

The next year, while playing at the Dubliner in the small Spanish beach town just outside of Barcelona called Sitges, Zevon wrote "Roland the Headless Thompson Gunner" with the pub's proprietor and landlord, the former mercenary, David "Lindy" Lindell. "You have to picture this six foot six, deranged John Wayne kind of guy, a retired jungle pilot pounding on the bar and waving a gun in the air with his other hand, while I'm strumming on a guitar," Zevon recalled to journalist Fred Schruers in 1978. Taking Lindell's factual and stirring soldier-of-fortune accounts, Zevon used his literary instincts as a frustrated novelist to lay out the gruesome tale of a vengeful apparition whose battles, like the world at large, would never cease.

The title track came fairly quickly after Marinell called Zevon "excitable" as an answer to his friend's query as to why no one would ever allow him to play lead guitar during any of their many jams. The line about the demented subject having "rubbed a pot roast all over his chest" was allegedly performed twice by Zevon as a gleeful response to his wife's and then a friend's perfectly prepared dish.

Much like Billy Joel following his breakthrough song "Piano Man," or Madonna after "Material Girl" hit the airwaves, Warren Zevon in the wake of "Excitable Boy" would forevermore carry the burden of being nicknamed after one of his own songs. Not that he fought it. He embraced his manic personality on- and offstage and used it to his advantage, keeping at bay those who might try and corral him while simultaneously attracting a rogue's gallery of miscreants to join his ramble. However much of Zevon's eccentricity is revealed in the song, the protagonist's exploits in "Excitable Boy" are told in the third person. It is another short story that unfolds with mini snapshots, sideways glances at a disturbed misanthrope who at once disgusts and enthralls. But unlike the melodramatic dynamics and menacing piano lines that adorn "Roland," a rollicking piano accompanies the terrible deeds of the demented urchin in "Excitable Boy," a hand-clapper of a piece with echoes of 1950s doo-wop with its *ooh-ahh-ooh*s, each one accenting the madness.

The chirping alto sax solo provided by much-sought-after session man Jim Horn could have found a comfortable home in any Eisenhower-era pop. Waddy Wachtel called on Linda Ronstadt, who brought along sultry-voiced Jennifer Warnes to provide the jaunty background vocals. "It was this amazing period in Los Angeles where all you had to do was ask a friend to come help you and they were there," remembers Wachtel. "Everybody wanted to be part of everybody's musical experience."

Sounding neither disturbed nor delighted by the proceedings, Zevon sings the song with the detached gusto of a newsman who is stoically resolved to present the gruesome minutiae of a crime scene, as it shifts from one excused incident after another. "Well . . . he's just an excitable boy," after all. This culminates without fail in murder:

And he took little Suzie to the junior prom
Excitable boy, they all said
And he raped her and killed her, then he took her home
Excitable boy, they all said
Well, he's just an excitable boy

Not even the ominous songs of contemporaries like Randy Newman or the provocative menace of Alice Cooper presented such carnage in quite the same musical style. Newman often draped his dangerous characters in baleful string arrangements and odd key changes, and the godfather of shock rock had the convenient cover of heavy guitars and odd sound effects, which everyone half expected would conjure the macabre anyway. Both Newman and Cooper also slid their disturbing ditties inside built-in alter-egos, one taken to dramatic heights by Newman, who always changed character with each song, and the other Cooper, the ultimate rock character. Zevon was always coy about where the grimness was coming from, and he was adamant that, unlike Newman and Cooper, who aspired to it, he was no satirist. "If Randy Newman sang 'God Bless America' straight, you'd know he didn't mean it," muses *Creem* magazine's Joe Goldberg in his review of *Excitable Boy*. "But Zevon has this open Great Plains voice that seems to give historical importance to whatever he sings."

It was as if Zevon cleverly juxtaposed a pleasant melody and sprightly rhythms to his sordid lyrics to enhance the cringe factor. Is this guy kidding, or what?

> *And after ten long years they let him out of the home*
> *Excitable boy, they all said*
> *And he dug up her grave and built a cage with her bones*
> *Excitable boy, they all said*
> *Well, he's just an excitable boy*

"I see it as being anything but funny," Zevon told *Songwriter* magazine in 1981. "On one level I'm asking the person who's listening to it, 'Wait a minute, what do you think is funny? What do you think I *think* is funny?' Maybe that way it's me trying to define myself as a writer, to force people to make a decision. And the decision is, if you think this [is] funny, you shouldn't be listening to my stuff, because you've really got it all backwards."

Zevon's new songs for the album were equally magnificent examples of this, especially considering that Waddy Wachtel demanded Zevon write more material to round out what Wachtel still refers to as his friend's best work. "There were two songs that totally had no place on that record: 'Frozen Notes' and 'Tule's Blues,'" explains Wachtel today. "The record thus far was really showing who this guy was, and those songs had nothing to do with that. They were too introspective and self-aggrandizing or whatever the fuck the term is.

"So all of a sudden Jackson goes, 'We're having a playback party tonight,' and I went, 'What are you talking about?' He goes, 'Well, the record is done.' I went, 'No. It isn't. It's not done as long as those two pieces of shit are on it.' But he has this playback party and side one was sequenced exactly the way it came out, great song after great song, and then side two comes up and it starts off with 'Nighttime in the Switching Yard' and then 'Tule's Blues' and 'Frozen Notes,' and by the time those two songs played people got up and left the party. Those songs *killed* the record. So I stood up and said, 'Zevon, I'm leaving town tomorrow and I'll be back in two weeks and I need two great songs from you.'"

When Wachtel returned from a short tour with Linda Ronstadt, Zevon presented him with "Tenderness on the Block" (with somewhat disabled assistance from Jackson Browne, who fell asleep trying to keep drinking pace with Zevon), and "Lawyers, Guns and Money"—two of his most celebrated songs and not coincidentally the final two songs on the record. "I went over to his house and he played me 'Lawyers' first and I loved it and then he played me 'Tenderness on the Block' and I was in tears," remembers Wachtel. "To him and me, and I still believe this, 'Tenderness on the Block' is one of the best songs ever written, and one of the finest records ever made. It's just so beautiful, and I got to play pretty guitars on it. We tracked those songs during a three-hour session in one morning with Ricky Marotta, Kenny Edwards, Warren, and myself. I had just come back with Kenny and Rick from being on the road with Linda, so we were playing incredibly tight, and they turned out to be remarkable tracks."

In true Zevon idiom, both songs were composed from the strange circumstances of violent conflict and near bedlam. "Tenderness on the Block" was written after another of Zevon's patented tantrums wherein he ripped a banister from the wall of his home. This prompted the obligatory call from a petrified Crystal to Browne, who was able to calm his friend enough to begin collaborating on the song. "Lawyers, Guns and Money" was ironically conceived during what was planned to be a "cooling-out" period in Hawaii recommended by Elektra/Asylum president Joe Smith. Asylum rep Burt Stein accompanied Zevon on a ride with a waitress who had promised some fun in a mountain cabin. It soon became apparent that the group would be breaking into a mountain cabin.

"We're in the Poipu Beach Hotel on Kauai, a place Warren insisted we stay despite literally twenty-five percent of the hotel being underwater, because the ocean had risen and the rest of the hotel had sunken," Stein joyfully recounted to me in August 2016. "Warren made friends with a waitress at the cocktail lounge and she had this plan and I didn't want to lose him in the hills on Kauai. So we get into the rental car and I'm driving, Warren's riding shotgun, the waitress is in the back seat, and we're rolling through a sugarcane field and I hear her say, 'I know my friend won't mind if we break into his house.' I look at Warren, Warren looks at me. I said, 'Warren, I can see the telegram right now: "Dear Joe, send lawyers and money,"' and then Warren says, 'And guns!' We quickly turned the car around and headed back to the cocktail lounge at the Poipu Beach Hotel. Warren jumps out, goes up to the bar, pulls out a pen, grabs a couple of cocktail napkins, and writes out 'Lawyers, Guns and Money'. The song was written *that* quickly. I still have those cocktail napkins."

"Lawyers, Guns and Money" is the quintessential Warren Zevon song: Musically, it stomps the terra, plodding along like a nineteenth-century Russian wedding march. It is both a folk song—featuring no pure chorus and one small but effective bridge filled with furious remorse—and a rock 'n' roll mea culpa. Once again, Zevon's narrator is the tale's victim, inadvertently finding himself in the throes of mayhem through no fault of his own, save for curiosity and misadventure:

Well, I went home with the waitress
The way I always do
How was I to know
She was with the Russians, too

I was gambling in Havana
I took a little risk
Send lawyers, guns and money
Dad, get me out of this

A wonderful staccato break in the action, the bridge builds upon the myth of the innocent bystander somehow being pulled into havoc and poking fun at his dreadfully appalling luck. Well, "poking fun" dramatically understates Zevon's crippling obsession with how much avoiding "bad luck" played in his daily life and steered his significant decisions throughout it. Despite his insatiable curiosity regarding all things intellectual, and despite his voracious reading, sophisticated demeanor, and spectacular proclivity for throwing caution to the wind, whether sober or not, Warren Zevon was inexorably hobbled by superstition.

It may have begun when his father pulled strings to get his son out of the Vietnam draft by having some nefarious doctor figure whip up some excuse, something Zevon gladly played along with by stocking up on several mind-altering substances that duly convinced the draft board that he was clearly unfit for duty. ("Dad, get me out of this!") Yet his guilt over so many of his generation who would fail to devise as clever an escape route and die in some godforsaken rice paddy forced him to avoid coming within eye-shot of any UNCLE SAM WANTS YOU sign for years.

Later in life, this quirkiness would manifest itself in a serious psychological condition known as OCD (obsessive-compulsive disorder). But when he wrote "Lawyers, Guns and Money," the idea of avoiding whatever he deemed "bad luck"—the potential purchase of a home, a bus ride, a particular airplane departure time, and any relationship, both professional or personal—was paramount. On the flip side, he would also immediately deduce when something had the air of "good luck" and without additional reasoning find himself heading in that direction— for a time, Zevon would only wear gray and drive a gray car or furnish his house in gray; then, once he had moved on from that color, it would never appear again in his life. "All of his clothes were blue and then everything was gray; he really evolved into a very superstitious person," recalls George Gruel, his good friend, confidant, and road manager during this period. "For instance, he had a lucky scarf in the studio. He would also arrange his pencils on the table and stuff like that, but it didn't bother him. Sometimes he'd go, 'Think my hands are clean enough?'"

The photographer for *Excitable Boy*, and brother of its coproducer, Jimmy Wachtel spent a great deal of quiet time with Zevon during this period and into the 1980s. The two often went to the movies or dinner and browsed bookstores, bandying about subjects banal and deep. It wasn't until later in their relationship that Jimmy became aware of this behavior. "At one point later in his life I went to his apartment when he was living up above the Whiskey on Carroll Drive, and for some reason I looked in his sock drawer and he had thirty pair of socks all exactly the same gray. I never forgot that. It was so bizarre."

"It was always about bad luck and good luck for Warren," his ex-wife, Crystal, told radio personality Allan Handelman in 2003. "When he would try and quit drinking he would drink Diet Coke or Diet Mountain Dew and open ten cans before he would find the 'lucky' one, and he could tell just by the way it sounded when he flipped the tab open."

Zevon would only ever smoke cigarettes that did not mention the word *cancer* on their packaging and practiced certain rituals when handling his ever-growing cache of guns. All of this would eventually serve as an essential personality trait and a singular focus for his entire life, lending further credence to the lines in "Lawyers, Guns and Money" where unheeded "bad luck" will cause a terrible injustice to the ignorant, or, more to the point, "the shit has hit the fan."

"Tenderness on the Block" is another third-person narrative that hits home for Zevon. "It's one of the most emotionally positive songs I've ever been involved in," he told *Circus* magazine at the conclusion of the sessions. "And very possibly that comes from being the father of a delightful baby daughter." It is a beautifully crafted piano number that warns clinging parents that their child is growing into young adulthood and therefore must make his or her own way, despite the potential dangers inevitably envisioned by the child's elders. In this case, it is a young girl who is heading into damaging headwinds. Jackson Browne provided the title, inspired directly by the birth of Zevon's daughter, Ariel, employing the double meaning of "on the block" as a neighborhood as well as a chopping block, denoting life's cruelties.

The song's inner dialogue reflects the author's mind-set, as depicted in the harshly worded compositions about the predatory women from "Poor Poor Pitiful Me" onward. The subject is primed to be the victim of bad choices and bad men who wish to do her harm, if not consciously, inevitably. Zevon speaks as the young man waiting to whisk the girl from her nest, as well as the father helpless to stop his little bird from plummeting to earth before her wings are ready for flight.

Although danger is ever-present, both the sweetness of the melody and the glimmer of hope in the lyric, specifically the measured answers to the concern of the parents at the end of each verse, about finding true love, provide the tenderness promised in the title. This is likely Jackson Browne's contribution, seeing how most of his work leaned into the glass-half-full philosophy, yet Browne was clearly influenced enough by the spate of darkly portentous material on *Warren Zevon* to assume a similar tone for the critically acclaimed *The Pretender*, which he would record almost immediately after wrapping up the sessions. "He's been there *forever*, man," Browne said of Zevon in a 1976 *Rolling Stone* interview. "I see him as having been there at various times in my life when I actually—and probably unwittingly—made a big change in direction. And he really influenced my thinking. Just look at 'The Pretender': That line, 'I'm going to be a happy idiot'—it's a little bit raw. That's not exactly the Browne touch, is it?"

Considering who Zevon was when he wrote "Tenderness on the Block"—a manic alcoholic sabotaging his life via random acts of insanity—and the demons of superstition that haunted his every step, the heart-wrenching conclusion that it will ultimately wound him to see his young girl walk out the door with a mind of her own was profound. It is Zevon's inevitable acceptance that one day a grown, independent Ariel will emerge from his shadow to find her voice was a real-life predicament that no amount of lawyers, arsenal of guns, or all the money in the world could solve.

Once Zevon's first tour of Europe concluded, he and his wife, Crystal (with infant daughter Ariel in tow), found themselves near their old stomping grounds in Spain, where she tried in vain to tame her drunk and boisterous husband. According to the stirring account in *I'll Sleep When I'm Dead*, he predictably flew into a rage before striking her and then disappearing for a week, which he began in Casablanca before ending up in Morocco. Zevon later claimed to have blacked out for most of it. His family sought refuge at Browne's residence, as they would again a few months later following another in a series of booze-addled violent incidents, the results of which produced the heartbreaking "Accidentally Like a Martyr."

The phone don't ring
And the sun refused to shine
Never thought I'd have to pay so dearly
For what was already mine
For such a long, long time

We made mad love
Shadow love
Random love
And abandoned love
Accidentally like a martyr
The hurt gets worse and the heart gets harder

Crystal Zevon solemnly shared its origins with me one winter Sunday morning in early 2017: "It was very tense, as he had been drinking a lot, and he became furious with me over not joining him for a charity tour in which Jackson told him no one could bring their wives, but Warren argued that [Jackson] was bringing the nanny for his two-year-old, Ethan. But Jackson's wife [Phyllis Major] had just died and I told him so, and we had this *big* fight and he got violent again, and when he passed out I took Ariel and went to a friend's and stayed there.

"When he returned from the tour he stayed with a woman who was working with *Rolling Stone* in San Francisco and when he came back to L.A. he moved into this bleak sort of basement apartment that was on Sunset somewhere near the Hyatt House for about three weeks. That's when he wrote that song. He asked me to come over and played it for me, and maybe a week after that he moved back home. It was his plea to say, 'Look what we have. Are we going to abandon it? Abandon love?'"

Never thought I'd ever be so lonely
After such a long, long time

The aching tone of the music is highlighted by Waddy Wachtel's masterful work on what sounds like pedal steel guitar but is a crafty aural trick he had perfected when working with the Everly Brothers and later with Linda Ronstadt. "I made my living in Los Angeles playing what I call 'phony steel' on a lot of records with the volume pedal," Wachtel explains. "As soon as I got to town I started hearing all this country music, and the guitar sounds are what did it to me."

"There was a deviousness about Warren which is one of my favorite things about him, but his singing was just about as flat as you can hit the nail on the head," says friend and fellow songwriter J. D. Souther. "He really sang directly and from his own peculiar voice, which was very touching. I always thought his ballads were stunning."

The *Excitable Boy* sessions proved no calmer than Zevon's private life. If anything, he would push the needle farther into the red. "I got used to him that way," says Wachtel. "I mean, that's how it was. He would show up to the studio [at] eleven in the morning drunk."

"Warren was drinking, and both Jackson and Waddy were trying to rein him in," recalls his friend and collaborator Jorge Calderón, who along with Glenn Frey, Don Henley, J. D. Souther, and Kenny Edwards added background vocals as the Gentlemen Boys on the first two Asylum albums. "Warren would say, 'Jorge, let's go out and take a walk,' and we would head down Hollywood Boulevard and he would have a flask in his pocket, so they were telling me, 'Don't let him do that!' and I'm going, 'Hey, man, I'll tell him, but I'm not his babysitter.'"

The sometimes fractured atmosphere surrounding the recording of *Excitable Boy* was what Calderón described to me as "productive chaos," as once again it involved a revolving door of Los Angeles's rock elite carrying more drugs and booze than instruments. "Yeah, there were a lot of people, but it was all about the music and supporting Warren," stresses Calderón. "There was a lot of laughter all the time, because Warren was hilarious and everybody was in good spirits. There were drugs, of course, but I don't think there was any kind of *crazy* partying."

A good example of the "productive chaos" would be the no fewer than four different bass player/drummer combinations that took a pass at recording "Werewolves of London." So unbelievably easy to compose by all accounts, the song consumed half the album's budget. "Warren and I had a really objective view of that tune," explains Wachtel. "'Werewolves of London' had to *feel* serious. For the jokes to work, the track had to have nothing to do with being funny. And we were at the point of saying, 'Look, if it doesn't work we're going to throw the fucking tune off the album. We don't give a shit,' which would have been such a tragedy because it was our only hit, but we didn't know that yet, so I think it was Jorge who suggested Mick and John."

Finally, at dawn, after an unconscionable sixty-two takes using Fleetwood Mac's venerable rhythm section of Mick Fleetwood on drums and John McVie on bass, both of whom were riding high on the mega-success of *Rumors* and becoming increasingly inebriated, Wachtel and Browne chose take two.

"A big part of the immediate and lasting success of that record is that layered rhythm section," David Landau, Zevon's lead guitarist on the second leg of the *Excitable Boy* tour effused to me in the autumn of 2016. "Go listen to it and focus on the bass in particular. That is such a monster fucking groove for a typical three-chord song, and it's intricate. To me, that's a big part of why that record won't go away. Obviously, it has that hysterical lyric and it's the ultimate tailgate party sing-along, but underneath it, that track is just wonderful. And it's probably the best solo Waddy's ever recorded."

"Since it took forever to get that track done, I figured the solo was going to be the same, so I sent everyone away," recalls Wachtel. "I sat down next to the engineer in the studio, poured myself a big drink, rolled myself a joint, and picked up the guitar and said, 'All right, let me hear it once.' He played it and as the solo spot came, I just *played* it. I didn't try to *compose* one. I didn't think it out the night before. I didn't work on it. I didn't write it out. When it's time to solo, if you're a soloist you just *go*. It's like when you're jumping off of a submarine they tell you, 'Grab your nose and nuts and jump.' So I picked up the bottleneck and I just played it *fast*, not thinking it would be the one, but when I heard it back I went, 'Oh, that's pretty good. Give me another track.' And I put the harmony on it. I never got a sip of the drink. I never lit the joint. It took mere minutes to do one take."

While Zevon's debut album toed the edge with brutal precision, the songs that make up *Excitable Boy* career right over it. Twenty-three musicians and singers are listed as contributors. "The talent that surrounded Warren was just the best that there was in L.A. during that amazing time in Los Angeles when the stars really shined bright in Laurel Canyon," says Burt Stein. "That great Southern California rock was happening and I would see Warren in all these different configurations, with all these different people. It was almost like Woody Allen's film *Zelig*. It was all these musical luminaries and Warren right in the middle. He fit in perfectly, but yet not quite. He was always this fabulous character."

"We used the great Russell Kunkel and Bob Glaub to play as a trio with Warren on 'Roland the Thompson Gunner,'" says Wachtel. "I got there early and taught them that specific ending that has the final lines about Patty Hearst. So Warren shows up to the studio, and he's already fucking drunk, and they run the song down and it's going fine and he gets to the end and I'm standing in the booth and they played the ending *exactly* the way it's written and Warren jumps up off the piano and yells, 'Holy shit! Man, I guess you pay these guys the big money to really understand what you're fucking doing here, huh?!' It was a classic moment, and then I just overdubbed a little guitar and the Gentleman Boys sang the choruses."

Now, since this is an essay about the entire *Excitable Boy* album, I would be remiss in leaving out the spectrum of Zevon's greatest attribute as a lyricist: the ability to express the absurd and the astute, ofttimes all at once. This rare talent prevails on two songs, "Nighttime in the Switching Yard" and "Veracruz."

The first is the album's aforementioned "disco song," something of a cultural requirement in 1978, especially after the Rolling Stones gave it a go with "Miss You," a revitalizing hit for a band that was in dire need of one at the time to remain relevant. Zevon, just beginning to break his way into the mainstream, had no reservations about going this route. He was nudged there by Wachtel, a huge Stones fan (he would later accompany Keith Richards in his late-'80s X-Pensive Winos band) who was intrigued by any musical genus and heard the possibilities when Zevon presented him with what was otherwise a pretty dreary double-entendre blues number about midnight trains and mainlining junk.

While showing off the elastic bass playing of Bob Glaub, who kicks ass on this record, specifically on this track, "Excitable Boy," and "Roland the Headless Thompson Gunner," "Nighttime in the Switching Yard" is a slice of midtempo funk that expertly opens side two and shifts the mood from the achingly somber "Accidentally Like a Martyr" that concludes side one and the serious tone of "Veracruz" that follows it. The guitar work by a highly motivated Wachtel along with Danny Kortchmar is a wonderfully understated but effective sonic device that replicates a train moving down the tracks. It never fails to strike me as funny: the little break when the backing vocals join Zevon's monotone "Listen to the train whistle whine"—holding out the last word like a train whistle whining—the laughably derivative *Doot dat doot dat doot dadoot*, and the repetitive "See that train, the midnight train, goes both ways," which has about one hundred possible meanings but only illustrates one for its coauthor, Jorge Calderón.

"An unknown secret about that song is when we were working on it Warren told me it was based on one of Lindy's crazy tales," Calderón told me in early September 2016. "The guy at the switch is a heroin addict and he's ODing, so he nods out at the time to switch. There are hints to it like, 'Get it out on the main line,' but we never actually *say* it. I actually wrote a verse for it, but then Warren decided it extended the song too long, so we didn't use it. But later on he told me, 'If you ever do a version, just put in the verse about him.'"

On the complete other end of the spectrum comes "Veracruz," the album's truest folk song and its one political voice (unless you consider "Roland" political, which it may certainly be, absent its macabre underpinning. Zevon certainly did, as he would often get letters from and be approached by Navy SEAL veterans about the deeper meaning of the song and be moved to tears). The events covered in the song, while taking place at the dawning of the American century, reflect a counterbalance to the world of modern mercenaries working for the U.S. government covertly reshaping the globe. Zevon makes clear that the responsibility for the aggression falls in the lap of the leader of the free world, as its victims are represented by a single woman, Maria, who effectively represents the plight of humanity beneath the sovereign might of nations. In another interesting lyrical twist, Zevon anthropomorphizes the town—as he does the Hollywood Hawaiian Hotel, Gower Avenue, and Carmelita Avenue on his first album—as its nineteenth-century Mexican ways expire:

I heard Woodrow Wilson's guns
I heard Maria crying
Late last night I heard the news
That Veracruz was dying

While Zevon would not play in this kind of ideological sandbox for another couple of albums, the song also serves as a mini–history lesson and provides another Spanish music bed for him to tell a sordid tale (the other being "Carmelita," wherein the narrator hears mariachi static on his radio as a portent of impending peril). A Mexican port town, Veracruz was invaded by the United States in 1914 at the behest of President Woodrow Wilson over what turned out to be misinformation about the arrest of nine U.S. sailors during the height of the Mexican Revolution, which would eventually deteriorate into the Battle of Veracruz when the U.S. Army invaded the city virtually unopposed.

Someone called Maria's name
I swear it was my father's voice
Saying, "If you stay you'll all be slain
You must leave now —you have no choice

Take the servants and ride west
Keep the child close to your chest
When the American troops withdraw
Let Zapata take the rest"

The viciously enigmatic Emiliano Zapata Salazar, another in a long line of deranged antiheroes in the Zevon canon, was the key figure of Mexican's peasant revolution that raged alongside the American invasion, providing Zevon with a triangulation of violent interests that clash in Veracruz while also giving voice to the pawns of a greater tragedy.

I heard Woodrow Wilson's guns
I heard Maria calling
Saying, "Veracruz is dying
And Cuernavaca's falling"

Cuernavaca is the largest city in the Mexican state of Morelos, where Zapata's revolution would foment, proving that tiny Veracruz would stand no chance and furthering the desperation of the song's protagonists. This once again brings to mind Zevon's cornered narrator from "Desperados Under the Eaves"—*desperado* being the Spanish word for "out of hope," a concept both songs cover, via the hotel as prison in the former and here through the doomed town of Veracruz. Once again, as he would repeatedly express in his art, Zevon sees both circumstance and geography as enemies of refuge and freedom, with escape the only solution. The difference for the victims of Veracruz is the absence of responsibility and hence of the resultant guilt found in his other songs.

The event has completely overwhelmed the townspeople. They are described as neither revolutionaries nor sympathetic to any side. They just want to be left alone to live their lives. Inspired by what Zevon told *Circus* magazine was "a first-person story from a Mexican landowner who'd gotten caught in the revolution," Zevon related the incident to more modern times. "I gathered it was kind of a Bay of Pigs, where America blundered into what was already a complicated political shit storm."

The similarity to "Desperados" is in the defiance of the song's Spanish verse, where the soon-to-be refugees have accepted their current fate, but find solace in proclaiming that they'll be back. The song, written from the Mexican perspective, is filled with warnings about the assault and the harried escape of the townspeople while they curse the destruction that would cause the narrator and his family to flee their home, but it contains a declaration sweetly sung by Zevon's close friend and collaborator, Jorge Calderón, in Spanish:

Aquel día yo jure (On that day I swore)
Hacia el puerto volveré (To the port I will return)
Aunque el destino cambio mi vida (Even though destiny changed my life)
En Veracruz moriré (In Veracruz I shall die)
Aquel día yo jure (On that day I swore)

I heard Woodrow Wilson's guns
I heard them in the harbor
Saying, "Veracruz is dying"

During our lengthy conversations in late 2016 and early 2017, Calderón spoke highly of the song that sparked a musical alliance that would last three decades. Zevon had become exasperated when he was told that Waddy Wachtel hated what he was then calling "Veracruz Is Dying," because he didn't want any damn song on the record that had *dying* in the title. Jackson Browne, though, loved it and prompted Zevon to approach Calderón to add a touch of authenticity to the track. "So I took it home and I listened to it and I went into this Spanish thing both musically and lyrically," remembers Calderón. "He then gave me a cassette of him singing, 'Take the servants and ride west, *na na nan a nah*.' He was missing that line, so I said, 'How about 'Keep the child close to your chest?' and he went, 'Yes!' So that was it, and he loved the Spanish part, which became a refrain."

Nearly four decades have passed since his yeoman's work arranging, producing, prodding, and playing on *Excitable Boy*, yet Waddy Wachtel still gushes as if it were yesterday: "The album really came out the way one would hope—the songs, the arrangements were very clear. Greg Ladanyi did a fantastic job of engineering, and collectively we all heard it the same way, and where we didn't we learned that the other one was right. It was an extraordinary experience and sonically amazing."

Excitable Boy was released on January 18, 1978, to another avalanche of rave reviews. Zevon's soon-to-be friend, respected music journalist Paul Nelson, gushes in the March 23 issue of *Rolling Stone*: "Warren Zevon's *Excitable Boy* is the best American rock & roll album since Bruce Springsteen's *Born to Run* (1975), Neil Young's' *Zuma* (1976), and Jackson Browne's *The Pretender* (1976). If there's not enough firepower in that statement, let's cock the hammer on another. Thus far, the Seventies have introduced three major American rock & roll artists—Browne in 1972, Springsteen in 1973, and Zevon—and I have every confidence the music of all three will be even better in the future."

"Linda Ronstadt asked me to go with her to Tucson to see the Stones, and before we left, someone told me that *Excitable Boy* was the most popular record on the Stones tour," says Wachtel today with pride. "When I showed up with Linda, Keith [Richards] picked me up in the air. Woody [Ron Wood] and everybody were yelling accolades about the guitar playing on the record and it was just such a great feeling to know [that] these guys, who Z and I loved so much, loved what *we* were doing. You know, when you're writing that stuff it's so nebulous that sometimes you wonder if anyone is going to ever hear *any* of it. Then, of course, 'Werewolves' hit."

Thanks to the unlikely ascent of "Werewolves of London" hitting the Top 40 in April of 1978, where it would remain for six weeks, peaking at No. 21, the album would reach No. 8 on the *Billboard* Pop Albums chart for two weeks that spring (May 13–27), sitting two spaces behind its producer Jackson Browne's breakthrough hit album, *Running on Empty*, and becoming by far Zevon's highest charting album. Certified gold on April 17, 1978, it went platinum in 1997, the only one of Zevon's albums to do so. Also alongside *Excitable Boy* in April was Linda Ronstadt's *Simple Dreams*—featuring two Zevon songs ("Carmelita" and "Poor Poor Pitiful Me") and the masterful guitar work of Waddy Wachtel—which would reach the top of the Pop Album chart. Additionally, Ronstadt's version of "Poor Poor Pitiful Me" would find a home in the much-hyped pop-comedy film *FM*, also released that April.

Particularly noteworthy in the early months of 1978 was the unlikely chart ascent of Randy Newman's equally quirky and absurdly controversial "Short People" from the 1977 album *Little Criminals*, which would eventually reach No. 9 on the *Billboard* albums chart. The single—which perhaps not so coincidentally also features the omnipresent Wachtel on guitar, not to mention members of the Eagles and J. D. Souther—by the otherwise fringe Newman caused a stir among the confused and humorless and managed to become the No. 2 song in the country by January 1978, where it would be denied the top spot by the sudden emergence of the Bee Gees' "Stayin' Alive" from the album that would dominate the year in pop music, *Saturday Night Fever*.

Perhaps both the successes of "Short People" and "Werewolves of London," two strangely themed satirical throwaway songs by cerebral artists, proved the truth of what Waddy Wachtel told me in 2017: "When they told us 'Werewolves' would be the single, we both went crazy. We were like, 'You got to be fucking kidding me!' We thought for sure 'Tenderness on the Block'—being the most amazing song anyone has ever written, performed, or heard—would have to be the single because it was just so artistically beautiful, but they went right for our dirty joke. We were both saying, 'What the fuck is wrong with these people?' We were completely offended, but they were so right and we were so wrong.

"First of all, 'Werewolves' is funny as hell and very brilliantly and cleverly written, but I think it's Warren talk-singing that sold it. He wasn't trying to be the *singer*. He was more the storyteller, and the *a-oooh* was nice and high. I learned that when you have a low voice like Warren's it's a very hard sell. But the combination of the humor, the way he presented it vocally, and the catchy chorus worked perfectly."

Wachtel may have been thrown by the label's choosing of "Werewolves," but it was not altogether that outlandish, as Zevon admitted in a 1995 *Goldmine* interview. "People were playing 'Werewolves' by then, so we were not completely innocent of the idea that the song had at least some kind of potential. 'Cause people would roll on the floor when I'd show it to 'em."

"It's really a comedic masterpiece," concludes Wachtel.

Beside Browne and Zevon, captured on a live radio recording from the 1976 tour in Bryn Mawr, Pennsylvania, in which the audience is shouting for "Werewolves" throughout the set, among those having performed the song live prior to its recording is the multitalented T Bone Burnett, joined by members of Bob Dylan's Rolling Thunder Revue on several dates, including December 4, 1975, at the Montreal Forum. (Burnett would go on to cowrite "Bed of Coals" with Zevon and sing backup on his final album, *The Wind*.) This lively version has been bootlegged several times and includes references to Jack Nicholson, Patty Hearst, Frank Sinatra, Rick Danko, Linda Lovelace, Marilyn Chambers, Lon Chaney Sr., Lon Chaney Jr., Sammy Davis Jr. and Jimmy Hoffa, among others.

Still, it is somewhat odd that after two albums of intensely arranged provocative melancholia, it is a novelty song about celluloid monsters with *a-oooh* as the chorus that would catapult Warren Zevon into the mainstream and forever come to define him in pop culture. Zevon's favorite director, to whom he dedicated "Hasten Down the Wind" many years hence from the stage with "To Marty Scorsese, who makes the best films in the world, with love" (he would also dedicate the live album *Stand in the Fire* to Scorsese), would use the song to great effect in his 1986 film *The Color of Money*, starring an aging Paul Newman, who would go on to win the Academy Award for Best Actor, and Hollywood's hot young star, Tom Cruise. The iconic scene of Cruise, a pool shark plying his trade with gleeful arrogance, dancing about the table to "Werewolves of London" helped drive the song back into the popular transom and provided a second boost to the songwriter's then staggering career.

It would seem Zevon would be forever haunted by the "dirty joke song" he cranked out ripped to the tits on weed and vodka with his friends in 1974. It would also be his guardian angel, his life raft, his beacon in the night.

A year after the chart triumph of "Werewolves," Crystal Zevon writes of hearing three gunshots at 2 a.m. from her husband's studio that was built in a guesthouse on their property. She found an inebriated Zevon standing with his back to the window holding a still-smoking .44 magnum (the one, ironically, pictured on the inside sleeve of *Excitable Boy*). When she slowly approached him, he had a look on his face "of a four-year-old boy who just saw his puppy run over." As she took the gun from his hand, he smiled. In front of him was the *Excitable Boy* cover propped up on the couch with three bullet holes in it. "It's funny. I shot myself," he said nonchalantly.

When I recounted the story, she recalled: "He had made a vow to stop drinking and failed immediately. I think that it had as much as anything to do with 'I can't even trust myself' as anything else. He had been at Bruce [Springsteen]'s concert and made a total fool out of himself in front of Bruce and Jann Wenner [cofounder and publisher of *Rolling Stone*] and he had no memory of being there. You see, he saw himself as this misunderstood, underappreciated genius. But when he realized that he was acting out in ways that were unbecoming of that title it became, 'Well, then you're nothing.'"

Yet despite the demons that "Werewolves of London" wrought and the sudden and only mass pop success he would ever enjoy generated by the album, Zevon would embrace both through the years and included the song and several others from *Excitable Boy* as staples in his shows until his untimely death in 2003. Poking fun at his otherwise potent and multilevel career as a serious songwriter being overshadowed by the few months "Werewolves of London" captured the imagination of the music-listening public, Zevon appeared as himself on a 1993 episode of HBO's hit series *The Larry Sanders Show*, a behind-the-scenes parody of a classic *Tonight Show*–style talk show starring comedian Garry Shandling. Throughout, Zevon is scheduled to be the musical guest and insists on playing anything but "Werewolves of London," but of course, it is the only song the producers want him to play.

When asked by journalist Steve Roeser in the late '90s if he could get away without playing "Werewolves" at one of his shows, Zevon curtly responded, "There's no reason why I should. There's no justification for it." Later on in the interview he expounded on this point: "If you're too bored or too cool to play some old song that you know they want to hear, then it's fucked up. It's like, 'I'm too cool to make you happy.' Not for three minutes!" His son Jordan concurred with his father's thoughts on his showbiz philosophy two decades later: "He was very savvy about the business. That's why he called his fans 'customers'—because he really understood that this was supply and demand."

It is a lasting credit to Warren Zevon's artistry that he was able to rationalize his success with "Werewolves" as a one-off whose time had come. He would not be so seduced by its popularity or that of *Excitable Boy* as to blithely repeat it. There would be no "Frankenstein Bop" or "Vampires on Parade" or really anything resembling "Werewolves of London" again. His follow-up, *Bad Luck Streak in Dancing School*, saw a change in producers, a subtler sound, and an enviable reach at more serious composing. He neither ignored nor copied *Excitable Boy*. He accepted it is a snapshot of his career. It certainly changed his life and for a time made him a rock star. It reached beyond critical exaltation and the envy of his friends and compatriots, bringing about new challenges and putting a spotlight on his increasingly ruinous decadence and pitch-black humor.

Excitable Boy altered a songwriter's being. It sure as hell did for me, as well as a ton of people who came to discover and love Warren Zevon for the rest of his journey.

Original handwritten orchestral charts from an unpublished Warren William Zevon symphony.
Photo and design by Suzan Alparslan

"Bad Luck Streak in Dancing School"
(interludes and symphony)

You don't have to firebomb Dresden to prove you can fly a plane.
— WARREN ZEVON (excerpt from his private diaries)

Sometime in the early 1970s Warren Zevon began work on a symphony or a series of classical pieces that may or may not have been connected into one seamless piece. The hearty George Gruel wrote in his 2012 photograph memoir of his time with Zevon from 1978 until the early 1980s, *Lawyers Guns & Photos*, that classical music was not only the songwriter's first and lasting love but that Gruel personally watched Zevon work endlessly on various "symphonies." This work would, in the words of journalist and friend Paul Nelson, hang "like a stone around his neck." Zevon admitted as much to *Circus* magazine while promoting his previous and most successful album, *Excitable Boy*: "I work on my symphony, which I keep claiming will come out any day now."

When rock journalist Robert Palmer visited Zevon in 1982 while he was living in Laurel Canyon with TV actress Kim Lankford, he noted in the *New York Times* that "on the electric piano sits the voluminous score to an unfinished symphony" and that "Mr. Zevon has been writing classical music since his teenage years."

Classical music may not have completely captured Zevon's musical affections, but it was definitely his initial seducer. "The music that first turned me on was classical music—Stravinsky, Beethoven," he told VH1 in 2002. "It took me quite a while to get around to rock 'n' roll." Not long after the 1956 incident when his father hurled a knife past his mother's head in an epic battle over what would be his first piano, Zevon would find solace and confidence in the instrument. He was, some might say, a natural. Others later hinted that he could very well have been a prodigy, a notion he quickly dismissed. "You have to be good, not just enthusiastic," Zevon told KGSR radio host Jody Denberg in 2000. "I studied piano for a while, but I always wanted to play it, and I started writing classical music and getting into some classical music young enough to be called a prodigy. If I'd been, you know, prodigiously talented or succeeded in any public way."

It was the Dana Junior High Music Department that would initially decide that the young Zevon showed the kind of promise that would benefit from an audience with Robert Craft. Craft, a composer/conductor/critic, was in his thirties when the preteen Zevon was introduced to him while in the company of the celebrated Russian composer Igor Stravinsky, then in his eighties. The story of their time together reviewing scores by such classical luminaries as Karlheinz Stockhausen and Luciano Berio garnered Zevon plenty of press over the years, which he downplayed to Denberg: "It's always exaggerated. But that's the nature of things. Sometimes you just stand back and smile and let it be exaggerated. It's flattering."

Years later Zevon remembered studying composition while watching the two heralded professionals work on chart orchestrations, feeding his need to comprehend the technical framework of how serious music is created. In a memoir excerpted for Crystal Zevon's oral biography, Craft describes the then thirteen-year-old Zevon as "self possessed and articulate far beyond his years," a boy who would pass judgment on the music he sampled with "acute arguments." He would even go as far as to call Zevon his "intellectual superior." Zevon also revealed to an interviewer in 1980 that Craft would evaluate his playing and give him critical notes. If nothing else, both Craft and Stravinsky were duly impressed by how the young man could drink scotch with the elder composer, displaying little to no effect from the alcohol.

This, by any measure, is a pretty auspicious introduction to classical music— not to mention alcoholism—and one that Warren Zevon carried with him into his early years of professional musicianship, first dabbling in folk (he is adamant about how much Bob Dylan would play a part in his musical maturity) then later becoming a pop tunesmith (inspired by working with consummate professionals like the legendary Everly Brothers) and finally a celebrated songwriter. Jackson Browne repeatedly stressed that Zevon's experience in arranging for orchestras was clearly evident in the studio, but ultimately it was the structure and chording of his songs that gave his work a classical sheen.

It is during those fleeting afternoons in the company of musical royalty that the foundation was laid for an artist who for the rest of his days would repeatedly return to the classics, obsessing over song structure while choosing terms like *cadence* and *voicing* to explain his torturous process. When I played Zevon's work for my dear friend Peter Blasevick, a classically trained pianist, he made sure I understood how Zevon's use of intricate bass notes combined with traditional chording vividly elevated what by all measures would be a folk/rock song into a far more melodious and redolent musical expression. This dedication to expressive songwriting incorporated the harmonic sensibilities of, among others, Béla Bartók, Sergey Prokofiev, and

Dmitry Shostakovich, as well as, of course, Stravinsky. These influences would lead Zevon to envision his potential as a composer above and beyond his contemporaries, even if this dream would be sidetracked by a modicum of stardom, indescribable substance abuse, and a wild persona that would be his eventual undoing.

"He was an unstoppable musical creature," cites Waddy Wachtel. "Just listen to the innovative way he subtly inserted things into his songs that would *have* to come from a different genre of music. The voicing in 'Frank and Jesse James' is very Aaron Copland, which almost anyone else would miss. They would do a simplified, straight-ahead version of the chords, where Warren makes sure that the bass notes are intentionally incongruous, creating this beautiful intention."

The man that Zevon called "a fellow classicist" throughout their friendship, J. D. Souther agrees: "Warren and I had classical music in our DNA. And I think his stylistic writing, combined with that voice, made it just a little more difficult dish than some people were willing to taste, but it was always rich in nutrients, which made his songs always sound very determined, and somehow, for me, it made his vulnerability all the more poignant."

During the height of what would be his only time in the glare of celebrity following the quirky 1978 breakout hit "Werewolves of London" from the certified gold *Excitable Boy* album that would reach No. 8 on the *Billboard* charts that year, several magazines clamored to get a piece of him. One such feature appeared as the cover piece in the March 1978 issue of *Phonograph Record* penned by Tom Nolan, who would later go on to author books on jazz great Artie Shaw and Zevon's literary godfather, Ross Macdonald. In the midst of painting a portrait of a suave singer-songwriter at home sipping vodka and tinkling random Beethoven at the piano—the antithesis of the hard-drinking, madman rock 'n' roller—Nolan delves into this duality when he references Zevon's "long-suffering, unfinished symphony." He continues: "Warren is knee-deep in these scores he's been working on for years, fragments of some incomplete work he toils away at laboriously, note by note. Maybe it's some kind of pipe dream or maybe he's stumbling towards some new kind of form, but that thirteen-year-old would-be classicist inside of him still yearns to express himself . . ."

As if predicting Zevon's next project and linking it to his subject's distant but hardly forgotten past, Nolan spends the next few paragraphs getting inside Zevon's head, describing his fantasies of infusing classical motifs into rock 'n' roll and his frustration over how the two are generally considered mutually exclusive art forms. "But it wasn't this way in the 19th century!" writes Nolan, channeling Zevon's thoughts. "There was no distinction between music that was entertaining and music that was . . . inspirational. Popular and classical were the same thing . . ." Nolan goes on to describes Zevon stalking his keyboard and playing a passage from his mentor Stravinsky's *Persephone* to prove that the classical form could indeed be fused with others.

Peresphone could very well have been described as the rock 'n' roll of the classical set when it debuted in 1934. With a libretto by André Gide, it was for its time— really, for *any* time—a unique presentation of symphony as spectacle, featuring a speaker, various solo singers, a full chorus, and dancers. Infamously, two decades prior to *Peresphone* Stravinsky would assault an unsuspecting Parisian audience with his avant-garde masterwork, *The Rite of Spring* at the Théâtre des Champs-Élysées. The then young and relatively unknown composer's violently dissonant and provocative arrangements were deemed so outrageous the performance nearly instigated a riot. Today this once reviled and scandalous piece is widely considered to be one of the most influential musical works of the twentieth century.

Stravinsky's radical musical choices intrigued Zevon for reasons beyond their bold play with style. He would come to see these works as courageous in a time when his dreams of becoming an experimental composer and conducting a full orchestra, demanding the attention of serious music observers while also challenging their preconceptions, would have been realized. As it was, he would be born too late. Zevon provided insight to his unrealized aspirations during a 1995 interview with *Goldmine* magazine: "I wanted nothing more than to be a classical composer and conductor. That's what I believed would be rewarding, and the very thought of it was exciting and romantic. The problem was that there was no such thing. And there really hasn't been any such thing since a cat named Anton von Webern [Austrian composer, 1883–1945] was around. He was like 'the last classical composer' in the same way that maybe Samuel Beckett was the last traditional writer."

This finally gets to the depth of what drove Zevon beyond classical or rock or any kind of music: literary legitimacy. Always a frustrated man of letters, Zevon expressed to journalist Steve Roeser that he yearned to accomplish with music what Hunter S. Thompson and Kurt Vonnegut, considerable influences on Zevon (the former would become a friend and collaborator), had done with the novel form: twist it, turn it, strong-arm it into biographical fiction cranked on biting wit and swirling tangents. This is where Zevon lived and breathed: He was the voracious reader, the writer of strange character portraits set to music.

Nolan continues in his piece: "Warren insists that there still exist formal possibilities in music, just as in literature; that there still is room for development, experimentation, innovation . . . new forms! Invented by people like Warren, who understands the relation between passages in Stravinsky and the heart of a primo Jeff Beck solo. Warren, who could take his very personal knowledge and create something totally unique, something only *he* could make."

"So what happens when there's no more literature is that there has to be something else," Zevon told *Goldmine* fifteen years later. "What happens when there's no more classical music is that, all of a sudden, bar music becomes elevated to the artistic stature of what classical music was in the 19th Century. So a conglomerate like the Beatles and their producer becomes every bit as important and of the same caliber and quality as the great classical composers of the century before. With certainly no depreciation in quality; artistic, spiritual, whatever."

Less than two years after speaking with Nolan, Zevon would come as close to this concept as he would ever again on the eventual follow-up to *Excitable Boy, Bad Luck Streak in Dancing School*. Both the album and its title track would reflect his duality as a musical artist: the dutiful and disciplined composer of classic symphonies, charting lush orchestrations with winsome string and wind embellishments, combined with the tongue-in-cheek "heavy metal folk singer" (his term), who howled bizarre tales of contemptible rogues while prancing upon the piano as if it were the last hours of Mardi Gras.

Not that the songs on *Bad Luck in Dancing School* were Zevon's first pass at arranging strings for his work, nor would they be his last. He composed and charted the tender orchestration that opens "Desperados Under the Eaves," as well as the aggressive accompaniment to its changes and the sweeping coda. Later, for the layers of keyboards used on his conceptual 1989 album *Transverse City*, specifically its opening title track, Zevon would summon inspiration from Pyotr Tchaikovsky's late nineteenth-century Russian suites.

Both Browne and Waddy Wachtel, his previous producers, cite 'Frank and Jesse James' connection with Copland's panoramic symphonies as a prime example of higher art. Additionally, many of Zevon's contemporaries recall it as a song he routinely played for them when he was in the mood to impress, while also believing it to be an artistic revelation that freed him of loftier musical notions. "'Frank and Jesse James' was a particularly important song for me because it was the first time I managed to overcome the intellectual restrictions of trying to be a composer and a songwriter at the same time, a combination that can sometimes be manifested in writing unnecessarily complex songs," Zevon told the *Los Angeles Times* in 1976. "I think it was a breakthrough in that I was able to write simpler songs. I realized that complexity is not what distinguishes a composer."

"Most of us operate in tonic thirds and fifths, but Warren loved fourths," concludes

J. D. Souther. "The animal of the fourth was much more interesting to him than a third or a fifth. You hear that in his harmonics, and he even liked sixths. It reminded me of old Quaker hymns or some of the stuff that Aaron Copland borrowed for *Appalachian Spring*. His songs never relied on that one-three-five harmony that we have all grown so accustomed to in pop music"

His piano lines and attention to melodic detail, so admired by many of his heralded contemporaries, had lent themselves to an exceptional aural plane. In 2001, while working with him on the *My Ride's Here* sessions, multi-instrumentalist Katy Salvidge was so impressed with Zevon's intricate string charts for his haunting "Genius," she would tell his ex-wife, Crystal, a few years later, "It was the most unbelievable arrangement I ever heard. It's probably my favorite string arrangement of all time. It was musically so advanced, and I could tell he wasn't a rock and roller."

Guitarist and bandleader for the ensuing *Bad Luck Streak in Dancing School* tour David Landau observed firsthand Zevon's creative and personal duality: "I think Warren had a sense that he was operating in a world of popular music and that there was this other realm that Stravinsky and some of these other great classical giants operated in, and I think that he liked holding onto the idea that he could do that. He would walk around with Stravinsky scores. Warren wanted you to know that he wasn't just the guy who wrote 'Werewolves of London.'"

As one structured piece, *Bad Luck Streak in Dancing School*, specifically its title track, eschews the façade of rock and folk and gets down to what classical music might sound like if melded into popular late twentieth-century form. This is of course assuming that Zevon's ideas were separate from those experimented with by the Beatles in the latter half of a career filled with elaborate compositions that drew on almost every type of music previously unavailable to rock performance, or what Frank Zappa expanded upon exponentially for much of a brilliantly eclectic arc within the Mothers of Invention and beyond, or what the prog rock syndicate, from the Moody Blues to the Electric Light Orchestra dabbled in during the anything-goes late '60s and '70s. By 1979 there had been well over a decade of shamelessly layering string arrangements and classical ornaments in pop music with sometimes miraculous if not overblown results. Zevon, never one to embrace the haughty psychedelics of prog rock's fascination with phantasmagorical imagery, remained dedicated to an obsession with expressing his love of classical music within three- to four-minute musical vignettes.

Zevon's actions at the time appear to back up his intentions. Beyond contemplating such a leap to journalists, friends, and colleagues, there is his overt professional move to break away from his most ardent champion and the producer of his previous two records, Jackson Browne. This is something Browne saw coming right before his work on *Excitable Boy*, as he would enlist the services of Waddy Wachtel to act as creative conduit between himself and the always volatile songwriter during the recordings.

By the time of the *Excitable Boy* sessions, Zevon's unhinged behavior, fueled by Herculean drinking jags and a myriad of pill-popping, was the epitome of rock 'n' roll lore. Friend and Elektra/Asylum rep Burt Stein recalls Browne's exhausted tone after weeks in the studio with Zevon: "When Jackson was about finished with the record, his comment to me was, 'All right, Burt. I got him to here. He's all yours now.' So he kind of passed me the torch and we ran with it."

Wachtel inadvertently instigated his inclusion in the studio by offhandedly commenting to a French journalist while on the road with Linda Ronstadt that during his time working as a session guitarist on *Warren Zevon*, he observed that Browne seemed "overwhelmed" producing the first Zevon album. Of course, he never considered the subject of his critique would actually read it. Upon returning from the tour, Browne contacted Wachtel and confronted him: "Jackson says, 'So I read your interview.' I went, 'You what?' And he goes, 'You know, the interview you did in Europe, the one where you said I had my hands too full and I didn't know what I was doing?' I went, 'Oh, you did?' And I could not believe [it] when he said, 'You're absolutely right, that's why I'm calling you. I want you to coproduce the next record with me.' I said, 'What are you talking about? You don't even *know* me.' He goes, 'I know you *now* and I know where I stand with you, but more importantly, I know where I stand with Warren and he will *not* listen to a thing I say now, but he *will* listen to you. But take it from me, after this album he probably won't listen to you either,' which is exactly what happened."

David Landau, who ostensibly acted as Wachtel's understudy during the *Excitable Boy* tour, realized the guitarist's strengths when it came to working with the mercurial Zevon: "Waddy was a pretty unflappable guy, acerbic and very aggressive. He had this in-your-face manner about him. Not in a mean way, but he lets you know he's there. When Waddy's in the room you *know* he's in the room. I was learning his guitar parts on the *Excitable Boy* tour and I studied that record inside out, but when I'd play it for him, he would say, 'Ahh . . . not quite.' There would be just the slightest nuance that I had missed and he wasn't wrong. He could be so supportive, but also so meticulous."

Landau told me about a key incident that occurred after a particularly sloppy show on the tour, in which Wachtel lit into Zevon in the lobby of New York's Gramercy Hotel. "Waddy was just ripping Warren to shreds for what he had done at a gig," recalls Landau. "The guy had coproduced his album, had gone out on tour with him in the midst of touring with Linda Ronstadt, and I don't know what Waddy was getting paid, but I'm sure it wasn't anything close to what he was normally getting with Linda. Basically, the theme of the rant was 'You want to destroy yourself that's one thing, but you're making me look bad!' Man, it was intense and brutal."

"For the most part, we were pretty solid during that tour, if not completely drunk, but that was the low point," says Wachtel today. "I don't remember too much else about that night except it was a horrible embarrassment."

Browne's decision to include Wachtel proved a shrewd one, as the guitarist's frankness as a musician/collaborator pushed his friend to loftier songwriting heights, resulting in Zevon's biggest chart success. But now, preparing for *Bad Luck Streak in Dancing School*, Zevon would come to find that complete creative control was much easier to demand following a gold record. With both Browne and Wachtel in reduced roles—Wachtel played on two tracks and Browne played on one and sang background on four—this would pave the way for his vision to be realized.

The statement is immediate and striking. *Bad Luck Streak in Dancing School* opens with a string quartet prologue to the title track, which is the first of three instrumental pieces that hold the musical elements of the entire song cycle together. Two of the remaining classical miniatures, also performed by a string quartet, stand alone as "Interlude No. 1" and "Interlude No. 2," both solemn requiems in a minor key that while acting as transitional bridges to the songs are in and of themselves musical diversions. While admittedly being nods to one of Zevon's classical piano heroes, Glenn Gould, whose technical proficiency, specifically in interpreting the work of Johann Sebastian Bach, is renowned, they mostly reflect an acute understanding of the work of fellow Russian-Jewish composer Modest Petrovich Mussorgsky. His *Pictures at an Exhibition*, a musical expression of movement through a museum and its varied moods of enjoying paintings by Viktor Hartmann (the name figures in the subtitle of the piece "A Remembrance of Viktor Hartmann"), provides the listener with an emotional progression through the exhibition. These "promenades" include diverse tempos that denote a stroll from one movement (painting) to the next. Zevon's affectionate homage to Mussorgsky appears in the main theme of "Interlude No. 2," a distinct melody reminiscent of the maestro's well-traveled reflective opening and repeated stanza for the piece. Here, like Mussorgsky, Zevon is cleansing the aural palette and providing a musical transition between songs.

"I've never seen him happier in the studio than when we were doing the violins or cellos," recalls George Gruel. "He was just beaming. We were playing his symphony, so to speak." Zevon would often prepare jokes and anecdotes to loosen up the jaded and dubious Hollywood string players.

The first of the album's interludes lulls the listener into a false sense of respite before barreling into the foot-stomping hayseed pastiche of "Play It All Night Long" with its mocking ode to country-rock stalwart Lynyrd Skynyrd's "Sweet Home Alabama" as "that dead band's song" and all the "sweat, piss, jizz and blood." The second, a more direct tribute to Mussorgsky's first "Promenade," ushers in the quietly contentious "Bill Lee," which uses another real-life pop culture character, this one from Major League Baseball, to present the outlaw iconoclast in one quick but effective verse and two very telling lines: "And sometimes I say things I shouldn't, like . . ." Zevon never completes the line, choosing instead to let the listener's imagination run wild above a seductive piano/harmonica run. Despite the disparate nature of the music, and the songs' pop culture subjects—the fatal airplane accident that killed members of a country-rock outfit and the rebellious, pot-smoking, wisecracking pitcher Bill "Spaceman" Lee—the opening lines of both songs are no less striking: "Grandpa pissed his pants again / He don't give a damn" and "You're supposed to sit on your ass and nod at stupid things / Man, that's hard to do," respectively.

It is the opening razor-sharp string arrangement, however, that prefaces the album while also ushering in the title track. The song begins in earnest with two snaps of what sound like a snare drum or enhanced handclaps. Neither would be the case, as George Gruel, present for the sessions, explained to me in 2015. "That *bap-bap* at the beginning of the actual song is a gun going off," he recalled, laughing hysterically. Zevon fired off his beloved .44 Magnum into a drum filled with sand, the sound of the two shots so shocking it could only be performed once. "We had no idea what was going to happen," Gruel continued. "Jackson was there and [coproducer] Greg Ladanyi, and we thought the compression might blow the windows out of the studio, 'cause the gun was like a hand cannon. But it worked!"

Thus the opening of this transitional record for Zevon displays both sides of the artist's complicated aura: the genius composer wrapped in the spastic eruption of the madman. It is something Paul Nelson marvelously described in *Rolling Stone* two years earlier: "While one hand steadily applies the Apollonian technique and obvious control of the classical artist, the other is compulsively jerking the trigger with Dionysian delirium."

The gunshots sonically herald Zevon's emancipation from the rigors of normal rock conventions, as his customary display of machismo had always been a dramatic response to the constant comparisons to the "L.A. Sound" that dogged him the minute he signed with Asylum Records. David Landau acutely observed this subtext when we spoke in the autumn of 2016: "Warren was always very conscious that he was in the midst of the whole L.A. scene and overshadowed by his patron saint, Jackson Browne. Although I think Jackson is one of the most brilliant songwriters ever, in terms of popular culture at that time he was the ultimate sensitive singer-songwriter. He was also responsible for Warren's career, and I think there was a real tension there, and Warren was so into his macho posturing with his handguns that I've always felt that a big part it was to differentiate himself from that: to not be seen in that light. I think he came by it honestly, but in that milieu, it really helped him distinguish himself."

Immediately after the gunshots, a distorted guitar riff, naked and commanding, gives way to a majestic swell of traditional rock instruments. Yet this raucous overture is steeped in classical overtones, rich and expressive in something akin to march time. It is a mini-symphony unto itself, as Zevon wastes no time getting right to the point. This is not going to be *Excitable Boy Part II*. It's a new decade and this is a new sound . . . well, at least an old sound *made* new. And just as Nolan had noted, this is a sound that Zevon believed only he could fuse into the culture, whether it would alienate the widening audience he had attracted with "Werewolves of London" or not. Zevon admitted a year later that composing the song had actually led to a seizure at the airport. "I thought I had a stroke," he confessed to music journalist Barry Alfonso. "I probably had been beating my head against the wall trying to write something I should have abandoned."

Perhaps the most conspicuous evidence that the album's production would vary dramatically from Jackson Browne's more direct approach is heard in Zevon's voice, which sounds far more distant and processed than on his first two albums. Where his vocals were clean and crisp and tended to dominate the backing tracks on both, here it blends into them, becoming more accompanying instrument than lead vocal. "I'm sorry to say that is a terribly dark-sounding record and the arrangements are not clear," opines Waddy Wachtel today. "It went exactly as Jackson predicted: As soon as we finished *Excitable Boy* he didn't want to hear from me. *Bad Luck Streak* is just not up to the standard it should be to me."

I remember being taken aback from the first track on the album in a way that I'm sure a number of fans were who may have been pulled in by *Excitable Boy*. This was completely different stuff. Well, as much as the sound may have been a departure, lyrically we are still very much in familiar Zevon territory: pain, anguish, guilt, beseeching penance, and trying like hell to pull oneself from the rigors of inevitable bad luck.

Bad luck streak in dancing school
Down on my knees in pain
Bad luck streak in dancing school
Swear to God I'll change

Zevon conjured the opening verse in 1978 during the *Excitable Boy* tour when he infamously tumbled from the stage in Chicago and suffered severe injuries that would force George Gruel to carry him onto the stage and place him on the piano stool for the rest of the tour. "As he lay in the orchestra pit, pain shooting through his knees, Warren recalled a quirky one-liner that he'd dreamed up a couple of days before," wrote Michael Branton in San Francisco's *BAM* music paper. "'It came to me as kind of a joke,'" Zevon says. 'I pictured a cartoon of a guy with his arms and legs in casts, holding a crutch, a bandage around his head, with the line 'Bad luck streak in dancing school.'"

While not sounding nearly as desperate as the solitary drunk of "Desperados Under the Eaves" or the smart-ass moaner of "Poor Poor Pitiful Me," the lyric and Zevon's passionate vocal performance are pure torment. As noted in the previous essay, Zevon did not fool around with the concept of "luck." He believed strongly in its control of his life and fortunes. As far back as his teenage pop duo, lyme & cybelle, during which he dressed as stephen lyme in only lime colors, then immediately upon its dissolution discarded all of its remnants and embraced the color blue while adopting the pop star persona of Sandy, Zevon believed "bad luck" was real and potentially lethal. And while there is a wonderfully satiric swipe at dancing school as a discipline similar to classical music training with its relentless repetition and adherence to stringent rules and forms, not to mention the demand of strict instructors, it is the ever-present looming "bad luck" that dominates the theme here.

Zevon would use the concept of "bad luck" perhaps more than any other theme in his work, save alcohol abuse and random violence, and even those were almost always tied to some kind of preternatural destiny. And while the lineage between the songs is explicit, it only scratches the surface of the subject. Again, as in the victim-themed songs "Poor Poor Pitiful Me," "Studebaker," and "Lawyers, Guns and Money," the existential outside sources that condemn many of Zevon's protagonists to predestined hardships suggest he was still working out its effect. The voices given to these narrators bemoan circumstance, whether historical or personal, asking the eternal question as to why such calamity could befall them.

"Warren looked at luck as something that's behind a cloud, because you can have it one day and not the next or think you're going to have it that day and it turns out to be the opposite," reasons perhaps his closest friend, Jorge Calderón, who was surprised to hear that his "quirky" behavior was later diagnosed as a disease. "I saw him as more of a realist. He loved to talk about luck of the game, because, as you know, his father was a gambler and he always had that in his mind: 'playing the hand' or 'putting your cards on the table.' That was part of his lingo all the time."

From "Frank and Jesse James," the very first track on *Warren Zevon*, as if preparing the thematic way for the remainder of his work, Zevon establishes that the titular characters' outlaw ways are not so much born of free will as they are a response to the greater circumstance of the American Civil War. Criminality is the pair's raison d'être, a drastic reaction to a nation torn asunder in armed conflict over morality, culture, and commerce. The song's most telling lyric, and an underlying theme to Zevon's bevy of compelling song characters, comes in the second verse, when we learn that a "raw deal" turned the James brothers from revolutionaries to marauders: "So no amnesty was granted / And as outlaws they did ride." What other recourse than to reject the system that denies you reprieve? And so the James brothers keep on "riding, riding, riding" to "clear their names," stopping only to continue their rampage as some demented form of social commentary.

Zevon follows this pernicious tribute by exploring the unwieldy happenstance of his parents' romantic wager in "Mama Couldn't Be Persuaded," in which he literally becomes a gambling chip. Then there is the man addicted to sexual depravity having to fend off the bestial women his lifestyle has attracted in "Poor Poor Pitiful Me" to the drug-addled cries of woe in "Carmelita" and alcoholic sighs of "Desperados Under the Eaves."

Zevon's next song cycle, *Excitable Boy*, brims with lovable rogues whose lives have been changed by the mercurial whims of fate—the murderous lunatic who is "just an excitable boy"; the headless Thompson gunner, a killer for hire who is "stalking through the night" after ironically becoming the victim; the powerless parent who must watch the sudden maturation of an innocent daughter being tutored by the streets in "Tenderness on the Block"; the man found taking home stray Communist waitresses ("How was I to know?"), gambling (again) in Havana and stuck somehow in Honduras (how did he unwittingly trek all the way to a war-torn Central American country?) in need of lawyers, guns, and money; the doomed family of "Veracruz" in the sights of Woodrow Wilson's guns. Hell, how does one accidentally become a martyr anyway?

These are figures caught in an objective vortex with no moral center, shifting and twisting as though, well . . . dancing.

Long after "Bad Luck Streak in Dancing School," Zevon songs returned time and again to the theme of mythical gods of chance raining down misfortune. More often than not, the ensuing tragedies have a specific source beyond the supernatural: a particular woman or the *presence* of a woman as a symbol for the erratic manners of fate. She moves like luck, with terrifying randomness, a frightening prospect for one so beholden to providence. This time he puts a name on the origin of his calamity and begs to be absolved of his "sins."

Pauline, don't make me beg

Pauline holds the key to the narrator's salvation. Within the context of the dance-school theme, she takes the part of the patrician instructor grown weary with his inability to meld into the greater whole. Sticking with the metaphor, the dance troupe that relies on him to learn the steps and understand the fluidity of the collective craft will suffer if he doesn't quit spiriting off the grid. The dance school represents structure, like polite society, with its rules and boundaries. Pauline is the systemic bane of the unrepentant contrarian, as was Zevon's mother, her strict Mormon values and disciplines set against his nomadic gangster father, who went his own way and played by his own rules—much like Zevon himself, although his internal battle between the studious, well-dressed gentleman and the snarling, macho werewolf would plague him until his dying day.

Dance is a discipline Zevon knew well, as he had indeed attended dance training to keep fit and, according to his friend George Gruel, took it quite seriously. "Warren took ballet lessons to get in shape, except the ballet dancers wore this reverse jock–type thing that spread your buns apart so you looked shapelier," Gruel recalls with laughter. "He would scream, 'This thing's fucking killing me!' As always with Warren, he went full tilt: he had the leotards and everything."

This, of course, also speaks to another classical framework that beckoned for Zevon. Photographed on the album's cover with ballerinas, he leisurely leans in a second-floor-balcony doorway, appearing aloof and fading into the woodwork. This reflects his unrequited need not only to immerse himself in higher art but to begin to exit the limelight he recently enjoyed thanks to the popularity of *Excitable Boy*. Again, in direct contrast to the previous album's cover featuring an ultra close-up of Zevon airbrushed to the point of obsession at his behest—a blatant act of vanity—here is the distant, naturally lit almost silhouette of an artist in humble repose. "We didn't set out to hide Warren specifically, but we'd already done 'the big face' on *Excitable Boy*, so we wanted it to be as though he were part of a scene," recalled photographer and designer Jimmy Wachtel when I pressed him on my theory in late 2016. "The true inspiration for that cover was Deborah Turbeville's soft, grainy style. That was a beauty. I wish I still had it, but it vanished somewhere. Somebody might have it hanging on their wall. Who knows?"

This may also further explain Zevon's desire to bury his vocals a little deeper in the mix than on the previous two albums. Once again, Zevon is quite literally pulling back, in both music production and image. It is the visual/aural equivalent of the artist rejecting his pursuit of stardom afforded by the success of "Werewolves of London" for deeper artistic pursuits and personal identification. He sings with gusto, "I swear to God I'll change!"

There is also a significant difference here from almost all of Zevon's lyrical excursions in that there is no backstory. If anything, the song is a mantra, as though there will be no explanation or regurgitating of the purported wrongdoing—fame, substance abuse, untrustworthy lover—just a repeated apology or promise to right whatever is wrong. The generalities of the remaining two lines in the song are some indication of his foibles, but only as broad allegation. These are lines that could be sung by a child who has been chastised for its behavior and not a man working with a sense of self or possessing true empathy.

I've been acting like a fool
I've been breaking all the rules

This song was written around the time when Warren Zevon was to first come to grips with his furious attack on anything pertaining to "normalcy"—family, friendship, professionalism—that would cause his marriage to fracture, turn him into a ghostlike figure to his children, make him a burden on his friends and colleagues, and give him the type of entertainment-business rep that alienates record companies, PR firms, agents and management.

Jackson Browne was convinced at the time that Zevon did not work with him again because he had confronted him about his excess drinking during the *Excitable Boy* sessions, which expanded to his erratic behavior with his record company and magazines that covered him.

"Warren suddenly looked like he could have a big career and I'm watching him just throw it away," remembers David Landau. As a result, there were interventions, rehab stints, and relapses. When pressed by me on the subject in 2015, his tour manager and drinking buddy George Gruel, who describes himself as "no saint either," found it hard to remember if he ever had a heart-to-heart with Zevon about his substance abuse and how it was negatively affecting his work and damaging those close to him. "He would sometimes say, 'I don't want to die, I just like getting fucked up,'" Gruel finally admitted. "And I can understand it. That's the way it was. He grew up with a Jewish father who ran a carpet store and never sold an inch of carpet. His mother was a Mormon, hypochondriac alcoholic. What a way to grow up."

During our discussion in the early autumn of 2016, Landau shared a rather harrowing incident that frames the kind of behavior that underscores "Bad Luck Streak in Dancing in School": "Warren had this fantastic suite at the Gramercy during the *Excitable Boy* tour. It was off-the-charts hip. It had something that belonged to *this* artist and *that* artist. And so I get this call one night around two or three in the morning from Crystal that Warren's been out all night drinking with the Clancy Brothers and came back really drunk. He was in a rage, waking her up by rubbing salad on her or something weird like that, and then he sort of hacked at his wrist with a piece of broken glass. When I walked in this beautiful room it looked like someone had set off a couple of hand grenades. He had absolutely trashed the place. Their baby, Ariel, was there. So I'm sort of confronted with this and somehow we end up getting through the night, and Crystal, in classic fashion, cleaned up the room, so that when Warren got up the next morning he had no idea what he had done."

"Nobody was as good at drinking as him . . . or as *bad* at it, I should say," adds Waddy Wachtel. "I'd never met a stone-cold alcoholic before Zevon. There were nights going back to our tour with the Everly Brothers where after the show he'd get so fucked up that he would be really insulting and I'd come close to punching his fucking lights out. If he'd been conscious he would have known it, but he was so gone. And he was taking quaaludes, too. I didn't even know what a quaalude was yet. One night he was so obnoxious that someone said, 'Oh, he took this pill on top of all the booze he's drinking.' And I said, 'I don't give a shit what he took. I'm going to fucking kill him.' Warren was *very* thirsty. Let's put it that way."

During the making of the record, Zevon, now estranged from his wife, was hunkered down at the historic and glamorous Chateau Marmont, where celebrities escaped to find the kind of cover needed to unleash demons and cause a ruckus. Gruel received a call in the middle of the night: "Can you please come disarm Mr. Zevon?"

"He's leaning out the window shooting at a Richard Pryor billboard," remembers Gruel. "He couldn't even see who it was. He was just shooting. It was fucking wonderful. I think it's fabulous. Then *People* magazine goes up to interview him and a mouse runs across the floor and he calmly says, 'I'll take care of it.' He comes out of the room with his hand cannon and vaporized the mouse. The guy from *People* says, 'Uh, I have to go now.' I seriously don't know how he lived as long as he did."

Nearly a full decade of decadence and debauchery, antisocial madness and overall dumbness had put Zevon on notice. He was quickly and savagely wrecking a career that had just begun to percolate. The unhinged *Excitable Boy* tour only enhanced his image, casting him as at best a wild child and at worst a borderline maniac. "He would drink vodka before the show and during the show, and sometimes it would be fine, because he was definitely one of those people who can *mostly* function," recalls his friend and guitarist on the tour, Jorge Calderón. "But sometimes he would be so out of it and slurring that it was painful to watch. We would tell him, 'Yeah, man, in San Francisco you fell off the bench!' It was embarrassing for him and everybody else. Then there was the time in Canada when he broke his ankle trying to climb up the speakers to make one of these rock 'n' roll jumps onto the stage and he was so hammered that he fell in the wrong position and screwed himself up."

"By 1978 he was a full-blown drug addict and alcoholic" adds Gruel. "I first met his wife, Crystal, in a hotel room in Portland and it was something like seven-thirty in the morning and she's holding an empty glass, and I said, 'What are you doing with that?' She goes, 'I'm gonna go down and see if I can get them to open the bar and get Warren some vodka.' And I said, 'Well, I'll do it.' So I did."

"When I left the *Excitable Boy* tour, Jackson and I went to see him at the L.A. Amphitheatre and it was horrifying," recalls Waddy Wachtel. "It was so embarrassing I snuck out, because I didn't want to be seen there."

Jordan Zevon, then only eight years old, recounts a backstage experience from the very same show: "My grandmother walked me to the backstage area and said, 'This is his son,' and they were like, 'Ehhhhh,' and she repeated strongly, 'This is his son!' Finally Crystal came along and realized what was happening and let us in, and they ushered me into this backstage room. I sat across from my dad . . . and he was just *completely* wasted, like a vegetable. And so I'm just kind of standing there, as you would awkwardly do as an eight-year-old, trying to kind of say, 'Well, school is good and I hope you're well.' And then the other side of the dressing room door opened and he went into a limo and *boom*, he was gone."

Bad Luck Streak in Dancing School is Warren Zevon at a crossroads. The songwriter was trying like hell to make amends. "The strongest part of making that record was living Warren's songs," the album's coproducer and late L.A. engineering legend Greg Ladanyi told journalist, Trevor Hards in 1980. "They came from a dark place in Warren. It was an emotional experience for everyone." And the dark place was beginning to play tricks on Zevon as he wrestled with, as Mikal Gilmore of *Rolling Stone* opined, "whether his best songs were evidence of a real and self-determined artistry or merely the product of an alcohol-immersed sensibility."

His son, Jordan, confessed to me: "I didn't really have any kind of significant relationship with him until *Bad Luck Streak*, when he got sober and I went to the care unit at Cedars-Sinai and I hung with him every day and we went to group therapy, because at the end of the day I was pissed, but I still wanted a dad. Before that there were certain moments I remember, like when he was staying at Chateau Marmont, because I think he'd been kicked out of the house, and it was '77 and he said, 'Well what do you want to do, son? Do you want to go see a movie? There's this new movie out. It's supposed to be really great.' I said, 'No, can you just play music for me?' And I remember that distinctive reaction of, 'Ugh. This is my work, but all right.' So we just sat around and played music. That opening-weekend movie that I missed was *Star Wars*. So in 1977, Warren Zevon and I could have gone and seen *Star Wars* on its opening weekend! But I just wanted him to play 'Werewolves' for me. I wanted that part of him to be *mine*, and not through all these other people; I wanted to have that moment for me, because at that point I hadn't really seen him perform or anything, and so I just wanted this special engagement."

Zevon's daughter, Ariel, who was forty when we spoke in the winter of 2017, told me she only knew her father through his music and would spend hours listening to his records and clutching the covers to be closer to him: "I adored him and I just wanted him to adore me. So, as kids do, you just glom on to where the love is, and I guess, not to sound cheesy, that love was in his music. I would listen to it to connect with him when he wasn't around, but I don't remember asking him to play music, because for me he was *always* playing his music. That was his life. His be-all and end-all was writing his music."

It is no surprise that classical music would ultimately help Ariel establish a bond with her mostly absent father during her formative years. "We connected fairly early on in classical music because I was studying classical flute as a kid growing up, and of course he really wanted to be a classical composer," says Ariel. "That had been his real ambition as a young musician. He carried it throughout his career and life. So when I started playing classical music, we could share that. When I was spending time with him he would play me classical music, and we related on those terms."

Cutting through the title track's classical motif is a ferocious guitar riff played joyfully by Zevon giving way to the heartfelt attrition of David Lindley's moaning lap-steel guitar played according to George Gruel at such an intense volume in the studio no one would dare wear headphones. As mentioned, Gruel also took candid photos attesting to the musicians' lightheartedness, many of which are included on the album's inner sleeve. Once again, a host of friends and colleagues, including Lindley, Jackson Browne J. D. Souther, Linda Ronstadt, and Jorge Calderón would join many of the Eagles, including newcomer Joe Walsh, to lend their talents to Zevon's work. It also appears by all accounts that while being repentant in song there was no sign that Zevon would be changing any of his loose-cannon ways. His attempts at sobriety, while sincere, were sporadic at best. This would be the third album for him in which professional edicts and social distractions would intersect to create some other thing entirely.

It is not without coincidence that Zevon would close the album with the rousing, almost Springsteenesque "Wild Age," another kind of confessional, this time with an auspicious absence of contrition.

You've seen him leaning on the streetlight
Listening to some song inside
You've seen him standing by the highway
Trying to hitch a ride

Well, they tried so hard to hold him
Heaven knows how hard they tried
But he's made up his mind
He's the restless kind

He's the wild age

Zevon was indeed still captured by the "wild age," as was his generation, as he sings later in the chorus, "No one can stop 'em." After the final verse, where he all but predicts an ignominious end to this unhinged behavior— "Mostly when the reckless years end / Something's left to save / Some of them keep running / 'Til they run straight in their graves"—he cries with reckless abandon, "Stay the wild age!" over and over again into the fade, completely contradicting his plea for forgiveness in the opening track. By the end of this experimental musical journey, here is the composer steeped in the sound and imagery of rock 'n' roll churning his genuflection to classical music disciplines into a fine mist.

Of course, Warren Zevon would make inroads to infuse classic themes in future projects, but not with the same passion and attention as in the writing, arranging, and recording of *Bad Luck Streak in Dancing School*. According to friends and colleagues, he would carry the remnants of his unfinished symphony with him until his death in 2003. It was never recorded. Maybe someday it will be.

"I truly believe his goal was to write a symphony," concludes George Gruel. "He had many unfinished movements. He wrote all the charts for *Bad Luck Streak in Dancing School* out over three days by hand . . . every part, even for the triangle and the timpani, and every part of the orchestra, even though he knew there wasn't going to be a full orchestra at the session."

"I think if Warren had lived another ten years he would have written something of some symphonic length," says J. D. Souther.

Ariel Zevon agrees: "He talked about writing, composing classical music all the time, all throughout his life. And he had a huge collection of older classical music, but he also listened to newer composers and the cutting edge of what people were composing in avant-garde classical music then. He got into *all* of that."

"I don't know whether he talked that much about it [symphony] with Jackson or with anybody else, but he did with me because we played each other little passages and little movements," remembers J. D. Souther.

"I can picture him now," remembers George Gruel. "Wearing a nice sweater or an ascot or a scarf or something, and he'd have all his pens and his classic score sheets laid out. Then he would play and write out all these charts and move back and forth from the charts to the piano. And this would go on all night long. Usually my spot would be to lie under the grand piano smoking pot and listen. He'd lean down every once in a while and say, 'Give me a hit.' And then right back to it."

Today, Jordan, who possesses all of his father's classical charts, cannot be sure of the aim and purpose of Warren Zevon's unfinished symphony. "I have a lot of sheet music that I've put down in front of people that were friends of mine that are good readers and even to them it was a little bit like, 'I'm not sure where this is going.' And my dad was not a scribbler. He had perfect penmanship and wrote these charts out perfectly, but they were so 'out there' that it even kind of perplexed those guys. So I think that there is something there that might have been really fantastic, but I have to be honest, I think at the same time that what it would have taken for him to develop those things would have been the free time away from the business and trying to sell records, and he didn't have the opportunity to have that part of his life pan out. It was still kind of, 'Give the people what they want.' Go on tour. Make some money. Pay the bills. I don't think he was able to get into a headspace where he could have said, 'Hey, I'm taking two years off and I'm going to work on this symphony.' But I'll tell you something: It would have been fucking amazing."

Warren Zevon ontage, October 2, 1982, at the Whalen Center for Music at Ithaca College.
Photo by Andrew L. Seymour

"Mohammed's Radio"
(live)

I sing as good as I can, and I dance as well as I want.
—WARREN ZEVON, Universal Amphitheatre, Los Angeles

Warren Zevon's live work was a jailbreak of unmitigated ecstasy that provided an uncompromising glimpse into his tortured soul with a rare understated honesty humming beneath it. Rock critic Dave Marsh described Zevon as an "assaultive performer." Artists with his kind of haunted, troubled, maniacal existence might see the stage as offering refuge from the relentless chaos of personal strife and the crush of celebrity. This, however, does not apply to Zevon. He left no baggage behind. Instead, he carried it onstage and unpacked it without shame beneath the glare of the spotlight.

This was never a choice for Zevon, for it's difficult to hide from his songs. They're works of intense construction with themes far off the beaten path. To take them on the road meant to own them, to funnel the songs through himself and out into the audience, letting his characters possess his performance. He was not an avoidance artist. He would never blink first.

Perhaps the best example of this is Zevon's most inspired live song, "Mohammed's Radio." Waddy Wachtel, who would play a significant part in the song's composing and would go on to arrange its live presentation, adds: "There is so much built into it—the dynamics of the gospel chorale to the chorus, and where it gets really soft in the verses. He would get so beautiful with it: 'You've been up all night listening for his drum . . .' And the *bah bah bah*. The orchestral dynamics in it strike your emotions very strongly, the way the chords lend themselves to the melody and the way they set up the arrangement, these strong punches in between delicate lines. It just works."

"I always loved that song," said Zevon's onetime touring lead guitarist David Landau, when I told him I was dedicating an essay to "Mohammed's Radio." "I have to tell you, it's funny that you think so highly of it. I hadn't heard the live version in many years, and after it started to circulate again I went back and listened to it and I was really struck by that tune in particular. It's such an unusual song, both in terms of structure and the lyrics. You'd be hard-pressed to find another song that you could say, 'Oh, yeah, it's like *that*.'"

"'Mohammed's Radio' is gorgeous," notes J. D. Souther. "It was a very inventive piece of music with a beautiful lead vocal on it and, I may say, some pretty nice harmonies too."

Zevon's endearing performance of "Mohammed's Radio" forcefully belies his discomfort with writing ballads that hail rock music as transcendent or spiritual. "I guess that song was like a rare, drunken, sentimental slip into something that I generally abhor, which is the whole idea of rock 'n' roll as some kind of spiritual, worth-dying-for phenomenon," he told *Goldmine* magazine in 1995. "I don't play that! Gimme a break with all the black leather and the pounding on the stage, and rock 'n' roll as an anthemic, magnificent . . . whatever."

Inspired by a "developmentally challenged local dressed as a sheik with a radio up to his ear" walking the streets of downtown Aspen that Zevon caught a glimpse of during a 1975 visit whilst sipping cocktails in the famed Hotel Jerome bar, the origins of "Mohammed's Radio" found its way to his collaborator LeRoy Marinell, who helped provide a backstory. Mohammed would become for Zevon and Marinell a symbolic figure, standing for everyone, which in a very real sense is not far off.

The name Mohammed, from the Arabic *hamid*, meaning "praise," is the most popular name on the planet. It is also the name with the most spelling variants (fourteen) of any other: Mahamed, Muhammad, Muhammet, Mohammed, etc. The last became something of a touchstone during Zevon's 1980 tour, in which he often substituted the song's original lyric, "You know, the sheriff's got his problems too" for "the ayatollah has his problems too," a timely reference to the Iranian hostage crisis in which Ayatollah Ruhollah Khomeini became America's great villain.

For 444 days from November 4, 1979, to January 20, 1981, fifty-two Americans were held hostage after a group of Iranian students took over the U.S. Embassy in Tehran. The incident would toss the United States into a Middle East cauldron from which it would never escape, from the arming of neighboring Iraq's despot Saddam Hussein to building the mujahideen defense force (a breeding ground for the Taliban and then Al-Qaeda) to thwart the Soviet Union's invasion of Afghanistan in the final days of 1979, through to the infamy of 9/11/01 and the ensuing Afghan and Iraq wars beginning in 2001 and 2003, respectively, and continuing today.

The xenophobic furor against Muslims would escalate over time, providing a sinister slant on the name Mohammed, which had more than a decade earlier driven a wedge in the social order when U.S. Olympic gold medal boxer Cassius Clay, fresh from his stunning upset of heavyweight champion Sonny Liston, joined the controversial black Muslim movement by taking the name Muhammad Ali. His subsequent refusal to register for the draft for the wildly unpopular and spectacularly mismanaged Vietnam War on religious principles ended in Ali taking on the whole of the United States government, resulting in his eventual banishment from boxing and the four-year stripping of his championship belt.

When Zevon recorded the song for his 1976 Asylum debut, Ali was back in the good graces of the nation and a shining hero for a generation. His conviction overturned upon appeal by the U.S. Supreme Court in a unanimous and landmark decision in 1971, he would once again be a conquering champion in the ring. This makes the choice of the name anything but coincidental. Mohammed triumphs. Mohammed polarizes. Mohammed stirs. Mohammed adds an air of mystery, holiness, menace. The name is spiritual, defiant, controversial, idiosyncratic, but more importantly, it is really musical.

Neither Zevon nor Marinell could hear what music was playing on their subject's radio, thus it becomes the sonar for *all* music that heals, provokes, and blesses. This is a song about *praising* music, about the power to turn desperate times into glorious arias, to transform crisis into infinite beauty. Hymns, *maqam*, be-bop-a-lula: This is the way of Mohammed and his radio.

Don't it make you want to rock and roll
All night long

Right from the start, Zevon used performance as a kind of all-encompassing affair. In his short-lived duo lyme & cybelle, he would, as stephen lyme, dress in . . . well . . . lime. He would brood. He would fawn. This was as much affectation as a visual expression of his inner discord. When he found his voice and put together what truly moved him—a lifestyle bulging with personal friction and intellectual combat—he strategically infused it into the music, as if he were exorcising demons and celebrating life all at once.

This idea of perpetuating the conceit of an artist, especially a rock 'n' roll artist bathed in imagery—living the persona beyond projecting it as idiom and later becoming its prisoner—was not lost on Warren Zevon. He understood his place in the pantheon of performance perhaps better than anyone. He expressed to journalist Steve Roeser in 1995: "I think you have to say, and I've always said this, 'Perry Farrell, Perry Como: same job, same fuckin' guy.' I don't care if he rubs broken glass on his chest or if he wears a white dinner jacket. It's the same fucking job! Don't be a hypocrite. If you can say something serious and important and moving, and something about your feelings and/or humankind, that's great. But as soon as it gets stupid, you better get 'em laughing, because otherwise, it'll be horrible. Hypocrisy and pompousness, which go hand-in-hand; that shit'll make your skin crawl."

Jackson Browne told *Rolling Stone* in 2003: "I asked him once, 'Do you consider yourself an entertainer?' And he said, 'Absolutely. If you're not doing that, you're not doing anything.'"

There would always be, as with everything in his life and art, a dark humor and deep pathos in Zevon's performance both in and out of the spotlight. He never left the house without them. They were his fedora, his walking stick, his stark-white Tom Wolfe suit, his charm in mild conversation, in correspondence with lovers, friends, and colleagues. Onstage it was a bazooka filled with serious ammunition, a passion play worth watching. It was as if Zevon put those songs on trial night after night, kicking them around the stage and taking them through their paces— laying them at the feet of the crowd, uttering Pontius Pilate's infamous line "What is truth?," demanding the audience join in his extortions of fear and aspiration played out in melody. And so when you placed the visual over the aural, it fit like a glove.

Zevon was the consummate performer. Long after he could afford to pay bands and his audience had slipped to merely die-hards and theaters turned to clubs, he worked the stage like a master, acoustic guitar in hand and a piano at which to adjust his frame and loosen his wrists. "Getting onstage is always novel to me," admitted Zevon to KGSR radio, Austin, later in his career. "I don't know why that doesn't go away. I'm like the goldfish in the Ani DiFranco song ["Little Plastic Castles"] that goes around the bowl and every time it sees the little plastic castle it's like it's seeing it for the first time."

From his very first tour in support of *Warren Zevon* in 1976, Zevon struggled mightily to curtail his day-to-day derangement of the senses and tame his penchant to explode in spastic revelry without warning, the literate commentator of the bizarre miraculously swinging from disturbing incoherence to a force of energetic wit and brilliance with shocking ease. Rock journalist Paul Nelson wrote of the tour's opening show at New York's Bottom Line: "Seeing the man onstage was like experiencing— what?—Jackson Browne's 'For Everyman,' the works of F. Scott Fitzgerald, Sam Peckinpah's *The Wild Bunch*, the New York Dolls, Norman Mailer, Clint Eastwood in *Dirty Harry* and Ross Macdonald's Lew Archer novels at an impressionable age. Rightly or wrongly, your life got changed."

During the tour, Zevon made several daytime appearances at local radio stations, where he would be asked to perform, answer questions, and trade zingers. Burt Stein, the head of the radio promotion team at Elektra/Asylum, tagged along to make sure this all went down without incident. Stein, whom Zevon affectionately described as "a deranged Dustin Hoffman–looking, iconoclastic recording company man who will alter all your ideas of recording companies" reminisced about this never-a-dull-moment gig when we spoke in the summer of 2016: "He would have a couple hits of his Stolichnaya vodka first thing in the morning, announcing, 'Starsky, you can never eat on an empty stomach!' He always called me Starsky, and he was Hutch. Now, I have to admit that on the road I wasn't always paying attention to what he was or wasn't doing, but I do know you could always depend on there being a flask in the inside pocket of his sports coat. Maybe he had a few in the morning, but he always had it together on the radio. He was very commanding and well-spoken. He had that great voice and he was always witty. The drinking never seemed to affect his performance."

Zevon honed his stagecraft from his time touring as bandleader for the Everly Brothers, learning valuable lessons on forging ahead despite personal issues. "We may have played the songs a thousand times before, but Phil and Don—no matter how they felt offstage—would always go out and perform them with passion," Zevon recounted to the *Los Angeles Times* during his first tour. "If anything, I learned that when you go out onstage, you give your all, even if you've been doing it for fifteen years and are sick of giving your all."

It was the famously combative but musically harmonious brothers who pushed Zevon to perform "Frank and Jesse James," a song he dedicated to their spirit of compartmentalizing inner conflict to avoid altering their professionalism. This above all emboldened him to publicly express his art. "The Everlys would let us do our songs in the show," the band's lead guitarist, Waddy Wachtel, recalls joyfully. "Warren had an arsenal of great songs and I had a handful of songs, so they said, 'Fuck it, let them sing.'"

Where Zevon truly found/lost/found his live footing was the *Excitable Boy* tour two years later. "Werewolves of London" had brought him to a wider audience and thus the halls were bigger. Backed ably by a smoking band of seasoned professionals led by Wachtel, including the accomplished bassist-and-drummer combo of Stanley Sheldon and Rick Marotta, and David Landau on rhythm guitar, Zevon took no prisoners. "It was going over really well, because people just loved that album," recalled Landau when we spoke in November 2016. "We also had material from the first album, and it was a really good band. Waddy was great onstage, a totally solid player and the perfect foil for Warren. Waddy and Rick had been touring with Linda Ronstadt, who was pretty much at the peak of her career." An excellent aural example of this outfit in action, with spectacular guitar work by Wachtel, can be heard on the 2015 CD release *Accidentally on Purpose*, a July 27, 1978, radio broadcast recorded at Sausalito, California's Record Plant.

It was during this tour that Zevon's persona, projected in the songs, became ever more exaggerated, as his alcoholism and drug abuse intensified. He'd barely been able to balance his art with his addictions on the first tour: Now, things began to unravel. "When we were promoting *Excitable Boy*, it was full throttle," recalls Burt Stein, again Zevon's liaison for the label. "He loved his drink. He was an alcoholic, but he was a functioning alcoholic. He would get done what he had to get done. After the show a lot of times, I was kind of off duty and didn't see much of all of that, but, again, he somehow kept it together."

"He would be weird in his hotel room and weird before the show, but once we went onstage, he would do what he had to do, because he always did," agrees his longtime friend, Jorge Calderón, who joined the tour for its second leg. "Music was always the most important thing for him."

"It doesn't help when you're an alcoholic and Stolichnaya offers to sponsor your tour," Wachtel shared with me in 2017. "We had boxes and boxes of vodka out there. We would come onstage with our own bottle, each of us, because I was drinking a lot then too. But no matter how much I would drink, you couldn't drink as much as Warren, because he was drinking *all* day. I would see him in the afternoon and he was already three sheets to the wind. But we'd put a set list together and we would go do it. I was pretty shitfaced myself, but I'm still capable of putting on a show. Still, some nights were a total fucking nightmare. The patter in between songs sometimes would get a little lengthy and stupid and he'd lose his place, but mostly on that tour no matter how gone he was after we'd count a song off he could pull his weight."

"I've worked with a lot of alcoholics, but I have *never* met anybody who drank the way Warren drank during that period," adds Landau. "If I drank the way Warren drank I wouldn't have made it to thirty. He had the capacity to do that and function up to a point, but the idea that Warren could be drunk and play amazing is part of his mythology. What I remember during that period was there would be nights when at the beginning of the set Warren would be sober and he would be sitting at the piano and his voice was clear and he was articulate, and he would have his vodka glass on the piano and right around the fourth or fifth song, as he kept drinking, you would start to hear his voice waver a little bit. It was a rare night on that tour when he started any show sober, but by the end of *any* set he was completely drunk."

This was the mystique of Warren Zevon: the growling, frenzied, leg-kicking, piano-pouncing, hop-hopping, sweat-sopped prowler, unrepentantly energetic and furiously menacing. His curly blond locks bouncing wildly above bespectacled dilating pupils framed by a wide-toothed grin, he let the songs wire through him like a circuit. They shoved him out there and forced an answer to the age-old query of what is artifice and what is real and where do the two intersect? Warren Zevon managed to traverse this duality at several junctures during each show that year; several of which he would fall off his piano stool and one in particular where he stumbled off the stage in a heap.

"There was the night in Chicago that he literally fell off the stage and sprained both his ankles," confirms Landau. "I thought that that was going to be the end of the tour. For several nights George Gruel needed to carry Warren out to the piano and put him down on the bench."

Jorge Calderón noted Zevon's near-manic state right away: "One of the first shows that I did with him in the second half of the tour, we're behind the curtain, ready to go, and he's talking to me and his teeth are blue. 'Why are your teeth blue?' 'Oh, I'm just chewing on some Valium. I always chew some Valium right before I go on, because I get the jitters.'"

"There was one show in San Francisco when he was fucking drunk *before* the show," recalls Zevon's burly and bearded road manager, George Gruel. "But he got up on that stage and performed. He even stood backwards to the piano and somehow played all the fucking chords properly."

To watch Warren Zevon work the stage in 1978 was akin to watching a high-wire act. He had turned rock 'n' roll into a righteous patrolling of "the edge." This was a man working somewhere between pure joy and apoplectic misery, stabbing at air and coming back with blood and tissue. It was a thing to behold, reminiscent of that classic Looney Tunes routine wherein Daffy Duck tries to out-duel Bugs Bunny in stage antics, a fatal piece of one-upmanship that results in Daffy swallowing a lit match into a stomach filled with explosives. As he floats up to heaven on boastful wings he regrets that he could only perform that kind of combustible finale once. You got the similar feeling that there was no way Zevon could keep up that level of fury. But you would be wrong.

His next tour in 1980 in support of *Bad Luck Streak in Dancing School*, affectionately dubbed by the band "The Dog Ate the Part We Didn't Like" (the name was inspired by a line from one of Zevon's favorite authors, Thomas McGuane), would continue to trade on Zevon's road craziness. This is when he began opening shows with George Gruel taking handcuffs off him and unleashing the "excitable boy" on a chanting audience. The look in Zevon's eyes during that tour reflects a strange fusion of speed and sleeplessness, an uncomfortable stroll on the border of insanity. I asked George if the stage would ever become a refuge for Zevon during these heady times. "Well, if you call snorting blow off the top of an amplifier a refuge, sure . . . yeah," he said, cracking up at the absurdity of such an idea.

However, it would be the first time Zevon would realize his lifestyle was harmful to himself and his closest friends, relatives, and family, informing his performance with a new balance of regret and disassociation. He now possessed an acute awareness that "the edge" had consequences, and therefore he could let you in on the joke that all this running-it-out-to-the-end *fuck-it* attitude had a shelf life.

There are several recorded documents of this tour worth exploring: The most well-known is the aptly titled *Stand in the Fire*. In an era when the live album had gone from overhyped bombast to subpar retreads of hits with noise, this is a living, breathing masterpiece. Featuring material from the first three Asylum albums and a few unreleased numbers, it was recorded over several blistering nights at West Hollywood's famed Roxy and captures the rough-and-tumble Zevon in the raw. Constantly exploring the immediacy of each band he was to play with—this one is arguably his finest—Zevon discovers a fresh take while forcefully stretching his vocals beyond the originals.

"Our goal was to play the songs as close to the records as possible, and Warren seemed to be one hundred percent into that," explained the band's rhythm guitarist, Zeke Zirngiebel, over the phone from Los Angeles in December of 2016. "This meant using the right instruments, like the lap steel. I shot my mouth off and said I could play just like David Lindley, which I couldn't, but in two weeks I learned as best as I could to play his parts on slide guitar, electric twelve-strings, and acoustics."

Zevon embraced the band concept and, according to Zirngiebel, was open to suggestions on arrangements and adding various instruments during detailed rehearsals: "Even though we knew this wasn't forever and that it would eventually stop and we would move on and he would move on, we still wanted to have the feeling of a *band*, the camaraderie of not having to look at somebody when you're playing. You just listen to them and know what to play off of them, and I think that kind of showed on the tour and on the live album."

Waddy's brother Jimmy Wachtel, who took the frenzied photos for the album's inner sleeve, including a classic (once again illuminatingly out-of-focus) cover shot of a raucous Zevon in mid-rocking fervor, recalls those seminal nights at the Roxy as he saw them from the pit in front of the stage: "That was a great show and it *sounded* so great. I had never really seen him perform with a rock 'n' roll band like that before. It's a very small club and it was exciting. I was right below him, so if he looked down he saw my camera pointing at him at all times. That's how I got that back-cover shot where he's at the piano and singing right to you."

"It was fantastic because every night was sold out, and as soon as we would go out onstage the crowd would just go nuts," remembers Zirngiebel. "When you get to play in front of audiences like that you feed off of it and it just makes you play all that much better. So it was kind of easy to forget it was being recorded and that it was a big deal, because we're in the heart of Hollywood at the prestigious Roxy and you could look out and see Jackson Browne and all these other people. You just play."

"There was a lot of buzz on Warren for those shows," concludes Wachtel. "He wanted to be a rock 'n' roll star and this was his chance. People were very excited. The place was packed with celebrities. John Belushi and Tom Waits got into a fight in the men's room, rolling around on the floor. It was a pretty wild time and a great rock 'n' roll moment."

Two visual representations from early in the tour exist: a black-and-white video from Passaic, New Jersey's famed Capitol Theatre and a color one from New York's historic Palladium. Zevon, dressed in a black suit, vest, and tie, all soon ripped off unceremoniously, leaving him in torn pants, stalks the stage like a wild animal, bursting into dance and leaping about seemingly beyond control. Paul Nelson would write of the latter: "Onstage at the Palladium, he's in fantastic form and gives such a kinetic, physical performance that some critics take him to task for exhibitionism. To me, these charges are small-minded and ridiculous. This is the first tour on which he's been in shape and sober enough to move. There's a celebration going on up there, and Zevon is trying hard to make up for all those drunken debacles in the past. Once you understand that, it's very touching."

Although Nelson would soon become personally aware that his distant assessment of Zevon's sobriety was badly skewered, his overall point is apt. These shows are a referendum on the performer's sense of awakening into an unalloyed child-like exuberance that is stark on both *Stand in the Fire* and the Capitol Theatre/Palladium videos. He is, of course, despite Paul Nelson's observations, fueled by coke and bringing the pain like no other: once again, something to behold.

Quick note: During an interview for this book, aide-de-camp George Gruel sent me a bootleg of an April 22, 1980, WMMR radio broadcast from the Tower Theater in Philadelphia that may be the most compelling ninety minutes of Zevon's live career. The band is smoking and Zevon is in fine voice and truly on the edge of the edge of the edge.

"We had moments on that tour where the band just levitated," recalls bandleader David Landau, whose guitar work on these recordings is remarkable. "I remember there was a performance one night where we did 'Excitable Boy,' and I had this sort of chicken-pickin' approach to the solo and for some reason I *really* got it right. It wasn't always easy to relax behind Warren, but on particular occasions we all did. And songs like 'Poor Poor Pitiful Me' and 'Excitable Boy' were just so fucking fun to play."

"I never played anything before when we had such a great command of dynamics, and it had a lot to do with the subtle way Warren and David led the band," says Zirngiebel. "That's not easy to do, turning and looking at everybody and feeding off each other, but it makes it much more interesting."

Along with Landau on lead guitar are the members of a Colorado group called Boulder: Roberto Pinion on bass and vocals, Marty Stinger on drums, the aforementioned Zeke Zirngiebel on guitar and vocals, and hauntingly gorgeous harmonies and keyboards by Bob Harris. "I remember thinking to myself when I was leaving to go home after the insanity of the *Excitable Boy* tour, 'I am never going to work with this guy again,'" says Landau today. "It was just too much. I was spent. But a couple of years later I'm in New York and Warren invites me up to his hotel room and I could see right away he had lost ten pounds in his face. He'd completely stopped drinking. He was working out and in the best shape he'd ever been in and he wanted me to go out with him on tour. Given that he was sober and I didn't have a problem with the music, I agreed, and then I heard Boulder, and they were really great."

Boulder burst into Zevon's earshot with a fiery cover of his "Join Me in L.A." off their debut album, which had just been dropped by Elektra. "George Gruel gave us a cassette with twelve songs on it and told us to learn them in two weeks for an audition," recalls Zirngiebel. "So we went into major woodshed mode and learned the songs until we could play them in our sleep, because we were determined to just blow Warren away with how well we played his tunes.

"So the big day comes and we get to this rehearsal studio in the valley and George is there, but no Warren. We set up and wait for a little while and suddenly the door bursts open and Warren comes bounding in and jumps up onstage and shakes everyone's hand and straps on a guitar and says, 'Do you boys know how to play "Johnny B. Goode"?' Then he looks at me and says, 'Okay, start the song.' So I start "Johnny B. Goode" and he sings a verse and then he goes around to each person to take a solo. Then he sings another verse and *boom*, the song's over. He puts his guitar down, jumps offstage, and starts running toward the door. Before he exits he turns around and looks at us and says, 'I'll see you guys in two weeks,' and he's gone. I mean, the drummer's cymbals were still swinging in the breeze. We're standing there with our mouths open looking at George like, 'Well, what the hell does that mean?' And he said, 'Well, I guess it means you got the gig.'"

This was indeed the right band for the right time, and "Mohammed's Radio" is the right song to portray it.

Zevon placed the number toward the back of his set, positioning it as something of a church spiritual. The opening piano chords, played sweetly, presage its sentiment. David Landau's guitar line (written and played originally by Fleetwood Mac's Lindsey Buckingham) dances across it, caressing the notes down into a bed for the vocals to lie over. Following Landau's soft musical landing, Zevon exhales the first lines wearily, as an actor would deliver an impassioned Shakespearean soliloquy:

> *Everybody's restless and they've got no place to go*
> *Someone's always trying to tell them*
> *Something they already know*
> *So their anger and resentment flow*

Whenever I hear this version I'm reminded of how fortunate I was to have seen Warren Zevon perform about a dozen times, and how each experience was new and exciting. I always felt as though he were singing the songs for the first time, as if he had just written them or was writing them right up there on the stage. The single spotlight shone down on him at the piano, as he leaned forward toward the microphone to testify. It was, ironically, religious to me, really the only religion that mattered. It was a true expression of the man and his song. Pure. Confident. Arrogant. I am also reminded of what the great Brian Wilson once told me about singing, how it was his favorite and most lasting art form. This is the conclusion of one of the most revered songwriters, arrangers, and producers in the history of popular music: *singing.* "An artist expresses," says the man who created the hedonistic ode to the eternal California wave as main composer and beating heart of the Beach Boys. And through phrasing and harmonies he could express something new each time. The human voice is, after all, an unreliable but clarifying instrument. Can you sing anything the same twice? Can Pavarotti? Sinatra? Zevon? What are you getting this time, on this night, on this stage? Who knows? Something magical.

Zevon begins the vocal with the one word he must utter, "everybody," as in, Mohammed and his radio *are* everybody and everybody *is* Mohammed with his (their) trusty radio—he is (they are) restless and have no place to go. *Where is he going with that thing?* Wandering? Like Moses in the desert? Like Mohammed upon his mountain? Like Kerouac on the road or Miles on the beat or Jesse James on the lam or a nation on the dole? Is someone always trying to tell Mohammed (them) something he (they) already knows? Is this what makes anger and resentment flow? Nothing new. Same old shit. Aphorisms and platitudes are poor substitutes for hope, and they rarely amount to a solution. Words are, in the end, empty. Truth and salvation come from the music, because all this anger and resentment flow into it, and it makes you (don't it?) want to rock 'n' roll.

I adore how Zevon holds the note on "already" and brings it down to the droning "know" as it twitters from his throat, carrying the burden of more than the radio. The 1970s were hard times. When he wrote the song, the fade of the 1960s still echoed. So many bemoaned it, but it was a new era and he was a part of it and he would not enter it bitching about botched revolutions, half-assed social upheavals, or failed countercultures. The spirituality lay in the music, and the music is not bound by time or genre or singer. And so he sings because he can and he must and he just has to tell you about Mohammed and his glorious radio that will not stop playing that *rock 'n' roll.*

As the band kicks in, the backing vocals for the first half of the refrain—specifically, Bob Harris's resoundingly beautiful harmonies—soar above Zevon's tender baritone and weave in and out of the notes like a solitary choir. It would be criminal to not mention the beatific vocal performance on the original studio cut by the always instinctual Stevie Nicks, which extracts the spiritual nectar from the song and sets the template for this entire arrangement.

Beneath it all, Zevon rhythmically tickles the piano notes higher and higher as prologue to the second half of the chorus:

I heard somebody singing sweet and soulful
On the radio, Mohammed's Radio

This is wonderful songwriting: The vocal is so unerringly illustrative of the lyrics. It gently whisks its emotions along, *telling you something you already know.* Shit, it's hard to ignore. It is a celebration of life in art, music as medicine, an elixir to the bad mojo. You heard it in your mama's womb. You brought it into the world with a shout that reverberated just as loudly each time something moved you, scared you, filled you with joy. These are the voices of the community and the celebrity and the icon and the plebian; they say, "Time to boogie. Strip off the shackles and get down to business—the business of living!"

The voices take on divergent visages, as if avatars in the swirling drama of life, from the lowliest village idiot to the president of the United States. On this recording, as mentioned, Zevon scats though the Iran hostage crisis with its two central figures: Iran's wicked Ayatollah Khomeini "has got his problems," and our beleaguered commander-in-chief has "the highway blues." Jimmy Carter's travels isn't Mohammed's, but it's not that far from where he will end up—where we all end up, Jack.

The band offers a handy slice of humor through its call-and-response vocals: "Walk it off, crybaby" comes after the line about the Ayatollah's "problems," and after having those problems being taken out on you, they respond with a stern "Take a nap, junior."

"I brought up a couple of phrases I used to use when I was a kid," says Zirngiebel. "One was 'Walk it off, crybaby,' and the other was 'Take a nap, junior,' which are things I would say to people when they were pissing and moaning about things you couldn't do anything about. George loved the idea, and he said, 'Yeah, you guys sing that.' So we sang it the first night onstage, and of course Warren turns to look at us like, 'What are you guys doing?' But after the show he said, 'I love it. Keep it.'"

I went and asked our governor 'cause I thought that he would know
You see, I knew he was up all night listening to Mohammed's Radio

It is entirely possible that Warren Zevon asked California governor Jerry Brown about the Iran hostage crisis, seeing how the eclectic Brown had been romantically linked to Linda Ronstadt. The two appeared on the cover of *Newsweek* on April 23, 1979, under the cover-blurb "The Pop Politics of Jerry Brown." The then forty-nine-year-old governor, fond of piggybacking on the generational appeal of the rock-star set, confessed to reporters he could never marry Ronstadt and maintain a future in politics—especially regarding the White House: In his initial bid for the presidency, he finished a distant third to Georgia's former governor in 1976. Imagine a first lady who loved to smoke copious amounts of weed and purportedly twice had to have her nose cauterized owing to cocaine abuse? Brown may have had a point, as a photograph emerged of the governor pictured with what appears to be a pretty stoned group of Eagles, along with David Lindley, Jackson Browne, and Ronstadt, sporting a wickedly lascivious grin, as she coyly lifts her dress to reveal a hint of garter. Of course, Zevon assures us that if Brown had any solutions to the Iran hostage crisis, they were likely drowned out by the all-night revelry of Mohammed's radio. *The man is hanging with rock stars, what do you think he's doing all night?*

I'm not sure this is relevant, but it's probably worth mentioning that the line about the governor replaces the original "In walked the village idiot and his face was all aglow." There is no telling whether this was a jab at Brown, a man the press pejoratively dubbed "Governor Moonbeam," or a playful coincidence. Regardless, the governor, whose two terms (1975–83) ended three years hence, would again be elected governor in 2011 following the two-term movie-star governor Arnold Schwarzenegger, and at the time of this writing still holds that post at the age of seventy-nine.

For her part, Ronstadt would deliver a spiritually charged version of the song on her 1978 *Living in the USA* album, an impassioned reading of the tale with a syrupy chorale. No one covered Zevon's songs more expressively or with more genuine reverence than Ronstadt. This would be the last of four of his songs she would make more famous than he ever could, while also instilling them with a female tenderness unforeseen in their composition. Her voice is unflinchingly seductive but also leaps on occasion into a strident pitch. Waddy Wachtel leads the musical ensemble and adds a signature melodic guitar line on both intro and outré, lending credibility to the recording.

Everybody's desperate trying to make ends meet
Work all day, still can't pay the price of gasoline and meat
Alas, their lives are incomplete

Coming down off the second chorus, the band's (specifically Harris's) harmonies ring out undeterred, fading into a refrain of the opening harmonious guitar riff that descends back into the second verse proper and heralds Warren Zevon's most cherished themes: desperation and incompletion. His voice cracks just a bit on the tail end of "everybody's" to allow an appropriate air by punching "desperate." The melody, so refined and insular on the 1976 studio version, with the tightrope rhyming of "work all day" and "still can't pay"—which will only be bested by the lines coming up in the next stanza—now becomes a fulcrum against the final punctuation on "gasoline." The disdainfully spat word superbly recalls the lines about Iran and Carter in one fell swoop. David Landau's raunchy bending of blues notes accentuates Zevon's guttural exclamation of "meat." The tension, once again, is aided by the band's building crescendo to the singer's impassioned testifying.

Another chorus, this one more chilling than the first two, kicks in again. But it is just a precursor to the second mini-bridge. This time the band floats beneath it, waiting there suspended for him to cry out:

You've been up all night listening for his drum

Solitary and booming, Zevon's voice wavers with every drag of every cigarette, every swallow of every pill, the burn of every gulp of vodka. He delivers a mystical reading of the line in classic Zevon style, switching from a story about Mohammed and our very DNA pumping from his radio speakers to an evocative description of your long night into dawn waiting, hoping, groping, "listening for his drum." That elusive beat is just beyond your (our) grasp. The medicine man is keeping it (us) at bay. Mohammed as Dylan's Thin Man, Lennon's Doctor Robert, Mick and Keith's Sister Morphine, all of them seducing us, distracting us from the horrors of the Iranian bogeyman and the befuddled president and the pop governor and his countrified girl. The background voices again step up and proclaim, "Up . . . all . . . night . . ." And then, one of Zevon's finest inside rhymes hit the solar plexus with concussive glee.

Hoping that the righteous . . . might just . . . might just . . . might just come

Goddammit, man, I *love* that! Every time I hear it, especially this version, I cannot help but whoop it up. Zevon sings it with such resolve. This is as black (as in African American, gospel-tinged, bayou yelping) as he gets. But it's within the rhyme, a moment of divine-intervention-meets-magnificent-happenstance that is fucking inspired stuff. Any writer worth his salt genuflects at "righteous" into "might just." And it is no throwaway line. It is the essence of the entire song: a generation of failed dreamers and doomed revolutionaries poised to find redemption in music. Somewhere out there the righteous might just come, no? They must! Nah, they *might.*

But of course two more spirited lines bring home this tour de force. The same melody that bemoaned the desperation of a heart without a home, the wandering spirit of a nation and its people working to barely make the grade, is now foretelling the army just over the hill. Who will come to our rescue? Ronald Reagan? Bruce Springsteen? Lee Iacocca?

I heard the General whisper to his aide-de-camp
"Be watchful for Mohammed's lamp"

Zevon's clutching for breath during the word *Mohammed* kills me every time. He sounds spent, but in a good way, as if there is only Mohammed, and everything around him falls by the wayside. When he blurts out "lamp" you can envision him slumping to the floor, the final bell having tolled. The army (nation) has stalled.

Stagnation. Paranoia. It is the waning, crucial years of the American century tilting at the whims of the oil man, the sinister sheik. But he comes as proclamation and purification. We wait not for him or what he brings. We wait for the music from his radio. This is the rock 'n' roll generation, having transmogrified from Elvis's evil hip-shake to the Beatles falling from grace and the dirty, scary, raucous new stuff happening in a dump on Manhattan's Bowery. We wait for the music to liberate us.

Listen for it.

The song soars from here into a beautiful sing-along reminiscent of a church revival, complete with a wonderfully balanced guitar crescendo from David Landau that bridges Zevon's strident sweep of the piano keys. "Gospel is a good word for it," concludes Zeke Zirngiebel. "That's why we tried to ramp up the choruses and have them big, and that's why I added the third part on the vocals. The dynamics of 'Mohammed's Radio' definitely made it one of my favorite songs that we did."

The voices rise as one. Ever present, Zevon keeps his baritone at an even keel, laying the groundwork for the band to push its needle into the high notes splendidly trickled out by Bob Harris, who has now taken Stevie Nicks's cue and made it his own. His roller-coaster harmony on the words *rock 'n' roll* is poetic. Landau's guitar is back, interweaving its wail with Zevon's piano flourishes, all leading to the a cappella coda.

The band slides slowly into the background and the two voices that have serenaded the previous choruses take a breath and complete their testimony. Zevon and Harris hang on every syllable, setting in motion the pitch and parry of only two words.

"Mohammed's . . ."

Down, down, down into the depths of their being.

" . . . ra . . . ra . . . radio . . . oh . . . oh . . . oh."

Up and out. Like a soul ascending to heaven. Like the spirit unearthed. Out into the ether once more.

With the music.

On the radio.

"Dirty Warren": Zevon with his "hand cannon" in 1979 at the house he rented with his aide-de-camp, George Gruel, on Mulholland Drive. *Photo by George Gruel*

"Ain't That Pretty at All"

My voice is in my sword: thou bloodier villain.
—WILLIAM SHAKESPEARE, *Macbeth*, act 5, scene 8

Violence.

Vi-o-lence. It has a musical ring to it. It even evokes a musical instrument: a viola or a violin. *Merriam-Webster* defines violence as "physical force used to inflict injury or damage" or "behavior involving physical force intended to hurt, damage, or kill someone or something." Its synonyms are equally aggressive and confrontational, while also wide-ranging: "brutality, forcefulness, ferocity, savagery, cruelty, barbarity, brutishness, strength of emotion or an unpleasant or destructive natural force, intensity, severity, strength, vehemence, power, potency, ferocity, fury, fire."

Most of these terms are abhorrent and tend to put off the more docile among us, forcing us to put up our defenses. Others, however, spark a sense of pride that humanity is capable of unyielding dedication to fight as vigorously *against* such injustices. It gives us a sense of comfort to know that those on our side, whichever side that may be, might exhibit the ferocity and strength to counter them.

For the American experience, especially deep in our origins, forged in aggression and defended as such, violence is part of the day-to-day ritual of a free society, an experiment in the human condition: a condition forced to face our violence and either fight back or be consumed by it. Violence looms as a constant threat, our inner core, as it also frames our proudest moments, those spent beating back tyranny, fascism, racism, and oligarchy. It is our bane and our tool, our curse and our blessing. And it is here that the essence of free will—the will to maintain life and liberty, to express our fears and aspirations—comes to the fore. Violence is not our most enviable trait, but it is one that cannot be ignored in either our history or our destiny.

The etymology of the word is derived from the Latin *violentia* (vehemence, impetuosity), or *violentus* (vehement, forcible), probably related to *violare* (violation, improper treatment), as attested from as early as the 1590s. But these are merely words, as violence is indeed an action. It, not affection, is arguably the very first action, as depicted in many cultures, and in the Judeo-Christian edict in which the Creator, God, rejects his offspring, Adam, by expelling him from a paradise he has refuted in favor of seeking knowledge denied him. Then there is Cain's murdering of his brother, Abel, out of an inherent sense of jealousy and the belief that in taking his sibling's life he would enhance his own.

In fact, the Bible is replete with stories of the Lord's vengeance, which variously takes the form of flood, temptation, torture, everything from the testing of Job to the denying of the Promised Land to Moses. Even the Christ of the purportedly more peaceful New Testament speaks of "bringing a sword" to a "fight" that ends in the Holy Temple, wherein a blow against the religious status quo is struck. Systemic state-sanctioned violence, celebrated as a sacred ritual, is then brought down upon Jesus Christ, who is depicted in the lore of Christianity as a sacrificial lamb, and whose endurance of unspeakable violence is noted as an act of sacrifice: the blood ritual as consecration.

Violence is not merely an outward action/counteraction. It can be perpetuated upon one's self apart from its ultimate act, suicide. There are the self-inflicted wounds of fear, guilt, anxiety, self-deprecation, or insecurity, all of which can sometimes manifest in an outpouring of violence, personal or societal. And of course it is reflected in art. Violence appears prominently throughout history, everywhere from prehistoric cave drawings to today's disturbing images flashed all over the Internet by the nanosecond. Depicting violence is the most effective tool to dig at the root of the human condition, one used by auteurs from Shakespeare to Quentin Tarantino, Dante to Edgar Allan Poe, Hieronymus Bosch to Jackson Pollock, Ludwig van Beethoven to Warren Zevon. Conflict is drama, and drama is art, and at its center is violence.

Explaining the preponderance of violence in his films, Martin Scorsese—perhaps America's finest filmmaker (Warren Zevon surely believed so)—told BBC.com in 2006 that it is the essence of his milieu, where he comes from and what he knows, and that it is also the very bedrock of drama, exploited for centuries by our most celebrated storytellers: "The action and conflicts that bring the characters together in these worlds is of a very explosive nature, it is very dramatic and it has that movement, life on the edge. Everything is almost a life-and-death decision, even though literal death isn't always the subject: Often it is a matter of spiritual death. And that's what attracts me to these worlds and these characters."

Scorsese, like most of the American nouveau directors of the 1970s inspired by the 1960s French and Italian New Wave movements, needn't explain his goal of denouncing violence by splashing violence upon the screen to confront audiences in regard to their baser instincts. His desperately poor childhood on New York's Lower East Side surrounded by violent corruption informed Scorsese's art, as similar circumstances inspired countless artists the world over: The dramatic shift from romantic to propagandized to nihilistic art and philosophy of Germany following the fall of the Third Reich or the reflective and revolutionary art that was shunned in the Soviet Union before the implosion of Communism in the late 1980s are symptoms of a shared experience, or simply a reflection of reality: Here, art *imitates* life, and subsequently, art *affects* life, as in perhaps Scorsese's darkest film, *Taxi Driver*, which would prompt displaced loner John Hinckley Jr.'s assassination attempt of President Ronald Reagan in March of 1981. To up the ante, Scorsese then directed a screenplay by Paul D. Zimmerman about the deranged kidnapper of an archetypal Johnny Carson celebrity character, called *The King of Comedy* (1982). Its star, Robert De Niro, and the director, who worked brilliantly together on *Taxi Driver*, were inspired by the murder of ex-Beatle John Lennon by another lone nut, Mark David Chapman, the previous year.

Interestingly, a shot in one of the film's final scenes appears to be a homage to the photo from the inside sleeve of Warren Zevon's breakout album, *Excitable Boy*, affectionately dubbed "Willy on a Plate." Designed and shot by Lorrie Sullivan and Jimmy Wachtel, it features Zevon's beloved .44-caliber Smith & Wesson as a purported substitute for his penis, hence "Willy." The gun is the vulgar substitute for "meat" on the bed of veggies and potatoes and would become a lasting icon for the singer-songwriter, followed later by Wachtel's "Old Velvet Nose" logo of a bespectacled skull with a cigarette dangling from its macabre grin.

A postscript to *The King of Comedy* and its stark commentary on the Lennon assassination is the back cover photo for Zevon's 1980 *Bad Luck Streak in Dancing School*, also taken by Wachtel nearly a year before the murder. Keeping up with the weapon theme from the previous record and the gunshots that prelude its opening title track, it features an Uzi beside a pair of ballet slippers surrounded by strewn bullets. Those working with a more literal vision and unfamiliar with the dark humor and multilayered subtext of the Zevon Corner construed it as a crime scene. "I got a call from Joe Smith, the head of Asylum Records, that I had to get my ass down there right away," Wachtel shared with me in 2016. "This women's group was up in arms saying that obviously we're intending to shoot ballerinas. This had never even entered into the equation. It was simply, 'This would be a cool shot, similar to the 'Willy on the Plate.'" So I had to go down and defend myself and the picture, which I did successfully, I guess, because they didn't sue the record company."

The exploitation of violence for violence's sake in American pop culture is so far-reaching and utterly daunting: One flinches at the very notion of it. It is everywhere. Films, magazines, political rhetoric, sports, musical genres, television, video games, cartoons, comic books, advertisements, social media—all are dominated by violence, its imagery and language, its combative and enticing nature. Here is where the villain runs free, and the villain is us, the greater society obsessed with a deep-seated yearning for dominance. The great social commentator and comedian George Carlin once mused that even American values have been infiltrated by violent images, noting how we declare war on everything: war on poverty, war on drugs, war on crime, etc. Carlin shouts, "We have the only national anthem that mentions rockets and bombs in the fucking goddamn thing!"

There is also the personal violence that permeates our neighborhoods and homes: domestic violence, gender violence, violence engendered by sexual preference or manner of dress or use of terminology. This has led to a dangerous backlash of censorship and political correctness, in which anyone and everyone is held accountable for the violent nature of a society they cannot begin to control. Here, alarmists see the potential for violence based on culture, race, nationality, religion, and all manners of choice in lifestyle. This, of course, begets a different type of institutional violence: the accepted and oft-heralded violence of social judgment, the conclusion that to form *any* opinion is in itself an act of violence. This distorts our innate yearning to be free, to express ourselves without oppression.

Vi-o-lence.

It is symphony and cacophony, but it is in itself a concussive musical outpouring of aggression and fury, variously evoked in the dramatic flourishes of crescendo or the bellowing wave of an aria, the streetwise beat of hip hop, and the gleeful belligerence of punk and speed metal. It is crudity and instigation, our revolutionary trip—the release of hormones, sexual tension, and youthful insurrection. Rooted in American music, jazz, blues, and rock 'n' roll, it stirs the melting pot and crosses the blurred lines of race and generation. For most of our lives rock 'n' roll has served to channel our basest and rawest expression. It is our joy and our rage. It is our libido and our passion and our indulgence and our escapism. What was once dismissed as a passing fad, a plaything for affluent postwar kids and a shameful practice of the delinquent, has had a lasting influence on generations. It has transformed from upheaval to exploitation, undercurrent to commerce, outlaw to establishment, yet never did it lose its sense of vi-o-lence.

Warren Zevon was keenly aware of this balancing act, as he explained to *Songwriter* magazine when pressed about his possible worry that he ran the risk of romanticizing violence in songs such as "Frank and Jesse James," "I'll Sleep When I'm Dead," "Excitable Boy," "Roland the Headless Thompson Gunner," and his only hit, "Werewolves of London," which featured the line "He'll rip your lungs out, Jim," gaily followed by "I'd like to meet his tailor": "The question of what songs mean and what they do is sort of terrifying, when you think about it, but then you begin to realize that there's such a thing as taking yourself too seriously," he said. "You back off and say, 'Isn't it a little pretentious of me to start wondering how I'm influencing society? Shouldn't I address myself to how well I'm doing the job of producing this piece of entertainment?'"

"I'm going to hurl myself against the wall!" sings Zevon with shameless glee in "Ain't That Pretty at All," and he follows it up with a brazenly self-aware acknowledgment of his all-too-human plight: "'Cause I'd rather feel bad than feel nothing at all!"

A song found smack-dab in the middle of 1982's *The Envoy*, a veritable swan song for Zevon's "rock star" period, "Ain't That Pretty at All" growls from the very id of the songwriter. It is musically strange—from its oddly formed time signature and grating keyboard sounds to its disturbingly relentless sonic badgering. *The Envoy* was promoted in two ways: as a serious album framing the neocon, international intrigue of the emerging Reagan era, as well as a series of songs penned and recorded by a songwriter freed of his raging alcoholism. It was not a comeback so much as a reminder. This was to be the bridge from which would take Zevon beyond his fringe folk career and past his later rock-star excesses, landing him in that most feared and yet cherished of categories: cult. "They describe me as a cult artist, which is fine with me," Zevon expressed to *Music Connection* magazine eight years later. "I'm fond of saying that any musician that can play what he wants is successful, no matter the size of the audience."

"Ain't That Pretty at All" is a violent song. Vi-o-lent. Musically aggressive. Harrowing. And funny. Very funny. Its humor, like that of almost all Zevon's cultural and personal anecdotes, is uproariously reflective of riot-meets-mob that decides to burn down the very edifice in which they are convening for kicks. It is a heaping slice of madness, as is the underlying theme of the more rousing Zevon numbers: songs about, influenced by, and in some weird and titillating way celebrating violence. The composer, however, framed his methods this way to KGSR radio's Jody Denberg in 2000: "I don't really think of my songs as particularly violent. I guess my favorite author overall is Aeschylus, and he was more violent twenty-five hundred years ago than anything on cable TV now. So was Shakespeare, all the time—*real* violent, in every sense. I just think that popular music as we understood it for a long time was limited to love songs for the most part, and it wasn't exactly what I was doing, that's all."

For a point of reference, and because it is fun to cite a third-century BCE playwright/philosopher whom the man who wrote "I've got a .38 special up on the shelf / If I start acting stupid, I'll shoot myself" might find a tad hostile, let's get some background.

Aeschylus lived and worked from about 525/524 to 456/455 BCE and is considered by Greek scholars and historians to be the "father of tragedy." An applied knowledge of the genre begins with his work, as an understanding of earlier tragedies is largely based on inferences from his seven surviving plays. His work spanned the centuries beside that of his more lauded contemporaries, Sophocles and Euripides; however, Aeschylus is credited with expanding character interactions during his plays to move away from a confronting of the chorus to forcing conflict among them. Succinctly put, it is right to credit Aeschylus with infusing conflict into drama, for without conflict, as Scorsese points out above, there is no drama. And Zevon is all about drama.

As illustrated time and again, Zevon lived his drama, and thus his life was constant conflict. When strife did not present itself, he created it. His vi-o-lence was his art *and* his life: One fed the other, and vice versa. There was a sense that for those working or living with Warren Zevon there would be collateral damage. This was the deal you made with him. You get the brilliance, wit, and charm with a heaping portion of insanity. Zevon quipped to Dave Marsh upon the release of *Excitable Boy* back in 1978, "My wife gets more exercise from shuddering than from picking up the baby."

This was in evidence every time Zevon brandished one of his many handguns, of which he was fond. The combination of alcohol abuse and firearms was to say the least a dangerous juggling act for friends, colleagues, and family. David Landau, lead guitarist on two tours and one of the axemen featured on "Ain't That Pretty at All," described it to me this way: "He had a fixation with guns, handguns in particular. Some of these stories were written about in *Rolling Stone*: the time he shot the bathtub and all that. But we were having dinner at his house one night and his little daughter Ariel was there and she was very young and he's drinking and he pulls his gun out at some point. This was already so alien to me, I can't even begin to tell you, because I'm a New York lefty Jew: The idea of owning a handgun, let alone waving it around your child, is just madness."

Zevon's notorious penchant for violent outbursts, his obsession with firearms, his rampant alcoholism and drug abuse, his crippling OCD, his battle between delusions of grandeur and feelings of self-loathing, and the torturous tussle with the muse to compose left little in the way of *not* digging close to the bone. "Ain't That Pretty at All" is a love letter to all that, a testimonial to a life fueled with and derailed by vi-o-lence.

> *Well, I've seen all there is to see*
> *And I've heard all they have to say*
> *I've done everything I wanted to do . . .*
> *I've done that too*
> *And it ain't that pretty at all*

This is where the rubber hits the road for Zevon. He lived the gory details and survived to tell the tale, with ample evidence of having "done that too," but he did consider the characters that inhabit his fourth studio album less masked than his first three. "It's my first attempt to communicate with people without using surrogate gorillas," he told *Rolling Stone* just before *The Envoy*'s release. "Not that I was hiding behind those things . . . but maybe I was. The album is still violent in the sense that that's my way of raging against the dying of the light. But I'm quite a bit past the gun on the plate."

Much like his friend and compatriot gonzo journalist Hunter S. Thompson, who coined the phrase "fear and loathing" and wore it as a badge of honor as he took on the "greedheads" in defense of the "doomed," Zevon yearned to express in song that which had never been broached before. "Hunter was one of the great influences in the way I went about writing songs a little different than the songs that I hadn't heard yet," he concluded to VH1 in 2003.

This brings to mind another of Zevon's literary and personal heroes, Norman Mailer and his *The Armies of the Night*, with its curious and stirring subtitle *History as a Novel/The Novel as History*, a conflation of personal experience with dramatic overtones, which would dominate the New Journalism of the late 1960s and 1970s. Another "close to the bone" art form, like Martin Scorsese's cinema of realism, it obliterated the objectivity of "reporting in prose" or "depicting in images" as a way to a greater truth. Zevon explained to VH1, retrospectively, in 2003: "For some reason or another I've been writing songs about death and mortality and violence, and I'm not sure why. Some of them are based on reasons of my upbringing, I guess, my background, but truly they're based on my reading habits. When I was a kid in the '60s, I read Norman Mailer and Hunter Thompson and a strain of American writers who tended to be kind of violent. During the war we lived in a culture—and we still live in a culture—where violence is all around us. And I don't know if I *chose* to, but I found myself writing songs about violent subjects more than romantic subjects. Now and then I like to think I have some good-hearted romantic impulses and express them in songs, but for the most part I write a different kind of song than that."

To that end, Zevon, like Mailer and Thompson, was intrigued and inspired by social upheaval, dabbling in radical thought as a mechanism for a more lasting agenda. In Mailer, Thompson, and other writers of their ilk, Zevon would find authors who shared his passion for the vi-o-lence of Raymond Chandler and his characters' desperate need for survival in a cruel world. Their conflicts are the conflicts of a wider, colder nature, where the asphalt jungle breeds contemptible deviants in an all-out war. They have, in essence, been to the edge and "done that too."

"I wondered why popular music was so square," Zevon told Steve Roeser of *Goldmine* magazine in 1995. "I had been reading Norman Mailer from the time I was twelve years old. I don't think it occurred to me that I was trying to make some kind of breakthrough in the popular song. It seemed to me then, and it seems to me now, that, for the most part, there were some kind of restrictions on the subject matter of songs. And it was quite the opposite in every other art form."

Originally presented in Truman Capote's novel about a West Kansas mass murder, *In Cold Blood*, in 1965, then followed by *Hell's Angels*, Thompson's exposé on the mythical outlaw biker gang, in 1966, and right beside Tom Wolfe's chillingly expressive *The Electric Kool-Aid Acid Test* of 1968, Mailer's book exploited conflict and violence as a battering ram to speak truth to power, specifically the bloody and immoral Vietnam War, which by that year had splintered the United States into pieces. It would be the beginning of the type of paranoia and apathy the body politic would feel about its institutions, from government to religion to the military: a new era of dread, a time ripe for war and assassinations, riots, and televised violence the likes of which the country had not seen since the Civil War.

There is wisdom, however spiteful and dismissive, in "I've seen all there is to see / I've heard all they had to say" when confronted with this type of truth-telling: a disregard for sacred cows and genuflecting reverence.

"There are things more insidious than violence, like hypocritical optimism," Zevon quipped to *Songwriter* magazine in 1981.

It is important to note that while the above writers and their books spanned the late 1960s with its cultural shifts in race, gender, music, and fashion, they were very much throwbacks, as was Zevon, similarly inspired by what journalist Barry Alfonso described as Zevon's "fascination with the theme of valor under fire." Men who harkened back to the grit of Mencken and Hemingway, they wrote prose filled with torrid lines of violent rhetoric and scathing humor aimed at the very readers drawn to its lurid subject matter. These were the men who railed against the growing hippie aesthetic, as did Jack Kerouac, who harbored a virulent disdain for all of it, despite his 1957 novel *On the Road* becoming a biblical guidebook for the "tune-in and drop-out" orthodoxy of the new revolutionaries that crowded campuses and joined underground cults.

One is reminded of "He Quit Me," Zevon's song included on the sound track to the 1969 film masterpiece *Midnight Cowboy*, which was based on the 1965 novel by James Leo Herlihy. Directed by John Schlesinger, the film, like the book, is a staggeringly realistic and disturbing portrayal of a country bumpkin lost in the seamy underworld of Manhattan beyond the plastic machinations of a late-arriving Madison Avenue depiction of the "Summer of Love," wherein the beautiful and naive revelers are easily hustled by the desperate and destitute. It would go on to win the Academy Award for Best Picture, despite its dubiously earned X rating. That same year, 1969, a real-life hustler/ex-con named Charles Manson emerged from this fractured movement to hijack the counterculture and turn suburban runaways into murderous drones. This is the milieu that is echoed by Zevon's wonderfully poetic "Desperados Under the Eaves," which gave voice to the forgotten subterranean outcasts who became the discarded victims of the peace-and-love sellout.

Noteworthy is that during one of my many discussions with Jordan Zevon, the subject was broached about the duality in his father's uncanny ability to impart humanity to the most despicable of characters with his personal abhorrence and ideological rejection of their violent nature. "Dad would sing about and explore internal darkness that exists inside all of us," says Jordan. "But he wasn't a dark guy. He had a moral compass that found humanity in those that he deemed worthy. I seriously doubt he tried to kick anyone's ass. He was his own worst enemy."

In his *Village Voice* review of *Excitable Boy* in the spring of 1978, Greil Marcus played with an interesting parallel between Zevon's undercurrent of violent images as social commentary and new punk icons the Sex Pistols, who had taken the rock world by storm with their virulent rejection of the dying hippie edict of the 1960s: "Right below the surface—with Zevon, the surface is usually a joke—Zevon's songs speak of a fascination with violence as a means to life, of a need to touch it, to come to terms with it. You won't get to the bottom of *Excitable Boy* simply by noting that its subject matter includes contract killing, the Congo civil war, revenge murder, psychos, the Mexican revolution, rape, the Symbionese Liberation Army, necrophilia, and mutilation, but you won't completely miss the point, either."

Although Zevon displayed the chops of a man of letters, he was no novelist, essayist, or journalist. He was a musician and songwriter, and to his advantage he added a stirring soundscape to his brutal soliloquies. Throughout his catalog are snippets of crude, raw, and penetrating violence of all measures: self-inflicted, societal, nefarious, and hilarious. None of it, according to Zevon's assessment in *Songwriter* magazine, was ever gratuitous, for that would be "worse than being bland." His violence spans the scope of humanity, from the Three Stooges to Caligula: darkly black humor that portends our frailties, what his biographer, Professor George Plasketes, calls "a sophisticated sense of violence." When I asked the professor to expound on this provocative phrase, he said, "If you listen to the most basic example, like on 'Excitable Boy,' you've got Ronstadt and Jennifer Warnes with the *Ooh . . . wahh . . . ooh* and this bouncy melody set against lyrics about raping somebody and 'building a cage with her bones.' I think there's a certain sense of sophistication that draws you in [with] this bouncy melody set against this wreaking of havoc, and yet I never found any of it gratuitous. Even the profanity in 'My Shit's Fucked Up' [*Life'll Kill Ya*, 2000] is refreshing. Instead of a doctor giving you this clinical diagnosis, he just looks at you and says, 'Hey, your shit's fucked up.' It's very blunt, but it's intellectual, it's humorous, and I think all those things add up to that sense of its sophistication without being pretentious. That's just part of what Jackson Browne called 'the berserk brilliance' of how he wrote."

There is the ballad of ruthless outlaws, "Frank and Jesse James," and the suicidal chick-magnet, "Poor Poor Pitiful Me." There's the hell-bent-for-mayhem antihero of "I'll Sleep When I'm Dead," the ghostly murderer-for-hire in "Roland the Headless Thompson Gunner," the psychopathic man-child of "Excitable Boy," the fashion-conscious beast of "Werewolves of London," and the cornered prankster of "Lawyers, Guns and Money." There are the merry mercenaries of "Jungle Work," the possessive father/cop and his double-crossing daughter of "Jeannie Needs a Shooter," the cold-blooded institutional musclemen of "The Envoy," and the young fugitives of "The Overdraft." There's the doomed drug dealer of "Charlie's Medicine," the accidental killer (and the sport that sanctions his actions) in "Boom Boom Mancini," and the paranoiac of "Trouble Waiting to Happen." There's the bloody trilogy of "Transverse City," "Run Straight Down," and "The Long Arm of the Law." There's the ticking suburban time bomb of "Model Citizen," the mysterious femme fatale of "Angel Dressed in Black," the aging radical of "Renegade," and the misanthropic looter of "The Indifference of Heaven." There's the vengeful maniac of "Rottweiler Blues"; the prescient doomsayer of "I Was in the House When the House Burned Down," "Life'll Kill Ya," and "You're a Whole Different Person When You're Scared"; the sadomasochist of "Hostage-O," and the misunderstood hockey goon of "Hit Somebody (The Hockey Song)."

"Ain't That Pretty at All" is the place where they all meet, a first-person rant bellowed over an ear-bending chorus of bizarre keyboard sounds played as if they are bashing up against some imaginary wall. They start and stop, contemplating impact, buttressed by a pounding offbeat drum that cuts through like Poe's raven summoning bad vibes, then descends, as the notes slump down utterly exasperated. This is followed by a guitar run that struts along fighting to be heard, but now adds a queer counterbalance before abandoning ship for the second verse. "That arrangement was the brainchild of Danny 'Kootch' Kortchmar," remembers guitarist David Landau. "He's playing the low-note guitar on there, which is something he likes to do if you listen to the stuff he's done with Don Henley—that *bowm, bowm, bowm*. I'm playing the eighth note, seventh chords up top. But I was really impressed with what he did with it, because on the one hand it's such a simple tune, but I felt he laid a solid foundation that Warren could just go nuts on."

Zevon sings in vainglorious splendor, acting out the words with the tone of a man on the edge of madness.

You know, I just had a short vacation, Roy
Spent it getting a root canal
"Oh, how'd you like it?"
Well, it ain't that pretty at all

The "Roy" is LeRoy Marinell, cowriter of many of Zevon's most manic tunes, back again to lend support to this ode to self-inflicted pain. "This is a perfect example of Warren and LeRoy getting crazy with a song, which they always did over the years, I love it," says longtime friend and songwriting partner Jorge Calderón. This time Roy gets into the act, asking Zevon knowingly, "Oh, how'd you like it?" to the age-old comedic axiom that something is so bad it can only be underwhelmed by a root canal, perhaps the most invasive and painful of procedures in the sadistic craft of dentistry. It so happens that when he was diagnosed with inoperable lung cancer, Zevon revealed to interviewers that he had failed to see doctors for decades to avoid the type of horrible news he was eventually handed. His one medical contact was his dentist, Doctor Stan, regarding whom he mused to VH1, "If Dr. Stan can't fix it, call 911. I'm done."

Dr. Stan is another colorful character in the cadre of confidants Zevon kept close during his professional life, while also hitting many touchstones. Beyond being

Zevon's dentist and only real physician, Dr. Stan was also Bob Dylan's cousin. A swashbuckling character who rode a motorcycle and proudly displayed signed photos of Mick Jagger and George Harrison on his office walls, the good doctor played, according to talent manager and later CEO of Zevon's last record label, Artemis Records, Danny Goldberg, "a paternal role that Warren coveted and appreciated."

Once again, without being too Freudian, Zevon uses the second verse to merge his dentist ("root canal") with his father ("paternal role") in a song about pain.

Zevon admitted to *Rolling Stone*'s Richard Skanse in 2000: "Sickness. Doctors. That scares me. Not violence—helplessness. That's why I turn to violent stories, I think. Nobody's ever asked me that, and I've never said that before, but I think that's true."

Gonna get a good running start and throw myself at the wall as hard as I can, man

Not satisfied with expressing inner turmoil, Zevon sets his sights on the outside world, poking holes in the ultra-glamorous, historic, and exotic cities across Europe. The band is all in, rollin' and tumblin' with reckless abandon. It sounds fun, but not loose. If anything, this is a song of precision, a complicated musical romp that sounds as if it were created by someone boldly imprecise—Zevon's yin scraping up against his yang again. "Rhythmically, there was always a surface difference to Warren's music, a rhythmic straightness to it," cites Landau. "Maybe that came from his classical background."

This becomes blatantly obvious once a woodblock clip-clop is introduced that gives way to growling complaints:

I've been to Paris
And it ain't that pretty at all
I've been to Rome
Guess what?

By this point, Zevon has abandoned all melodic parameters and begins to playfully crow over the cacophony:

I'd like to go back to Paris someday and visit the Louvre Museum
Get a good running start and hurl myself at the wall

Crashing sounds follow each hurl into the wall, prompting a charming moment in the song where a chanting sing-along seems like the best idea. It is now a mob-rules sentiment. All this rhythm and counter-rhythm and noise and guitar runs and clip-clops come together to make one single statement:

It ain't that pretty at all!
It ain't that pretty at all!

Returning to the role of rock 'n' roll as the ultimate musical sledgehammer, it is here that Zevon tips his metaphoric cap to the punk rock movement, which by 1982 had limped into the New Wave and British Romantic phase, characterized by the type of lifeless sheen he hated in his truth-telling. "It really is a punk song," notes Landau. "I think he related to punk. He liked the wildness of it and the primal aspect. You could hear it on the live album we recorded together [*Stand in the Fire*, 1980]. After 'Mohammed's Radio' or some of the other more introspective ballads, he needed to reach for something primal, whether it was 'Bo Diddley Was a Gunslinger' or 'I'll Sleep When I'm Dead.' He was pushing that band to *rock*. Playing music that loud and unrestrained gave him a chance to get that out."

The chanting of "It ain't that pretty at all!" in lieu of a singsong chorus was the calling card of such concussive acts as the Sex Pistols (reflected in Greil Marcus's parallels: "There's more violence in Zevon's repertoire than there was in [Johnny] Rotten's"), the Ramones, the Damned, Television, the Voidoids to name a few. A cover of the song by the 1990s alternative band the Pixies for 2004's *Enjoy Every Sandwich* tribute album illustrates this perfectly. The vocals slither in after squealing guitar feedback, a pounding drumbeat, and a thumping bass line that hint more at the song's punk aesthetic than does the manic keyboard attack on the original. This is evident when the chorus kicks in with a garage mantra sung in apathetic monotone by bassist Kim Deal and a screaming Black Francis, then swings into an homage to "Waiting for the Man" by the Velvet Underground (arguably the first punk band). The last two minutes of the song descend into pure noise, sounding more like a car accident than like anything musical.

If you stand back from the Warren Zevon catalog and see it as a whole, as I do, it is a novel with arcs and villains and conflict and a grand morality play. As stated earlier, drama is conflict. Still, it is hard to ignore this particular author's obsession with violence. That is not to say he is flippant or irresponsible in its use, but it is there, and at times it is rampant and overwhelming. And if you add his inordinate number of songs about death, it is a blowout. However, Zevon understood his place in all of this as an artist. "There's the notion some people have that I'd probably write a song about Jeffrey Dahmer," Zevon told journalist Gerrie Lim in 1993. "I don't know where they get the idea. Reaching that conclusion about me is like thinking that Clint Eastwood is actually a cop."

And while this is inarguable, Clint Eastwood did not write a word of his most famous "cop" film, *Dirty Harry*, an unflinchingly violent depiction of a rogue law enforcer that made him the most recognizable tough guy in cinema. He played a role. And although Zevon most assuredly believed he was playing many roles in his songwriting, he was the one conjuring its origins.

"Reconsider Me": Andy Slater with Warren Zevon in the studio in 1987. *Courtesy of the Andy Slater Collection, photo by Henry Diltz*

Sentimental Hygiene

If I cannot inspire love, I will cause fear.

—Mary Shelley, *Frankenstein*

On May 27, 1983, a thirty-six-year-old Warren Zevon took a walk around his new neighborhood in Philadelphia, where he had decamped during a break in a cross-country solo tour, ostensibly to move in with his new girlfriend, Anita Gevinson, a popular DJ on WYSP rock radio. According to many who knew him, however, the curious move from L.A. was more likely a way to distance himself from the constant hounding from friends and family about his voracious drinking and copious drug abuse. Idly glancing at the latest issue of *Rolling Stone* magazine, he was stunned to learn that Asylum had dropped him. His label since 1976, which had taken him in at the behest of his colleague and friend Jackson Browne, and had nurtured him through rough and wild times, from meager to increased record sales, nearly suicidal tours and everything in between, was kicking him to the curb. For the first time since returning to the states in 1974, Zevon was professionally homeless.

"I was freaked and enraged," he wrote in his diary later that day. "I called the N.Y. TV people and told them 'they didn't have enough money to pay me to work in a moral vacuum.'"

It had been a rough stretch for Zevon already. Beyond his dedication to unbridled depravity, he had seen *The Envoy* record sales go from paltry to nonexistent. He was deep in debt and forced to tour in a car. His three-year relationship with actress Kim Lankford ended as poorly as his marriage to Crystal, who was now living in Paris with his six-year-old daughter, Ariel. He hardly saw either of his children, and even those close to him, who had endured his radical shifts in behavior for years, had all but given up trying to "save" him. These included Browne, his then best friend George Gruel, and his longtime collaborator Waddy Wachtel. Even Jorge Calderón, perhaps his closest confidant, was left in the dark: "That period in Philadelphia, man, it was like a vacuum. I hardly ever spoke to him when he was out there—

maybe a postcard once in a while. I thought he was on the road, because I was out there doing my thing—playing with David Lindley on *El Rayo-X* and working with Ry Cooder's band. To tell you the truth, I'm part of that black hole that was left out of that."

Ariel visited her father during this period and describes Zevon's subsistence as being "dark and bleak," and although she cautions that these observations are through the lens of a six-year-old, they fill in this mysterious and desperate time in the songwriter's life. "I remember him sharing an apartment with his girlfriend at the time," Ariel told me with a tone of apprehension in her voice, even now. "I don't really remember her being there except when they were in their bedroom with the door shut, and the blinds were always shut, and I remember watching TV and making myself cereal and wanting to talk to my mom on the phone, but she was in Paris, and I remember being very unhappy.

"What stands out for me is watching *Rocky* and *Rambo* movies and horror movies with him, and I was this little kid and I still just wanted my dad to love me, so I didn't complain or say, 'This is really scary.' I just went along, and I remember not being able to sleep at night because I was so petrified from watching these movies, but not knowing how to tell him, being too afraid of his disapproval to say anything about it. It was a terrifying time for me certainly as a kid. And yes, he was obviously drinking. That had a huge part in all of it."

Anita Gevinson provides further evidence of Zevon's plight in her 2012 tell-all memoir, *You Turn Me On, I'm a Radio: My Wild Rock 'n' Roll Life*: "I admit I was a bad influence. My life with Warren started out as Bonnie and Clyde, and by the end it turned into *Who's Afraid of Virginia Woolf?* But I was only Liz on weekends. He was shitfaced Dick with the lampshade on his head every night of the week. And I covered for him because I loved him. I never told anyone how bad it got."

The relationship, according to Gevinson, was an ongoing train wreck, as Zevon descended from functioning alcoholic to mere alcoholic. Gevinson describes a broken man who by the end of the year was a veritable shut-in, wandering around her Philly apartment in a robe drinking vodka straight from the bottle. It would have surprised no one, including Zevon himself, if it all ended right there.

Enter Andy Slater, a twenty-five-year-old former music journalist who was working at Frontline Management, which was seriously considering dropping Zevon from its roster of talent. During a meeting in which company brass understandably ran down Zevon's list of negatives—mostly drunk, heaps of trouble, with no record label, and allegedly $180,000 in debt to the IRS—Slater took on the unenviable task of defending him.

Slater, whose California connection included handling Don Henley's affairs, passionately argued that despite a mountain of issues Warren Zevon was the management company's most talented client. Hiding his secret fandom since his college days at Atlanta's Emory University, Slater stood up and said, "Hey, this is the best writer we have!" Thirty-four years later, he continued the story for me. "The head of the company argued, 'He's in debt. He doesn't want to work. He doesn't have a record deal. He is off the roster.' I said, 'He's a great artist and maybe other great artists would want to come here.' And he says, 'Slater, you've been here five minutes. You know what? You manage him. Okay. Next topic.'"

Even after several futile attempts to connect with an unstable Zevon, who hung up on him repeatedly, and months of rejections from a series of A&R contacts and record companies, Slater was still game enough to convince Warner Bros. to part with five grand for demos of new material. With limited options regarding backing musicians, Slater contacted another Zevon fan from his college days, Atlanta native Peter Buck, guitarist for an up-and-coming indie rock band called R.E.M.

Founded in 1980 in the same bohemian music scene in Athens, Georgia, that produced the eclectic B-52's, R.E.M. featured a uniquely swampy sound enhanced by the melodically incoherent vocals of Michael Stipe. By 1984, the band had released an underground hit EP, *Chronic Town*, and a critically acclaimed debut LP, *Murmur*, featuring the infectious "Radio Free Europe." During this time, its instrumentalists—Buck on guitar, Mike Mills on bass, and drummer Bill Berry—decided to join local friend, Bryan Cook to form a side cover band they called the Hindu Love Gods. The group bounced around Athens playing old 1950s and '60s rock rarities for fun and became intrigued at the prospect of having Zevon sit in.

Eager to escape his dreary existence and rocky romance in Philly, Zevon jumped at the chance at an all-expenses-paid trip down south and began immediately hitting it off with Buck, Mills, and Berry. With Warner Bros. funds, the band cut some rough tracks of freshly penned Zevon songs, "Trouble Waiting to Happen" and "Boom Boom Mancini," along with a Bill Berry original, "Narrator," and an old Easybeats song, "Gonna Have a Good Time Tonight." The latter two were eventually mixed for a single. Not surprisingly, the demos were roundly rejected everywhere, sending Zevon back to Philly for more drama with his DJ girlfriend and a mini crisis in which he allegedly tried to kidnap his daughter that eventually landed him a minor stint in rehab in Minnesota.

"He called me from Philadelphia one night and said, 'I'm dying,' remembers his cousin, Sanford "Sandy" Zevon, who after Stumpy's passing became something of a father to Zevon. "I told him to take the next train to New Rochelle, New York, close to where we were living in White Plains. He gets off the train and he's completely disheveled, unshaven and unkempt, draped in a fraying and dirty gray overcoat with a beat-up guitar slung over his shoulder." Sanford's wife, Madeline, then studying to be an alcohol counselor, arranged to get Zevon to a rehab center in St. Paul. "He was absolutely whacked out of his mind, incoherently mumbling something about Spain with prescription drugs just falling out of his pockets," Sanford's son, Paul, recalls. "We had a hard time getting him on the plane, he was so frightened."

Predictably, the cure didn't hold and Zevon escaped back to Los Angeles, where he toggled madly between sobriety and drunkenness. Providing insight to Zevon's deteriorating state once he got back to L.A. is former touring guitarist Zeke Zirngiebel, who ran into him at Tower Video on Sunset Boulevard one evening: "He looked kind of ragged, but I walk over and I said, 'Hey, Warren,' and he turned around like he was going to throw a punch. Then he saw who I was and said, 'Oh, hi. Zeke Zirngiebel, right?' He was that person that everyone talked about again, the one that people had a hard time dealing with."

George Gruel, who was let go by Zevon during the latter's financial crunch, also remembers his friend's lost period: "By '84 I'd moved on and had other things to do. Warren was living in these business apartments in L.A. and I took him over some pot, and it was just sad. There were pizza boxes everywhere. I asked, 'Anything I can do for you?' And he said, 'No, I'm all right, man.'"

Despite all this, Andy Slater admits to being seduced by Zevon's wit and charm and an ongoing excuse for balancing a phalanx of pills as a strategic practice of becoming a "chemical engineer." Slater's reward for his attrition was an achingly tender ballad of remorseful reconciliation called "Reconsider Me." The song so moved Slater that he swore, against all odds, he would get Zevon a deal.

"Warren was a consummate writer," says Slater today. "There was never a misplaced word in his writing. It was simple and powerful, like Hemingway, so when I heard 'Reconsider Me,' a lot of it came together in that moment for me, because in a way it reminded me of all the great things that I knew about him, and yet there was something new in that song, as powerful as any he had ever written."

Soaked in melodic strains and the warmest of vocal deliveries, "Reconsider Me" is arguably Zevon's most honest expression of his damaged soul since "Hasten Down the Wind" a decade earlier. This time, though, instead of telling the tale under the cover of a third-person narrative, he writes as if sending a letter of apology to everyone he has ever wronged. Once again, he delivers the lines in a higher register than usual, with a tinge of trepidation: "And I'll never make you sad again / 'Cause I swear that I've changed since then / And I promise that I'll never make you cry."

If you're all alone
And you need someone
Call me up
And I'll come running
Reconsider me
Reconsider me

If it's still the past
That makes you doubt
Darlin', that was then
And this is now
Reconsider me
Reconsider me

The phrasing of the "reconsider me" refrain delivered in a near whisper is heartrending, as Zevon lifts the repeated line just slightly, raising his regret to a final, desperate plea. This is articulated beautifully with perhaps the song's finest musical moment, a wonderfully crafted bridge that is reminiscent of the most touching Rodgers and Hart or Lennon/McCartney couplets.

You can go and be
What you want to be
And it'll be all right
If we disagree
I'm the one who cares
And I hope you'll see
That I'm the one who loves you
Reconsider me

On the strength of this openly sentimental appeal for salvation, in early 1986, after Warren Zevon had spent nearly three years in exile, the newly formed U.S. wing of Virgin Records signed him as its first act. It didn't hurt that celebrated film director and Zevon favorite Martin Scorsese had recently decided to use "Werewolves of London" in *The Color of Money*, his sequel to the 1961 pool-shark film, *The Hustler*. Once again, Zevon's powerfully raw songwriting, unbelievably not destroyed by pills, drink, or random acts of violence, coupled with an indestructible novelty tune that had taken him ten minutes to write in 1974, rescued him.

"I'm shaking and I'm feeling shitty, but I'm pounding the piano twelve hours a day and singing and writing songs for myself—telling myself a lot of things in songs," Zevon confessed to friend and journalist Paul Nelson, alluding to the one thing that never seemed to abandon him, his incredible songwriting prowess.

The sessions for what would become Zevon's fifth studio album, *Sentimental Hygiene*, began in the final month of 1986 in Los Angeles with his new musical cohorts R.E.M. backing him. By then, Zevon had miraculously pulled himself together and was attending regular AA meetings, supported by new girlfriend, journalist Merle Ginsberg.

"There's no question that Warren was sober during the making of that record," Andy Slater insists. "He told me that he wasn't sure that his perspective and his ability to create the characters in his songs would be intact in the same way in sobriety as it was through the rest of his life. But as the songs came for the rest of the record, he realized that whatever gifts he had were not dependent on being in an altered state of mind. It was all there and it all came back, and maybe in a way it was more powerful this way."

Zevon even insisted on producing himself, continuing a natural progression that had started when he changed sonic directions for *Bad Luck Streak in Dancing School* after the success of his first two albums under the tutelage of Jackson Browne and Waddy Wachtel. Zevon also pushed Slater into the coproducer's role, making sure to keep the usual L.A. cohorts at bay. Only Don Henley, Wachtel, and Jorge Calderón would contribute sparingly to tracks laid down fast and furious by what amounted to the Hindu Love Gods in action. "All we did was play," Zevon confessed to John Soeder from *Scene*.

The new songs reflected Zevon's brighter and freer outlook while revisiting the anguish of getting sober and making amends. "I used to feel it was cheating to work at writing a song—that songs should just flow fluidly or spring from a bolt-shop of inspiration," Zevon reflected to *Rolling Stone* in the early '80s. "But now, when I'm working consciously on a song, I know what real work is. In a way it makes the process more frustrating, but it also makes it more exciting. I get these vague but real intense feelings about things I could write that are just a little beyond my grasp, so I have to work harder to reach them. That's real exhilarating."

To that end, only three of *Sentimental Hygiene*'s ten tracks feature cowriters, something Zevon had leaned on heavily since his debut album, and one of them, the biting music-biz screed, "Even a Dog Can Shake Hands," is a collaborative effort with Buck, Mills, and Berry that conjures the fun-filled musical abandon of "Poor Poor Pitiful Me."

All the worms and the gnomes are having lunch at Le Dôme
They're all living off the fat of the land
Everybody's trying to be a friend of mine
Even a dog can shake hands

The venom Zevon had saved for the many femme fatales that were absorbed into his untamed existence would now be duly aimed at a recording industry rife with sharks and sleaze, which, of course it had been long before Zevon hit the scene, but by the 1980s it was overrun with them. The selling and marketing of rock 'n' roll during the 1970s bloated into a commercial monster by the mid-'80s, with the advent of MTV, corporate sponsorship of tours, and classic bands from the 1960s like the Rolling Stones and the Who becoming multitiered conglomerates. Just as Zevon had dissected the L.A. music scene when it was fading into a haze of drug abuse, abject greed, and gnawing apathy in 1976, ten years on he was faced with a larger, more faceless beast, which had chewed him up and spit him out when he was on shaky emotional and professional ground.

Take your pick of canine in "Even a Dog Can Shake Hands": record execs, agents, managers, A&R personnel, booking agents, the pencil-pushing geeks behind the scenes manipulating art as commerce, selling image over substance and robbing the innocent and starry-eyed ("We'll do the rest for you / Find a way to make it pay"), as well as the aging songwriter on the fringe ("'Cause he knew you back when / Now they all want a piece of the band"). Fast-talking yuppies riding around Mulholland Drive yakking on car phones and sucking up their twenty percent, while professing undying love: "Everybody's trying to be a friend of mine / Even a dog can shake hands."

Sign page 42
We'll do the rest for you
Find a way to make it pay
Don't lose your head
You'll end up dead
Or you'll be living in the valley some day

You'll be making the scene 'til they pick your bones clean
No, they don't leave much for the fans
Everybody's trying to be a friend of mine
Even a dog can shake hands

R.E.M., although prolific in having released three more albums in the ensuing years since first meeting Zevon, had not yet broken through to the wider international audience it would soon garner in the late 1980s through the 1990s. By then R.E.M. would have mellowed its sound by introducing more acoustic instruments like mandolin and piano (both featured prominently on the band's biggest hit, "Losing My Religion"), which prompted Stipe to become more articulate in his previously garbled delivery. The 1986 version of the band was still steeped in hungry guitar riffs driven by a rock-steady backbeat, something Buck, Mills, and Berry displayed with great relish in their side outfit, the Hindu Love Gods. In fact, throughout the sessions the band would roll tape and cruise through raucous versions of old blues and folk standards like Robert Johnson's "Walkin' Blues" and Woody Guthrie's "Vigilante Man," with Zevon belting out raw vocals with rapt enthusiasm. This not only fused a cohesive recording unit but finely tuned the sound of a band cooking, the mantra taken from Mike Mills's edict, "We'll do it 'til the food arrives!" These funky side sessions to *Sentimental Hygiene* would eventually be released by Zevon's next label, Giant, to cash in on R.E.M.'s commercial breakout in 1990, bolstered by a threadbare cover of Prince's 1985 hit "Raspberry Beret."

The foundation of R.E.M.'s unrefined indie cred gains serious momentum on each track of *Sentimental Hygiene*, infusing Zevon's material with striking sound and fury. Unlike on his previous three albums, here there is only one ballad and very little piano. For his part, Zevon's electric guitar playing is pushed to the fore, as many of the songs were written poured through a cranked amp. This is evident from the first tracks, "Sentimental Hygiene" and "Boom Boom Mancini," two four-on-the-floor rockers that hit hard from the opening bars, portending a true "band" album, something Zevon acutely devised onstage (illustrated with unbridled verve in 1980's live album, *Stand in the Fire*), but had never attempted in the studio. Aside from a period-sounding keyboard supplement on the title track, this sound is the obvious result of the rough-edged covers Zevon joined in on a few years back.

In the Virgin Records promotions package, Zevon would describe "Sentimental Hygiene," another in a long line of wonderfully evocative titles, as "feelings so clean you can eat off of them." The song is a call-to-arms confessional that finds the protagonist caught in a storm of societal meanness, or, worse yet, apathy. It projects both a personal admission of building walls to prevent the pain of rejection and fear, while also sympathizing with human frailties.

Everybody's had to hurt about it
No one wants to live without it

It's so hard to find it
Sentimental hygiene

Battling to get sober against his baser instincts, Zevon had come to learn—perhaps through several aborted rehab assignments and recently AA—that the chaos of his life was self-inflicted. His inability to outwardly express any emotion beyond rage, jealousy, or wild abandon was just a cleverly fabricated defense mechanism. It is a subject he had broached in previous songs within several damaged characters who had given voice to deeper recesses of his own psyche. Both the song and title of the album are exclamations of his turmoil and resurrection, a return from the abyss that cannot be ignored, and with "Sentimental Hygiene," while the song is rough-edged and driving musically, he compassionately gives himself permission to absolve himself of his sins one at a time. Not unlike "Even a Dog Can Shake Hands," it also serves as an opening commentary about the times in which Zevon finds himself, wherein everyone seems to be going through the motions, "trying to get along," trading in true feelings for masks of pride in a mad pursuit of wealth and projecting an image of success to fill an emotional vacancy. The result is dead-end jobs that prompt lonely rides in expensive cars through sheltered neighborhoods with the stinging realization that none of it is enough to allow one to achieve true happiness or even an honest expression of sadness.

In his own smarmy take at an "expression of sadness," in "Trouble Waiting to Happen" ("Just when I thought it was safe to be bored"), Zevon reflects further on where he finds himself in the mid-'80s: a fading rock star in exile, aging beneath a mountain of regret and watching his fellow Californian musicians, like the Eagles' Don Henley and Glenn Frey, build popular solo careers, and Jackson Browne stepping out with his movie-star girlfriend, Daryl Hannah, basking in a level of success unavailable to him.

"I think us Zevons are a little more self-deprecating, so I don't think there was a 'Why them, not me?'" says his son, Jordan Zevon, who listened to his father wrestle with an explanation for his utter lack of popularity. "It was more 'What the fuck is wrong with me? What am I doing wrong? What am I missing?'"

J. D. Souther adds, "There was a standing joke between us, although there was some degree of bitterness to go with the humor, which was I always told him I wish I had his reviews and he always told me he wished he had my royalties."

"Warren had a decent-size audience, but he certainly didn't reach the peak that Jackson and the Eagles reached," observes veteran record executive Danny Goldberg, who would eventually sign Zevon to his final label contract at Artemis Records. "He was not a commercial singer. I happen to love his voice. I love that baritone. It's just so unique and it just gets to me, but it wasn't a perfect fit for the sort of crossover radio environment the way Don Henley's was or Linda Ronstadt's. I think his career is somewhat greater as a songwriter than as a singer. That's objectively what one would have to say."

Not coincidentally, "Trouble Waiting to Happen," with its wonderful piano homage to the ghost of "Excitable Boy," was cowritten with old companion J. D. Souther, one of the few compatriots from his 1970s L.A. past who deigned to visit him in his downward spiral. Zevon writes in his journal of the visit that prompted the composition of this personal exposé of his sometimes exaggerated public persona versus his actual downtrodden lifestyle: "It's hard to say how happy I've been to see him & how glad I am to have a real friend who understands me & whom I respect."

"I think maybe the one reason I went is because no one else did," recalls Souther, who told me he has written a short story recounting his time with Zevon in Philadelphia. "It was winter and I knew what effect that had on him and I wasn't exactly in the greatest period of my life either at that time. We were both getting really high and I was between records floundering around. It felt, from talking to him on the phone, that he was doing the same. So I just called him and said, 'What are you doing?' And he just said, 'Come as quick as you can.' So I did, and we had a very interesting time there and we worked on the song—both of us alternatively typing, while the other one played and back and forth. The song really is about our lives at the time. It was not an easy period for both of us and it probably bonded us more than any other period of our friendship."

The song's second verse, in which Zevon expresses his shock and dismay at being dumped by Asylum and, in effect, being discarded by the entire L.A. scene that had moved beyond him, is its most autobiographical. Not that it was ever *his* "scene" in a sense, but it was one that nonetheless took him to its bosom, where he was once celebrated and revered by its artists and by the critics who recognized his brilliance as the outsider. This is perhaps why it was so easy to ostracize him. They fed voraciously off the Hollywood teat while he mocked them mercilessly in song, tossed the career they afforded him away in a torrent of antisocial behavior, and then went east to wallow in his excesses. But he could never escape it entirely. It came in phone calls with news from the front, sometimes right at his doorstep, infiltrating his airtight, booze-addled, pill-popping cocoon.

The mailman brought me the Rolling Stone
Trouble waiting to happen

It said I was living at home alone
Trouble waiting to happen
I read things I didn't know I'd done
It sounded like a lot of fun
I guess I've been bad or something
Trouble waiting to happen

Beyond receiving his notice of unemployment in *Rolling Stone*, Zevon is referencing a cover story the magazine ran in March of 1981 that detailed one of his many failed attempts at sobriety. Filled with firsthand accounts of its subject by respected rock journalist and friend Paul Nelson, "The Crack-Up and Resurrection of Warren Zevon," whose title is based on that of F. Scott Fitzgerald's 1936 *Esquire* essay on the pressures of fame, is considered to this day to be one of the most honest accounts of a rock 'n' roll artist's personal destruction. Nelson spent a remarkable two and a half years in and around the Zevon hurricane, reporting in the gonzo style made famous by Hunter S. Thompson in the pages of the same publication in the early 1970s. Nelson conducted a series of long-form interviews in which Zevon acknowledges that his alcoholism is a fast track to a "coward's death," yet still in the throes of being a perpetually lying junkie, he presented a false image of himself as a figure of health and propriety. His friend, confidant, and road manager George Gruel confirmed as much in 2015 when he told me that Annie Leibovitz's brilliantly stylized *Rolling Stone* cover shot of Zevon being pulled limb from limb by disembodied hands was taken while everyone was on a three-day bender. "That woman liked to party," laughs Gruel. "It was just like one big movie."

Nelson, who truly loved and respected Zevon, as the sentiment was mutual, had participated in a traumatizing "intervention" after the symbolic assassination of the *Excitable Boy* cover. He was joined by Zevon's wife, Crystal; her parents; Jackson Browne; cowriters LeRoy Marinell and Jorge Calderón; and photographer Jimmy Wachtel in participating in what Nelson describes as "an execution with a happy ending." Zevon's brother in conflict and mayhem, Waddy Wachtel, was also invited, but declined for reasons he shared with me in February of 2017: "It would have been so hypocritical for me to be part of the intervention. I mean, we *lived* together on the road and in the studios, and our abusing of drugs was also very close. So I wished everybody good luck, but I could not be there because if I'm there he'll go, 'This is ridiculous if he's here.' It would have invalidated the whole thing."

Jackson Browne, who'd confronted Zevon regarding his increasing substance abuse back when they recorded *Excitable Boy* together, cites this conflict as putting a strain on their personal and working relationship, and was now encouraged by the fact that his friend was publicly admitting via a press release that he was indeed an alcoholic.

The group would eventually meet in the antiseptic confines of the Pinecrest Rehabilitation Hospital in Santa Barbara, where Zevon had checked in to be treated for alcoholism.

"I put it together," Crystal told me, in an emotional retelling of events. "The intervention was originally planned to *get* him into treatment, so after he finally got in the car with me after the night he shot the album cover I was hugely relieved we weren't going to have to do this thing, because I was terrified by the idea of it. For my parents, who were very normal and traditional—they grew up in the same town in Kansas and were boyfriend and girlfriend from high school and got married—this was totally shocking. But then the therapist told me it would be better to do it at the hospital in a safer environment, where he needed to be. So I called everyone and said, 'It's on.'"

Soon eight of the closest people in Zevon's life were facing him, each unburdening their souls about how he had hurt them as well as himself.

Jorge Calderón shared with me his chilling recollection of the afternoon in a deliberate, almost reverent manner one mild mid-September day in 2016, the timbre in his voice stressed by the memory: "Crystal called me and told me that she wanted me to be part of it. I was like, 'Oh my God.' I'm thinking to myself, 'What are we going to do here?' I really wanted to help, but in the back of my mind I was thinking, 'I'm going to drive up there to Santa Barbara and do this and he'll never speak to me again.'"

"All of us felt the same way," agrees Jimmy Wachtel when I told him what Jorge had said. "I think Jorge, LeRoy, and I drove up together. And I distinctly remember him coming into that room with the shock of seeing all of us. It was kind of heartrending. We were there to do good, but it was so shocking for him to be confronted by everybody."

"I knew all of these people had to write down Warren's worst atrocities and share them, but I didn't realize that I had to," says Crystal. "During the run-through, the doctor said, 'Crystal where's your list?' So I had to sit there on the spot with everybody in the room and write down things that had happened. I think because I didn't have any time to think about it, it was totally uncensored and probably more gut-wrenchingly honest than it would have been had I written it earlier. I probably would have tempered things, but I didn't. The way Paul expresses it in his article, when it came to my turn . . . it's actually bringing up tears right now just even thinking about it."

"Everybody had a story to tell of what he had done when he was drunk and I can't remember what I said," Wachtel continues. "I don't remember any specific phrase or incident, although there must have been some. You see, I was never frightened by him. He never did any violent stuff around me. Although there was a period when his daughter was born when he was bringing home guns and shooting them off, drinking an amazing amount of alcohol, which was obviously very dangerous. But everybody was kind of crazy then anyway, so it wasn't out of the ordinary. It was a seriously druggy, crazy era in the '70s. It's hard to say who was crazier than the next."

Zevon later would tell Jackson Browne that he would never forget the way his once relentless benefactor appeared to filibuster, never qualifying if he thought that perhaps Browne was struggling to find the right words or that he flatly refused to do so.

"When it came to me, I just said what I had to say . . . stories on the road and how hurtful and embarrassing it was for me to see him like that," Calderón remembers. "Crystal had told me that he had crazed tantrums and had thrown things in the room while Ariel was there in the crib. Finally, I said, 'I'm doing this and I hope that you can stop, because you're a fine person when you're not under the influence.'"

"It was very shameful," adds Wachtel. "That's the expression I remember . . . shameful."

"I remember watching his face as I read," Crystal continues. "I looked up a few times and there was this rage, and I just knew right then that we would never be together again. But then as I continued to read . . . he broke. I watched his face just kind of crumble and his expression soften. And when I finished there was this *long* silence and then all of a sudden everyone stood up and we were all crying and hugging. And he just held on to me and then he thanked everyone. It's a brutally honest process."

"I drove back to L.A. that day and I told my wife, 'I'm not going to see him again. He's going to hate me forever for doing this,'" says Calderón. "But on the contrary: Crystal told me, 'No, he loves you and respects you more than ever and he says that of all the people that were there, what you said really resonated with him. You're his friend!' And actually our relationship got better after that. I was amazed and grateful that that happened, because I didn't want to lose him as a friend, regardless of what we did musically. The writing of songs was always great, of course, but the friendship was better."

"It was intense," Crystal says with a deep sigh. "One time years ago I found what I had written in a box somewhere and I think I must have thrown it away, because I haven't seen it since."

"It helped him, I guess," Wachtel concludes. "He did stop drinking . . . for a while."

Nelson's intense study of Zevon's battle with alcoholism, including his own cringingly excruciating details of the intervention in which he paints Zevon as "dazed and pale, like a small animal who'd been struck on the head," would end up as a forty-five-page, 20,000-word manuscript that was cut considerably to fit into a *Rolling Stone* main feature. This was nonetheless something of a triumph, considering the magazine's founder and publisher, Jann Wenner, had sworn as far back as 1978 that he would never allow a single word to be published about Zevon after enduring one of Zevon's obnoxious drunken displays at a Bruce Springsteen concert at New York City's Palladium.

Despite Zevon's continued substance abuse, for perhaps the first time it was Nelson who forced him to cop to being on a suicide jag in the most agonizing terms. The last few paragraphs of his epic feature are filled with declarations of real pain, as Zevon recounts a conversation with his friend, author Ross Macdonald, aka Ken Millar, about his conflation of artistic expression and alcoholism: "I drank to *force* the fun, to get rid of the anxiety and guilt I'd had all my life. For the first time, everything made a crazy kind of sense to me. Since what I felt guilty about was also destroying me, crime and punishment were taking place simultaneously, so I must have thought I didn't have anything to worry about. If somebody reprimanded me for my conduct, I could tell them, 'Don't fret, I know I'm being bad, but I'm punishing myself for it.' Ken Millar made me realize that I wrote my songs *despite* the fact that I was a drunk, not *because* of it."

Up until his death in 2006, Nelson was haunted by the full piece having never been given a proper presentation. Ultimately, it would appear years later in its entirety in the posthumous collection *Everything Is an Afterthought: The Life and Writings of Paul Nelson*.

Of course, as Jimmy Wachtel observed, the intervention and Zevon's sobriety were fluid exercises. This sentiment is echoed by Calderón, who would help his friend turn this personal conflagration into art: "After the intervention he did eventually get sober, but he fell off the wagon a few times in between in those years. Like the time I visited him at the Chateau Marmont and he was deep into his Mr. Crazy Rock 'n' Roller character and he tells me, 'Well, I got myself a gray Corvette!' And I said, 'Oh, that's great, a Corvette, huh? So, what, are you going to drive your Corvette over to Detox Mansion this time?' It just came out of me. And he said, 'Detox Mansion. We've got to write that!'"

Continuing the theme of survival, "Detox Mansion" is the first track on the second side of the album and expounds on Zevon's experience on what he sardonically dubs "Rehab Mountain" on "Last Breath Farm," where he and the other patients "learn by heart" that "it's tough to be somebody and it's hard not to fall apart." Reading like a diary, the lyrics, sung with rhythmic guttural force, tell the tale of a celebrity drunk tank. "Raking leaves with Liza / Me and Liz clean up the yard" places the narrator side by side with two classic Hollywood casualties, Liza Minelli and Liz Taylor, both of whom had checked into the freshly minted Betty Ford Clinic in the early 1980s. "I think I've always tried to avoid poking fun of anything I wasn't right in the middle of," Zevon surmised to rock journalist Anthony DeCurtis during the making of the record.

Sitting on a fourteen-acre ranch in California, the institution, founded in 1982 by the former first lady of the United States, was the forerunner for the modern rehabilitation trend that would soon be standard fallout practice for the famously damaged. Over the years it has treated the drug and alcohol addictions of giants from around the entertainment world, notably Mary Tyler Moore, Tony Curtis, Robert Mitchum, Johnny Cash, Drew Barrymore, Stevie Nicks, Andy Gibb, Ozzy Osbourne, Etta James, Chevy Chase, Gary Busey, Richard Pryor, Don Johnson, Lindsay Lohan, Steven Tyler, and Jay-Z. Indeed, as Zevon describes, the stay involves rudimentary chores like doing laundry and yard work.

In 1985, Taylor, while being complimentary of the support she received there, spoke openly about her harrowing experience inside by reading from her 1983 journal to the *New York Times*: "I feel like hell. I'm going through withdrawal. My heart feels big and pounding. I can feel the blood rush through my body. I can almost see it, running like red water over the boulders in my pain-filled neck and shoulders, then through my ears and into my pounding head. My eyelids flutter. Oh God, I am so, so tired." It was Taylor who would prompt an exhausted Liza Minelli, who had been on a legendarily notorious roller-coaster binge since the late 1960s and claimed in *People* magazine to suffer from "drug jitters," to check in to Betty Ford a year later.

"Detox Mansion" is one of the heaviest rock songs in the Zevon canon, although Calderón recalls it starting off as a country foot-stomper transformed into a blues song before the boys in RE.M./Hindu Love Gods got ahold of it. It swings from the open, with an edgy guitar crunch, a snapping snare, and a rumbling bass line. Once again, Zevon, with able assistance from Calderón, who added the "it's hard not to fall apart" section, transforms a painfully pathetic experience into a musical tour de force, at one point shouting, "Hot dog!" before a screaming slide-guitar solo kicks in.

The band concept continues unabated as the cold ending of "Detox Mansion" tumbles forth into a snare pop that begins "Bad Karma," a song Zevon had been authoring with his actions and planting seeds of inside his work for years. It is another tale of cosmic vengeance being brought down on the head of poor, poor pitiful Warren. This time the humor is full tilt, with an accompanying sitar accentuating the Indian flavor of karma. The song offers a spiritual Hindu/Buddhist take on "every action has a reaction" and the effects of good and bad deeds on the fortunes of humanity. In layman's terms, Lady Luck—or the lack thereof—rears her head again for Zevon, who plays with his OCD as if it is a determined Wile E. Coyote ready to pounce on his sleek but hunted temporal Road Runner: "Bad Karma / Coming after me / Bad Karma / Killing me by degrees."

Was it something I did
In another life?
I try and try
But nothing comes out right

I took a wrong turn
On the astral plane
Now I keep on thinkin'
My luck is gonna change
Someday

The third hard-core rocker on the album is "Boom Boom Mancini," an old-fashioned boxer tale. It is both a devastatingly romantic take on survival as a brutal match of strength and guile pitting man against man in the looming square-circle, and a pugilistic metaphor for the rigors of life as blood sport. For decades authors, playwrights, poets, and filmmakers have mined the "sweet science" to dissect the human condition within the boxing ring. Among others, Jack London, Arthur Conan Doyle, Ring Lardner, Nelson Algren, Dashiell Hammett, Damon Runyon, and O. Henry have challenged readers to reevaluate the significance of boxing among the lower classes against the physical and psychological damages of the game. Celebrated films such as *On the Waterfront* (1954), *Requiem for a Heavyweight* (1962), *Fat City* (1972), *Rocky* (1976), *The Champ* (1979), *Raging Bull* (1980), and *Million Dollar Baby* (2004) have less to do with the sport than with what its rigors reveal in its characters.

The symbolism of boxing is rich with its vicious combination of raw emotion, pure violence, and singular heroism lending itself to dramatic themes of good versus evil, overcoming difficult odds, and enduring relentless punishment. "It is the ultimate elemental sport, not dependent on artificial appendages like balls, rackets or bats, nor on the help of teammates," writes Marcel Berlins in a 2007 essay in the *Guardian*, "Why Boxing Makes for Top-Class Writing." He continues: "Physical suffering is integral: it is the only sport specifically aimed at inflicting and receiving pain (which is perhaps why you 'play' cricket, tennis, football, etc., but you do not play boxing)."

Zevon deftly treads the tightrope between straight sports commentary, à la the poetic ruminations of a 1920s Damon Runyon, and the symbolism for his own personal failures in the glare of 1980s celebrity. The song's key lines reverberate with dual meanings: "Some have the speed and the right combinations / If you can't take the punches, it don't mean a thing" and "The name of the game is be hit or hit back," both of which I have used time and again to describe the brutal details of politics throughout decades of column writing. The idea of taking a beating and getting up, of continuing on until the bell rings or the opponent is vanquished, can be used for any and all of life's moments of truth. For Zevon, it is his own bout with alcohol and drugs and his battle to overcome professional strife. He sings "When Alexis Arguello gave Boom Boom a beating / Seven weeks later he was back in the ring" with the grit of a man who understands this implicitly, for it mirrors his own experiences with the cold and calculating music business, which pronounced him obsolete. Here, he is with an up-and-coming indie rock band, kicking up some dust and making the kind of noise that inspired him as a kid. But mostly, the song reflects another of life's contradictions: that sometimes there is no "good and evil" and, more often than not, no clear-cut decision regarding the elusive "right and wrong."

Zevon's subject for this passion play is Ray "Boom Boom" Mancini, a twenty-five-year-old light middleweight champion, who was described by Pat Putnam in a 1984 *Sports Illustrated* article as possessing "brute force coupled with a big heart and a stout chin . . . although he's also capable of a fair amount of rough-edged ring artistry, certainly more than he's given credit for."

More "brute force" than "artistry" is at work in this song, as the narrator sings with rapt eagerness of Mancini's upcoming bout with Bobby Chacon, a fighter ten years Mancini's senior and one Mancini vanquishes under the cloud of controversy. Complaints arose when referee Richard Steele stopped the fight at 1:17 of the third round after those in Chacon's corner could not stem the gush of blood from the fighter's left eye, which would require ten stitches. Zevon opens the tale with a refrain brimming with anticipation for the tussle. ("Hurry home early—hurry on home / Boom Boom Mancini is fighting Bobby Chacon") There is a thirst here for battle, or at least to participate vicariously in it as voyeur, to witness true manhood in action, not a fabricated, marketed, corporate-massaged version of it, to fill Zevon's "moral vacuum" with something real: one man hitting another until one of them falters. In the ring, as in Zevon's view of his art, which he believes has been exploited and ignored to his ultimate consternation, there are no blithe interpretations or middling gray areas. Here, there is the prospect of a clear winner and loser.

This is also a personal song for Zevon, whose father was a boxer in his pre-gangster/gambler years. I share a similar history with him, as my grandfather boxed in the late 1920s as a bantamweight in New York City. The opening line of the first verse is telling, as Zevon superimposes a biography of his subject with himself: "From Youngstown, Ohio, Ray 'Boom Boom' Mancini / A lightweight contender, *like father like son.*" There is a certain unnerving pride that comes from being born into a boxing family. It resonates with lower-middle-class street values, instills in your DNA a sense of the conflicts to come, framing every confrontation as a kill-or-be-killed edict. Thus, the song swiftly turns from the prospect of a fight that will be stopped to save the fortunes of a boxer to one that is not stopped and thus ends in tragedy. The central theme for Zevon is a true-life incident in which Mancini "killed" his opponent Kim Duk-Koo in the ring during their November 13, 1982, bout at Caesars Palace, Las Vegas, setting the sports punditry alight in a torrent of outrage.

What looked that steamy desert evening like merely a technical knockout in the fourteenth round of a one-sided affair would alter the sport of boxing forever. The champion, Mancini, as Zevon sings in the second verse, returned six weeks after his first professional loss and a severe beating at the hands of Alexis Arguello to defeat Manuel Abedoy. Then, as the story and the song go, seven months later Mancini claimed the light heavyweight title by knocking out Arturo Frias "in round number one." It is then that the champ takes it to the South Korean Kim, felling him with a right cross. Kim, who many experts at the time believed was grossly overrated and probably did not merit a championship bout, would suffer a cerebral hemorrhage and lapse into a coma. Surgeons at the Desert Springs Hospital operated on Kim to remove a blood clot from his brain, but, alas, five days later, the twenty-three-year-old contender was dead. Less than a year after the tragedy, Kim's mother committed suicide by drinking pesticide, and the match's referee, Richard Green, deluged with media scrutiny, shot himself dead.

The outcry was as sweeping as it was vitriolic, forcing the sport to reduce championship bouts from the mandatory fifteen rounds to twelve, a change that endures today. Investigations were launched and debates raged, but the indisputable idea of boxing, two men standing toe to toe relentlessly punching each other, remained. The entire exercise of "regulating" a violent contact sport was ultimately one of futility, much like the later feeble attempts by the National Football League to keep a sport in which concussions are as common as touchdowns from being taken down by lawsuits. And it is this delicate balance of cruel reality and its collateral damage that seems to Zevon to be the height of hypocrisy. Many who spoke up after Kim's death were those who'd derided a referee's decision to stop a fight too early— ironically, Mancini versus Chacon—and after years of cashing in on the blatantly obvious brutality of the sport now displayed moral outrage at its nadir.

Similar ridicule had come down on one of the sport's leading voices, controversial broadcaster Howard Cosell, when he unleashed an on-air diatribe against boxing during his network's coverage of the Larry Holmes versus Randy "Tex" Cobb heavyweight contest, which took place only two weeks after the Kim incident. Bearing witness to the relentless pummeling Holmes levied on a bloodied and battered Cobb that evening, Cosell crowed with revulsion, "What is achieved by letting this man take this kind of beating for fifteen rounds? I wonder if that referee understands that he is constructing an advertisement for the abolition of the very sport he is a part of. From the point of view of boxing, which is under fire, and deservedly so, this fight could not have come at a worse time." Critics cited Cosell's sudden disgust with the sport to be disingenuous in the face of his usual blustery promotion of it. Cosell, who surmised during the event that he had called some three thousand prize fights, would never call another.

> When they asked him who was responsible
> For the death of Duk-Koo Kim
> He said, "Someone should have stopped the fight, and told me it was him."
> They made hypocrite judgments after the fact
> But the name of the game is be hit and hit back

Once again, Zevon offers no moral judgment on the incident he has chosen to dissect, nor does he deny sympathy to the characters he portrays. Instead, he offers a sneering rebuke to those who would stand apart from the fray and dare interject gratuitous opining, despite failing to understand those engaged. In this, the song is similar to "Frank and Jesse James" and to the later "The Indifference of Heaven." In many ways, "Boom Boom Mancini" is a microcosm of the Zevon lyrical gospel, and perhaps explains why so many deeply related to his art, as much as it clarifies the reasons for his lack of broader appeal. Many songwriters of his generation made a living espousing ideologies and supporting causes, even when many had little to no connection to the events or movements beyond exploiting them for subject matter. Here, Zevon *becomes* Mancini from the inside out, as he also keeps hitting us (pun intended) with the third-person chorus of bloodlust, "Hurry on home!" Life offers us a daily beatdown, so is it so bad to be seduced by the darker edges of our violent nature? This is a notion Zevon explored time and again, as I explain more completely in the previous essay.

During the recording of *Sentimental Hygiene,* two rock legends joined the proceedings. Most notable was Bob Dylan, a man whom Zevon had credited more than once over the years with having "invented my job." According to both Zevon and Andy Slater, Dylan showed up unannounced during the sessions wearing shades and motorcycle boots and waited patiently in the studio lobby. Zevon would tell David Letterman months later while promoting the album that he failed miserably to make small talk with his hero, sheepishly asking Dylan what he had been doing lately, only to receive the cryptic, "Travelin'." Dylan also had his seventeen-year-old son Jakob in tow. In an interesting twist, years later after Zevon's passing, Jakob would perform "Lawyers, Guns and Money" for the Zevon tribute album *Enjoy Every Sandwich* with his band, the Wallflowers, whom Andy Slater managed.

Dylan told Zevon he was a fan and was interested in hearing his new tracks. On a particular folkie number, "The Factory," replete with union-style protest allusions, Dylan blew furious harp echoing the angst of Zevon's protagonist, who is "kickin' asbestos in the factory!"

Soon Neil Young, who had been working on new material at the same studio, was duly solicited to play searing lead guitar on the title track. Former Stray Cats lead man Brian Setzer added his chops to "Trouble Waiting to Happen" and Tom Petty's right-hand man and Heartbreakers lead guitarist Mike Campbell offered up his talents for "Reconsider Me." Zevon's connection to Young, a fellow alumnus of the Laurel Canyon artist colony, is an interesting one in that it was the infectiously simple G-C-D chord progression in "Werewolves of London" that was first exploited for southern rock stalwarts Lynyrd Skynyrd's 1974 hit, "Sweet Home Alabama"—a song that was a direct answer to Young's 1970 critique of rampant racism in the region, "Southern Man." Zevon would infamously reference Skynyrd's most famous song and its three members who would die in a 1977 plane crash, in his hillbilly pastiche "Play It All Night Long" on 1980's *Bad Luck Streak In Dancing School*: "Sweet Home Alabama, play that dead band's song / Turn those speakers up real loud / Play it all night long."

Funk impresario George Clinton arranged *Sentimental Hygiene*'s weakest track,

"Leave My Monkey Alone," with a guest appearance by Red Hot Chili Peppers bassist Flea. A video of it ran intermittently on MTV to lukewarm attention. In pushing the song, Virgin, perhaps considering it another potential novelty hit for Zevon's "second act," may have done little to expand his audience, but the album did, however, prove Andy Slater's faith in what he heard with "Reconsider Me": his client's ability to crank out a worthy album that would bring him back from professional purgatory.

"I sort of like starting my career over every seven years or so," Zevon quipped to *Rolling Stone* just before the album's release. "Or I sort of *have* to, whether I like it or not."

However, despite Virgin's million-dollar investment on the recording and promotion of *Sentimental Hygiene* (which included a press release that cast his two-year stint in a vodka-soaked, near-catatonic state of reclusivity as a time when he "ate cheese steaks and watched Sixers games on TV"), the ensuing American and European tours, and glowing reviews from adoring music critics who immediately tapped into Zevon's critique of the decaying and soulless modern music business set alongside his honest accounts of battling alcoholism while facing middle age and obsolescence, the album stalled on the Billboard charts at No. 63. Yet, it did end up being his third most popular release, behind *Excitable Boy* and *Warren Zevon*.

Sentimental Hygiene put Warren Zevon back in the game, but the game had changed. When Andy Slater pulled him from the brink, gone were the comforts of the Asylum label and its catering to introspective artists raising an alternate voice against the initial tide of big business that grew from rock's first exploitative era. And Zevon, quite evidently, did not change with it. Beyond his finally embracing sobriety and getting down to producing his first and really only straight-ahead rock album, Warren Zevon still provided his audience with the type of brutal honesty and wickedly penetrating characters that he always had. Smack in the middle of a decade of corporate excess and a music industry obsessed with image and fashion over substance, he got down to business with one of the seminal rock bands of the era to sound a warning alarm that needed sounding. It did not set the world on fire, but neither was it ignored. Most important for Zevon, it resurrected a severely damaged career and may have saved his life. If nothing else, it would embolden him to make a more in-depth and creatively overt social statement with his next collection of songs.

Georgia O'Keeffe in repose, in her home at Ghost Ranch, 1968. *Alamy/Everett/CSU Archives*

"Splendid Isolation"

I hate flowers. I paint them, because they're cheaper than models, and they don't move.
—GEORGIA O'KEEFFE

The geography of Warren Zevon's art lies on a thin line between irony and commentary. If he had anything resembling a comfort zone, this was it. How he arrived there was always a mystery.

More often than not, he began writing songs from a provocative line he may have read or picked up in idle conversation and then from there built out verses that frame an eventual story line. "He wrote all the time and he wrote whenever it came to him and he had different ways of writing," explains Crystal Zevon. "Some songs like 'Werewolves of London' or 'Mr. Bad Example' or 'Excitable Boy' came very quickly. Of course, those were collaborations. Other songs like 'Veracruz,' 'Desperados Under the Eaves,' or 'Accidentally Like a Martyr,' where he'd get an idea or a title or a line, he would work on sometimes for *years*, but it was *always* there. Sometimes it would be downright agonizing, but when he was writing, and he wasn't too drunk, there should be a caveat there, he was a hundred percent *there*."

His traveling companion George Gruel provides further insight: "There's this thing called 'Notes on Songwriting' that he gave me that explains his writing style, and it really was how he did it: 'Keep going regardless, remember a title becomes a chorus, a chorus becomes a verse, a verse becomes a line.' He would sometimes start with music or he'd hear some obtuse line, because he read so much that something would always end up inspiring him."

"He had a very unique vision that was literary, cinematic, incredibly romantic, and sensitive," cited his biographer, Professor George Plasketes, when we compared notes on our adoring exposition of Zevon's lyrical prowess in the early autumn of 2016. "His tender things are as tender as anybody's works out there, and also *really* funny. If you even take some of those lines, which I know you've done, 'You've got an invalid haircut,' and 'In walks the village idiot,' and 'I'm dragged behind a clown mobile.' Where does that stuff come from?"

David Landau, who worked with Zevon on two tours as a lead guitarist and played on *The Envoy* album, expounded on Plasketes's points when we spoke later that fall: "What always struck me about Warren is a lot of songwriters play with linguistic clichés, phrases in the language that come up all the time and maybe they'll put a little twist on it. Warren wasn't trying to do that. Warren wanted to *create* phrases. He was looking to put the language together in a slightly different way."

This exercise in clever wordplay, what Bruce Springsteen once described as "Zevonian dialect," was most prevalent in his song titles, which presented insights into the lyrical theme while implying misleading preconceived notions and inspiring imagination before a single note was played. "Every time we would write together, it was title first," explains Jorge Calderón, who would compose fourteen songs with Zevon over three decades. "We'd get a title and then he would write it on the top of the page and our job was to fill in the song." Perhaps the best example of this is a song Zevon recorded for his 1999 Artemis Records debut, *Life'll Kill Ya* (another fantastic title, by the way). "I had a postcard of Elvis's TV room at Graceland, which has three TVs on the wall and a big, goofy-looking porcelain monkey in the middle," says Calderón. "So Warren says, 'What is *that*?' And I said, 'A porcelain monkey in Elvis's TV room.' And he immediately went, 'What!?' and wrote down the words 'Porcelain Monkey' at the top of the blank page. Then he said, 'This is the next one we're writing.'"

Zevon chuckled to a VH1 interviewer in 2003 when he was pressed to elucidate on all this: "The creative process is sort of goofy and mysterious and impossible to explain, and if it's not *those* things, then it's something else that *isn't* the creative process—the craft we spend our lives learning: the technique of figuring out what do to with those wacky ideas."

Two of Zevon's most delectable titles found on his 1991 album *Mr. Bad Example* would be used for a novel and two films: "Quite Ugly One Morning," which inspired a 1996 crime novel by Scottish author Christopher Brookmyre and was adapted into a TV movie in 2003, and "Things to Do in Denver When You're Dead," which would become the title to a 1995 Gary Fleder film.

Just to name a few of my favorites: "I Was in the House When the House Burned Down," "Gorilla You're a Desperado," "The Indifference of Heaven," "Poisonous Lookalike," "Roland the Headless Thompson Gunner," "Hostage-O," "Monkey Wash Donkey Rinse," "The French Inhaler," "My Shit's Fucked Up," "Accidentally Like a Martyr" (yes, I named this book after it), "I'll Sleep When I'm Dead," (his ex-wife named her book after it), "Something Bad Happened to a Clown,"

"Macgillycuddy's Reeks," "Lawyers, Guns and Money," and "Fistful of Rain." I bet you could reasonably formulate a decent idea in your head—never mind a pretty damn cool movie—about any of these songs just from their titles.

"I would never in a million years have written a song called 'Macgillycuddy's Reeks,'" admits Pulitzer Prize–winning Irish poet Paul Muldoon, who worked with Zevon on two songs that would end up on Zevon's 2002 album, *My Ride's Here*. "I used it in a book about County Kerry and he said, 'We have to have a song called "Macgillycuddy's Reeks!"'"

"I think any writer worth his salt would write stranded on a desert island just to entertain himself," Zevon told WMMS DJ Matt the Cat in 1976. "If you don't feel that way, you shouldn't really do it, or at least you shouldn't be foisting it off on other people."

This brings us to "Splendid Isolation," a clever folk song about shunning society for a slice of self-absorption that his son broached after months of unanswered calls from the author. "If you are wondering if 'Splendid Isolation' is a song that explains the Zevon gene pool, then you are correct," Jordan said, apologizing for his apparent reclusiveness. "We don't like to be bothered. The family crest is a 'Do Not Disturb' sign."

As discussed in an earlier essay, Zevon's queer social interactions were evident in his enigmatic relationships with women, colleagues, and family, which formed a kind of protective isolation. "It was *always* awkward, but that awkward sort of becomes the normal," his daughter, Ariel, explained to me. "I'm awkward. He was awkward. It was *all* awkward. Visiting him on these Christmases in this weird gray apartment where it would be me and Jordan and him and maybe a current girlfriend and then my ex-husband was always great, but *filtered* in an odd way."

"Warren had a very odd background, and I think he spent a great deal of mental and emotional time and energy reconciling his relationship with his parents," adds Crystal Zevon. "When we were married they wouldn't come to visit. I finally insisted they come after Ariel was born and bought them a ticket, so they kind of *had* to come. But they didn't even stay overnight. They came. We had lunch. They left. There is an awkward picture of the baby on Warren's mother's lap sitting on the couch, very stiffly."

"Today I live on a class-four road a mile away from the last house in the sticks of Vermont where I'm trying that whole 'Splendid Isolation' thing," concludes Ariel. "I'm trying my darnedest to get myself as isolated as I can. Because the more isolated I become, the less lonely I feel, and I think that's sort of a Zevon paradigm. Honestly, I can't make any other good sense out of it. Jordan has a different way of doing it. My dad had his own way of doing it in his little Kings Road apartment, but it's all kind of the same quest for solitude."

Long before "Splendid Isolation," Zevon had laid out his modus operandi. We know from whence he came and where he will go. The voice that sings, "Splendid isolation, I don't need no one," has no message any deeper than what it displays in the clearest possible terms. "If I could think of a way to sum it up it would be, 'Love me, love me, love me . . . leave me alone,'" says Jordan. "It was, 'I want to appeal to you and I want you to love me and I want to connect with you, but then I need to go back into my space and reflect about what I did right, what made me connect with you, or at least just what this whole healing process is all about.' I think that's where it came from."

When translating the biting humor of Warren Zevon's theoretical anthropophobia into a literal construct it is important to remember that this is a man who opened his first major release, *Warren Zevon*, with a mythical ballad about two murderous racists. The very fact that he chose historical figures rather than merely inventing characters tells you all we would come to know about Zevon's art. He understood the folklore of Jesse James and what it evokes in the listener. Then he plays with those preconceived notions. There are the "deeds"—factually indisputable and a matter of record—and then there is the "art," which involves recounting and refiguring them. It is the blurring of the lines that works like gangbusters for Zevon in this formula, as in his use of the fictional titular character in "Roland the Headless Thompson Gunner" and of the very real American diplomat Philip Habib in his 1982 song "The Envoy." He deftly zigzags from personal to social commentary and back again with ease, leaving us with something greater. He would achieve this also in his sports-figure odes "Bill Lee," a song about personal rebellion (evoking a kind of social isolation) and "Boom Boom Mancini," a song about the moral vagaries of the human spirit (here taking the form of judgmental isolation).

As a matter of distinction, it should be pointed out that Zevon did not, in fact, throw the title Splendid Isolation" together in a wonderfully quixotic mishmash, like, say, the delectably evocative, "Seminole Bingo," another favorite title of mine, nor was it entirely an insight into his peculiar social habits. This nugget is the work of turn-of-the-century Canadian politician George Eulas Foster. In an introduction to a book covering Britain's minimal involvement in European affairs during the mid- to late 1800s, Foster praised its effectiveness, as espoused by Conservative Party prime ministers Benjamin Disraeli and Robert Gascoyne-Cecil, Third Marquess of Salisbury, and their reluctance to enter into permanent European alliances in an era of increasing global competition.

Historians argue that "splendid isolation" was imposed on Britain because the empire could no longer abide the constant threat of war with Germany and Russia. It was a practical reaction to a world that was fast outgrowing it, or more to the point, that no longer feared it or, most important, relied on it. In other terms, it is a psychological retreat from progress by a nation balanced by crumbling traditions. Splendid isolation would mark a new, industrial age of self-reliance for England, but at its core was fear; fear of deterioration, weakness, and uncertainty. If Britain were a man, it might be an anachronistic figure swallowed up by the times that threaten to leave him obsolete. Thus, he must curl up in a ball and ignore the outside world.

British political history aside, literary examples of the insular figure versus a corrosive society are numerous in the works of Charles Dickens, Thomas Mann, Mark Twain, and Franz Kafka, as they are echoed in the early twentieth-century musical protests of Woody Guthrie and Pete Seeger and, later, during the era of civil rights, in the voices of Marvin Gaye and Bob Marley. It is where we find the centerpiece of Zevon's song: at the crossroads of man and society.

"Splendid Isolation" should not be taken out of context as a significant, maybe *the* most significant, statement in the greater whole of the concept album it appears on, though its instrumentation—already sounding folkie, with its minor-key, acoustic-guitar and harmonica intro—presupposes a stark "human" contrast to the otherwise electronic keyboard and drum-machine-laden "inhuman" musical presentation throughout the rest of *Transverse City*. The latter was a specific theme Zevon attempted as subtext to this tried-and-true precept of science fiction as prophet crying out against the hegemonic course of soulless progress all around: "A place we can't remember / For a time we can't forget" ravaged by ecological corrosion and economic collapse. That all of this predates the kind of computer-age stuff Zevon is going on about in *Transverse City*, or, more to the point, the advent of the Internet and/or cyberspace deconstructed in the record ("I will upload you, you can download me," from the song "Networking") falls on the imagination of author William Ford Gibson.

Zevon had been reading Gibson's 1984 novel *Neuromancer*, which popularized the term *cyberspace*, first used by the author in his 1982 short story "Burning Chrome," and it roused many fears in him. The plot foreshadows a world much like ours today, dominated by social media, the Internet, and the trading of human relations for the wonders of immense technological advancement, not to mention the eradication of privacy, intimacy, and "splendid isolation." *Neuromancer* gave linguistic form to what a decade later would become the Information Age, and as the songs on *Transverse*

City make apparent, scared the living shit out of an already paranoid Warren Zevon, whose distrust of irrational concepts of luck and destiny dominated his personality and the themes to many of his songs. In most cases, these *were* the themes to his songs. With *Transverse City*, he was to dedicate an entire album to this paranoia, but with the very serious notion that it was not merely paranoia but a possible calamitous outcome to the inevitable shift in human interaction from visceral to viral.

These kind of technology-run-amok themes were nothing new to rock music. Pete Townshend's infamous bout with his enormously intricate *Lifehouse* —which presumed the idea of an Internet long before W. F. Gibson—nearly splintered the Who, and his inability to complete the concept would haunt him for decades. Then there is the god-awful prog-rock-pop concept album *Kilroy Was Here* by Styx, with its hilariously abysmal "Mr. Roboto," which also mined similar sci-fi fears of technology becoming ascendant over human emotion. However, Zevon's perspective, culled from a literary source (Gibson was celebrated as one of the finest science fiction authors of the 1980s and his short story "Johnny Mnemonic" inspired the 1995 film of the same name), is unique. Here is a man, as stated, who has written extensively about the grim realities of progress and his atavistic place in it. Zevon is the throwback, the anachronistic outlaw, a persona Jackson Browne once compared to something out of Robert A. Heinlein's 1961 sci-fi epic *Stranger in a Strange Land*. In his September 9, 2003, eulogy in the *Wall Street Journal*, novelist Jim Fusilli wrote that Zevon was "blessed to be a musician out of sync with his times" and that he "revealed universal themes that transcended time and geography." Here we have an artist "blessed" with an out-of-touch sensibility taking on the looming curse of modernity.

So just what were W. F. Gibson and Warren Zevon railing against, exactly?

The antihero of *Neuromancer*, Henry Dorsett Case, is not only a cyberspace hacker but a drug addict who through a series of underground machinations has his liver and pancreas "modified" to biochemically nullify his ability to get high. That Zevon, an addict who would tell the world he suffered from an aggressive form of cancer twenty years later, related to Case so completely is eerie, but it is hardly out of step with his obsession with death. There is not one Warren Zevon album that does not have at least one song about death, and in almost every instance, the subject is masked in dark humor. There are two ways to confront it: to be stricken crippled by it or to mock it. Zevon chose time and again to at the very least chuckle at the existential enormity of nonexistence.

The eponymous character the Neuromancer is very much a metaphor for destiny or luck, as he controls the movement of the characters through a matrix. For Gibson, it is the idea of a technological world where humans are worth no more, and in some cases are worth less, than characters of artificial intelligence that adds to the drama and alters the moral universe of his plot. In fact, Gibson does such a fantastic job of creating a world devoid of morality that his universe indeed dehumanizes even the human characters, all of whom are addicted to a cocktail of drugs. Their emotions are swayed by their addictions, which allow them to survive in a world not of their making.

In *Transverse City*'s second track, "Run Straight Down," Zevon does a masterful job of syncing his heavily affected spoken-word vocal opening with guitar feedback and a searing keyboard note as he spits out chemical and organic compounds, fumigants, pesticides, and industrial carcinogens contaminating the landscape in a disturbing robotic mantra. The song's narrator walks through the "wasted city" thinking about entropy, setting the scene for the rest of the album. *Entropy* is one of those double-meaning words Zevon relishes, underlining the mechanical thermodynamics of a tainted environment and a state of disorder brought on by, in his worst OCD nightmare, a disturbing lack of predictability. He sings with dread, "I can see it with my eyes closed / Run straight down."

The more you delve into the plot of *Neuromancer* and its themes, the easier it becomes to see why Zevon connected to the book on every level. These were the very thoughts that tortured him and inspired him and lent much fodder for his musical tales of mayhem and mischief, longing, and disillusionment. It is a world from which isolation would undeniably be splendid.

In 1978, Zevon told *Rolling Stone*, "When a guy gets complicated, he gets unhappy. When he gets unhappy, his luck runs out."

In 1989 he wrote:

I want to live all alone in the desert
I want to be like Georgia O'Keeffe
I want to live on the Upper East Side
And never go down in the street

Splendid Isolation
I don't need no one
Splendid Isolation

The absolute beauty of juxtaposing the desolation of desert life with Upper Manhattan, a stretch of the most densely populated patch of land in the United States, knows no bounds—although the idea of being lost in an island city of millions is not unlike that of being alone in a desert, especially when one never wants to "go down in the street." The opening stanzas reek of paranoia, yet are sung with a calming tone. Once again, placed in the context of the rest of *Transverse City*, with its vignettes of random violence of terrorism, bloodless corporations, and a nation lost, it stands to reason that the narrator would welcome his isolation. It is hard not to conjure, as I did when I first heard the song, Paul Simon's haunting "I Am a Rock," in which the native New Yorker also uses "island" as a metaphor for isolation, for it promises that such sequestration will lead a person to "feel no pain."

For the voices of Gibson's book and Zevon's venomous interpretation, the drugs could never be enough of a numbing agent as the solace of blessed loneliness. And yet it is not loneliness itself that Zevon chooses to express. Once again parsing his words carefully, this is a song about being *isolated* not *lonely*. Remember his daughter Ariel's confession: "The more isolated I become, the less lonely I feel." And his son Jordan's description of his father's "Love me . . . leave me alone." Perhaps this desire for isolation comes willingly or at the very least is forced upon him by the cruelty of a society devoid of true emotions. Unable to express this angst, it is better to withdraw, as did late nineteenth-century England in regard to its foreign policy, framed by George Eulas Foster.

It is in the second verse, and its switch from the acceptance of the artist in isolation, the 1920s painter Georgia O'Keeffe, to the 1980s King of Pop, a damaged, fragile soul crushed by the immense weight of stardom, that this theme of "retreat into comfort" emerges.

> *Michael Jackson in Disneyland*
> *Don't have to share it with nobody else*
> *Lock the gates, Goofy, take my hand*
> *And lead me through the World of Self*

Michael Jackson, the biggest pop star on the planet when Zevon was composing the songs for *Transverse City*, makes an appearance huddled in a fantasy world of his own construct, both mentally and physically. It is a reflection of the fantasy world of Disney—the icon of a generation of dreamers being force-fed insipid tales of wishing on stars to become real boys or awakened princesses—a wholly corporate translation of dreams. The cultural shift of celebrity paranoia from a recluse painter to a pop star resplendent in his arrested development lends a real-time, news-ticker touchstone to this folk song nestled inside a science fiction–inspired concept album. The "World of Self" the lovably foolhardy Goofy leads the increasingly bizarre and plastic-surgery-deformed Michael Jackson through is not entirely fictitious. Jackson's descent into the darker corners of eccentricity would eventually lead him to create his own Disneyland on his sprawling Neverland Ranch (another allusion to Disney's Peter Pan, the boy who never grows up), a Los Angeles property to which he allegedly lured young boys for either sexual favors or to satiate psychologically irrational behavior. On a lighter but no less stark note, Goofy has been described as never having had an identity, as he appears to be a "dog" yet has a dog named Pluto: a "World of Self" worth exploring for sure.

The song's bridge is self-explanatory. There is no fancy poetic license or metaphor or symbolism here. This is where Warren Zevon goes when he is at his most confessional. In an album replete with modern keyboard sounds and haughty references to technology and societal paradigm shifts, this is the solitary figure warm in the knowledge that without love there is no loss and there is no pain of separation.

Don't want to wake up with no one beside me
Don't want to take up with nobody new
Don't want nobody coming by without calling first
Don't want nothing to do with you

By 1989 Zevon's personal life was in shambles. His marriage to Crystal had been over for a decade. The three-year romance with actress Kim Lankford had dissipated in the lurch of several failed attempts at rehab followed by unhinged binges, and his current girlfriend, Annette Aguilar Ramos, seemed promising but would eventually turn out to be, like all the rest, transient. His professional fortunes, while resuscitated by the *Sentimental Hygiene* comeback, were still very much in flux. The solemn, if not baleful, acceptance of solitude in the song's bridge is echoed by the insecure beseeching chorus of "They Moved the Moon," which strategically comes right before "Splendid Isolation" in the story.

They moved the moon
(I feel so strange)
While I looked down
(Everything I depended on)
When I looked away
(Has been rearranged)
They changed the stars around
(I was counting on you)

And so the man seeking refuge in self-imposed solitary confinement cannot stave off hurt. Loneliness, the *emotion*, infiltrates the *act* of isolation. In fact, it is the result of cutting one's self off from true feelings. Zevon's use of the geography of space to express isolation is not unique to pop/rock, as evidenced by David Bowie's strung-out astronaut in "Space Oddity" or Elton John's (actually, lyricist Bernie Taupin's) disassociated space junkie in "Rocket Man," or, in film, Stanley Kubrick's soul-crushing, time-lapse expanse of Arthur C. Clarke's puzzling *2001: A Space Odyssey*, wherein a computer attempts to murder humans. Yet it ruminates on the idea of leaving the planet we inhabit to dream of a socially isolated place beyond the stars, darkly envisioning a generation of cyber-heads using virtual reality and social media to replace actual lives and the emotions that come with living them.

Zevon's commentary on the plight of the 1980s in his previous album, *Sentimental Hygiene*, whose title refers to "feelings so clean you can eat off them," leads to a crushing realization at decade's end: Soon even the most remote sensation will be sublimated by machines that may bend to our every whim but also rob us of our humanity. The album's trilogy of personal angst in the shadow of so much inhumanity—"They Moved the Moon," "Splendid Isolation," and the final track, "Nobody's in Love This Year"—perfectly balances a dystopian screed with heartache and longing. There is, reasons Zevon, a price to pay for shielding emotions, whether they are boxed in by the march of progress or protected in an emotional fetal position.

> *We keep walking away for no reason at all*
> *And no one says a word*
> *We were always so busy protecting ourselves*
> *We never would have heard*
> *And the rate of attrition for lovers like us*
> *Is steadily on the rise*
> *Nobody's in love this year*
> *Not even you and I*

Thus Zevon ends his trek with the final verse of "Splendid Isolation," the image of the agoraphobic recluse, a Howard Hughes character walled off in some mansion buttressing his psychosis from hidden dangers.

> *I'm putting tinfoil up on the windows*
> *Lying down in the dark to dream*

I don't want to see their faces
I don't want to hear them scream

While Zevon played with international politics in previous songs, specifically, "Veracruz," "Roland the Headless Thompson Gunner" and "The Envoy," *Transverse City* is his first openly political statement. The connection to nineteenth-century British foreign policy aside, he plays with sociopolitical memes of the 1980s and beyond, most pointedly an expanding and ravenous consumer age tumbling toward ruin in "Down at the Mall" ("We'll put it on a charge account we're never gonna pay"), an oppressive police state in "The Long Arm of the Law" ("Nobody move, nobody gets hurt"), the dehumanization of machines in "Gridlock" ("The radio's tuned to the traffic news / And everybody's choking on monoxide fumes"), and the Soviet "glasnost," the precursor to the fall of Communism in his father's home of Russia in "Turbulence" ("Turmoil back in Moscow brought this turbulence down on me").

It is quite extraordinary how far ahead of the curve Zevon was with these observations, now that smartphones have allowed us to replace conversation and human interaction with texting, Facebook, Twitter, Instagram, etc; the advent of a doomed generation of creditors snapped the Western hemisphere's banking culture in 2008; and the creation, perpetuation, and ignoring of climate change has resulted in an alarming increase of flash floods, droughts, and melting of polar caps in the early twenty-first century. And then there was the implosion of the Soviet Union around the time of the album's release.

"I find it ironic that I've written songs about genocide, war, rape, incest and addiction and they seem easier to take than new songs about shopping centers, traffic and pollution," Zevon pondered to journalist Steven P. Wheeler while promoting the album. "These songs seem to depress people more."

Zevon was not a political purist. He may have even considered his worldview staunchly conservative, more in a libertarian bent, and thus viewed sweeping and immediate change with a jaundiced eye, but he was also keenly aware of the cold and calculating injustices of capitalism. His friend Billy Bob Thornton described him as a "moderate radical." On one hand, he could mock his daughter's liberal assistance of inner-city kids and on the other give all the money in his pocket to a homeless wino. He shouted at his wife that he was to the "right of Reagan" but reveled in hobnobbing with the man Reagan slaughtered in the 1984 presidential election, Walter Mondale, when he dated his daughter, Eleanor. He joined in author/activist Hunter S. Thompson's crusade to free a woman wronged by Colorado law enforcement and gleefully performed at independent Minnesota governor Jesse

Ventura's inauguration. He even openly campaigned for his friend Steve Cohen, a Democrat who in 1982 became Tennessee's first Jewish senator since 1958. Cohen would eloquently eulogize Zevon at Zevon's funeral. Yet in each of these cases, Zevon was most likely assisting a friend rather than making an overt political statement.

"Political stuff was not something Warren would do on his own," says Crystal Zevon, a vocal activist today. "I was very political, and Jackson was political, and he did agree to go on a Save the Whales tour of Japan once."

"I'm not a politician; I avoid being a political spokesperson," Zevon emphatically concluded to the *Music Connection*'s Steven P. Wheeler in 1990. "To me, the concept that every artist is a potential politician is sort of insane and certainly dangerous. I always thought rock 'n' roll was supposed to be against that sentiment."

Jackson Browne, a tireless activist, reconciled Zevon's lack of political commitment to his grander and perhaps more lasting desire to express the concerns of the common man through the universal fear of survival, using his trademark black humor to ease the anguish. "He was able to laugh about the modern world and horrify you at the same time," Browne told David Fricke of *Rolling Stone*. "He could depict the place where those things meet, where you find the desire to go on living in spite of it all."

"Warren was an *incredibly* complex person; to this day I don't feel I ever fully understood him," says David Landau. "First of all. he spoke very slowly and deliberately. There would be a lot of pauses in any conversation you were having with Warren about any subject. I'm sure you've had the experience of talking to someone about something where they're talking very slowly and maybe they leave a long pause and you know exactly what they're going to say and maybe sometimes if you feel comfortable you will even complete their thought just to speed up the conversation, because it gets frustrating. You would *never* be able to complete Warren's thought. You had no idea what he was going to say. It could be the most normal sentence in the world, but there would be that pause and you're waiting for him to finish thinking, 'Oh, he's going to say *this*.' He never said *this*. He always said something that you didn't expect. It was a remarkable thing."

Like all true intellectuals, Zevon was a freethinker with an instinct to call bullshit when and where he found it and embrace causes that reflected his sense of moral decency. A jester pessimist by nature, Zevon faced his fears beneath the comfortable mask of storytelling, a fun exercise for a frustrated novelist like himself.

"I think a lot of people that are as bright or perceptive as Warren Zevon would tend to run the risk of pushing it down someone's throat," reasoned Taylor Goldsmith of Dawes when we discussed Zevon's lasting message to another generation. "He's not necessarily a nihilist, but he's able to take this attitude of 'It doesn't really mean that much, so don't get yourself carried away, but it's worth it because it's fun.' He's able to capture that as a songwriter in a way where most guys get a little carried away with thinking that they're here to save the world through their guitars. Zevon transcended that, but he does know how to communicate the human condition, that balance between the seriousness and self-righteous attitude with the one that just wants to hear a good joke."

Or, as Zevon pinpointed during a KGSR radio interview with Jody Denberg in 2000, "If you define that you're being ironic, you're automatically *not* being ironic."

Brothers in Arms: Mack (Kevin Kline) and Simon (Danny Glover) from a production still from Lawrence Kasdan's *Grand Canyon*, 1991. *Alamy*

"Searching for a Heart"

I think probably the greatest and most dangerous adventure is love.
—WARREN ZEVON

Scene: A corporate cafeteria. Afternoon. Dee, a young blond woman in her early twenties with a razor's-edge sexuality bordering on the frenetic, unburdens herself of the emotional fallout from a one-night stand with her married boss. Listening intently is her thirty-something coworker Jane, a beautiful and wryly confident black woman. Dee asks, "Jane, do you ever feel like you're just *this far* from being completely hysterical twenty-four hours a day?" Without so much as a pause, breaking into a knowing smile, Jane answers in a world-weary tone: "Half the people I know feel that way. The lucky ones feel that way. The rest of the people are hysterical twenty-four hours a day."

For the briefest of throwaway moments in any workday, two people distinct in age, race, and wisdom are nevertheless connected by a singular grim philosophy that frames the very foundation of civilization. Volumes of philosophical rhetoric fill great libraries in grand halls across the globe with similar observations. Hundreds of poems, psalms, and ballads long to express it, and this is what I believe filmmaker Lawrence Kasdan was aiming to portray with his brilliant *Grand Canyon*, an ensemble piece about deeper troubles among the economic, racial, generational, and sexual landscape of early-1990s Los Angeles. No one, the film argues, is immune to the struggle of the human condition, the desperate search for meaning in a rapidly changing and ever-complicated society that is seemingly constructed to hide it.

Grand Canyon is a story of our struggle to not be completely overwhelmed by day-to-day survival in our professions, our families, our lives. When life is happening, it often happens beyond our control. In fact, control is a myth. The whims of a much greater chasm dog our pursuit to bridge racial, economic, emotional, and sexual divides, pulling us further away from our center. It is indeed "Grand Canyon–size." Parents/children, police/gangs, Hollywood culture/the culture of violence, love/hate: people trying hard to be people, a city under siege. It is a time filled with doubt. How did we get here?

Darkness in the morning
Shadows on the land
Certain individuals
Aren't sticking with the plan

The music used in the film, beyond a sweeping sound track by James Newton Howard, consists of two Warren Zevon songs. Of course. Who captured the dichotomy of the Western dream set against an underlying yearning to be whole better than he? Kasdan uses the quintessential Zevon classic "Lawyers, Guns and Money" to great effect in the film's opening sequence in which the central character, Mack, a forty-something professional (who we find out later had the aforementioned one-night affair with the troubled Dee), gets lost on the seedier side of L.A. after a Lakers game. Driving away from his exclusive courtside seats in his expensive car, he begins to realize he is lost in a very dangerous area for forty-something white guys in expensive cars. He nervously sings along with the line "the shit has hit the fan," which will soon ring true. However, it is the other song in the film, "Searching for a Heart," that will bring us face-to-face with "*this close* to being completely hysterical twenty-four hours a day" without surrendering to the despair the songwriter normally depicts with uncanny directness.

Grand Canyon and "Searching for a Heart" are brethren, not unlike Kasdan's characters, who hail from glaringly disconnected backgrounds of race, gender, and generation, but who will nonetheless affect each other in ways that they might not recognize, yet cannot escape.

Zevon did not write the song for the film and there is no indication that it inspired the screenplay, but beyond the inexorable marriage of song and image that made "Everybody's Talking" the perfect ode to *Midnight Cowboy* or Simon & Garfunkel's "The Sound of Silence" forever embedded in *The Graduate*, it resonates within its central themes. It speaks to the ache for connection, a true journey to find a heart—not *the* heart, but *a* heart. Once again, Zevon's choice of a single conjunction changes the entire meaning, and consequently the film it adorns. It is a search amidst the chaos for any connection—cultural, personal, spiritual—putting Kasdan's tale in pinpoint perspective.

Although *Grand Canyon* was released in 1991, it is ostensibly a film about the 1980s. Eight years after the writer/director's ode to the decay of the hippie dream and the lost kinship of youth in an epilogue of a 1970s fallout, *The Big Chill*, Kasdan, along with his wife, Meg, set his sights on the decade of excess when those same flower children began to run things . . . into the ground. The all-for-one edict of the 1960s rolled through the Me Decade beneath the pall of 1970s drug abuse and rampant self-indulgence: The cold realities of the 1980s and the detached generation to follow were startling to those who had come of age in the age of Aquarius. This was, Kasdan reasons, not how it was supposed to go. Zevon made a similar argument with his "comeback" album, *Sentimental Hygiene*, which critiqued the soulless trade of meaningful expression for the quick buck: marketing over art, emotion sold for image. Then, with *Transverse City* Zevon imagined its grim future. This loss of connection felt by a generation that once believed itself organically inseparable in the understanding that love conquers all and that the solidarity of social upheaval would prevail is devastating.

"Searching for a Heart" boils the universal need for love down to its core, to the desire to find love, to understand love, to be rescued by love. Humanity orphaned by its purpose, looking for a way back to Eden.

And it is a powerful love.

Creating a combination of "Studebaker" and "Mama Couldn't Be Persuaded," two songs about his parents and his childhood, Zevon is in full expression mode here, shaping his hopes and fears into poetic form while also unfolding a personal testimonial. He hides his intent, providing Kasdan a musical vehicle for the visual and emotional deconstruction of his characters' lives, while also coming clean about his often misguided but always sincere mission to find a kindred spirit. "Searching for a Heart" is, in essence, a love song about love, much as *Grand Canyon* is an inspirational film about finding inspiration. In both expressions this "search" can take strange turns and lead us to new ways of homing in on our desires. For Zevon, it is his masking of true feelings in violence and machismo, a defense mechanism against revealing mature emotions and coming to grips with his yearning but this time with an acquired wisdom. There is light at the end of the tunnel, even if the protagonist prefers to move beneath a cover of grief.

Leaving in the evening
Traveling at night
Staying inconspicuous
I'm staying out of sight

And I'm searching for a heart
Searching everyone
They say love conquers all
You can't start it like a car
You can't stop it with a gun

The chorus, sung as a refrain of each verse and remaining in the minor key that kicks it off, is what takes the song from the personal to the universal and also, getting back to Kasdan's film, puts all the lives dissected therein within a social construct. As he did effectively in most of *Transverse City*, Zevon juxtaposed his fear of a decaying culture with his sense of isolation, of feeling both shunned and welcomed: Here he is a man in need of love who sees his plight as our own. The use of the vehicle ("start it with a car") again, as in "Studebaker," and his fascination with firearms ("stop it with a gun"), as in "Jeannie Needs a Shooter," lend credence to the hovering threat of violence in *Grand Canyon*—gang wars, police retribution, street justice, predatory sexuality, corporate greed, Hollywood insensibilities, materialism, youthful rebelliousness, passive-aggressive coping—that manifests itself in the spiritual impairment of those living in its shadow. When Zevon sings, "*They* say love conquers all," or, later, in the bridge, "*They* tell me love requires a little standing in line," he removes himself from the opining and, through this literary device, embraces detachment, for he is indeed "searching everyone" for some sign of emotional association. Taking the lyrics literally, he can be searching someone—as if a police officer searching a person for contraband—or searching *for* someone: a woman searching for a lover who defines her, a child searching for a parent's approbation, etc. Here is the man who wrote "Sentimental Hygiene" telling us once again that we are all in need of something beyond our scope, especially if we do not activate the radar needed to locate this missing tether to humanity. However, unlike in "Sentimental Hygiene," Zevon sings with a tenderness usually reserved for his torch songs, tales of broken promises and missed opportunities, regretful odes to the mercurial woman whom he cannot figure out.

Following up his heart-tugging performance of "Reconsider Me," here Zevon and coproducer Waddy Wachtel, back in the fold, use a mist of keyboards floating on a hypnotic beat to accompany his crooning, a defenseless, raw expression that belies his otherwise raucous and sardonic persona. "I love that song," Wachtel said when I told him I was dedicating an essay in this volume to it. "It's really beautiful. I think he did some of his finest writing on that album, and 'Searching for a Heart' is a completely helpless love song. It just reeks of *heart* to me."

To wit: Much like the black-and-white music video that would promote "Sentimental Hygiene," the one for "Searching for a Heart" attempts to soften Zevon as a voice of reason behind all of the color film scenes splashed upon seminal moments of the lyric. It opens with dramatically angled shots of Zevon lighting and smoking a cigarette against a dark background, his noir character exposed to the modern video era. Soon we get glimpses of *Grand Canyon*'s two polar characters, the aforementioned Mack (Kevin Klein), upper-middle-class, middle-aged professional, who believes he is happy but acts to the contrary, and Simon (Danny Glover), lower-middle-class, middle-aged man, who knows he is not entirely content but who, we will soon find, is working diligently at being so. Mack is white and Simon is black. Mack, perhaps owing to his race and station in life, has known little struggle to be where he is. Contrarily, Simon has seen plenty of struggles. For although Mack lives a mostly inexpressive, uneventful life, Simon's is filled with challenges: a deaf daughter away at college and a down-on-her-luck sister abandoned by her husband with two children, the oldest of which, Otis, is a member of a street gang. It is Simon who rescues Mack and his fancy car from a jacking ("the shit has hit the fan") that could easily turn into murder before his tow truck arrives just in time. The scene also stirringly depicts the clash of two generations, as the young, nothing-to-lose street thug with the gun stares down the grizzled older man brimming with wisdom, who just wants to "go my way." To escape this potentially deadly trap, Simon symbolically genuflects to the kind of "street law" that has engulfed much of Los Angeles by this time. He reluctantly shows the kid with the gun a modicum of the "respect" a gang leader craves to allow the teen to retain his illusion of having power in a world that has rendered him feeble, thus saving himself and Mack. Simon compromises his machismo for survival, providing Mack a glimpse into a confrontation he has only seen on the nightly news from his cushy suburban detachment.

Before a single word is sung in Zevon's romantic grand gesture, we see a slow-motion sequence of Mack leaving the Lakers game in a fog, alone in this sea of "beautiful people" gliding effortlessly back to their cushy lives. As he has been for most of his life, he is blissfully unaware he is mere moments from panic. Then there is Simon, looking up through the flashing lights of his tow truck, not sure if the gang will refuse his offer of "respect" and decide instead to execute both him and Mack. One character is utterly oblivious that his existence hangs by a thread, while the other is not. This, of course, foreshadows the "*this far* from being completely hysterical twenty-four hours a day" office discussion between the frenzied white girl, Dee, and her older more philosophical African American confidant, Jane.

Once the song kicks in, we are introduced to the film's other characters: the young gang member, Otis, whose uncle Simon receives the chance to move into a new apartment courtesy of Mack, in return for his heroism, an opportunity that will help his family escape the "bad" neighborhood for a "good" one. Otis, who did not want to "escape," is seen peering from behind a fence (his prison), as he knows the affluent, suburban Caucasian environs will inevitably reject him, as they do later when he is halted by police for innocently running along the streets of his new neighborhood. Zevon sings, "Certain individuals aren't sticking to the plan," providing us insight into young Otis's justified fears that he will never be fully accepted by white society, and as it was for the young thug from earlier in the film, his only defense is the illusion of a violent street subsistence beyond the law that has failed him. One is immediately reminded of Zevon's sociological trip down Gower Avenue in the early 1970s, where economic and cultural divides are as stark as the blazing California sun, a divide *Grand Canyon* unflinchingly portrays.

The film montage continues as we see Mack's wife, Claire (Mary McDonnell), finding an abandoned baby—a blatantly obvious nod to Moses in the reeds along with the repeated biblical myths of the aging woman being blessed with an unexpected child. Beneath the image, Zevon is singing, "Searching for a heart / Searching everyone." With her marriage to Mack fading into the kind of complacency that drives him to bed a young coworker, Claire also suffers from her teenage child leaving the nest for summer camp and no longer needing her. She will bring the lost baby home and confront Mack about adopting it, thus rediscovering her lost worth and familial identity.

The second verse about "traveling at night" unveils Kasdan's Big Brother symbolism of the constant hovering police helicopters, faceless automatons that aimlessly attempt to curtail the urban plight below, as detached as Zevon's protagonist, who is "staying inconspicuous, staying out of sight."

Zevon introduces a strategic shift-in-mood chorus, as the minor key smoothly ushers his lament into a more upbeat and positive major key for a refrain full of hope and solace.

They tell me love requires a little standing in line
And I've been waiting for you, lover, for a long, long time
I've been pacing the floor
I've been watching the door
Meanwhile I'll keep searching for a heart

The charming melody actually lifts the song into the realm of potential hit that effectively leads the listener out of the darkness and into the light. Yet, in true Zevon brilliance, it smartly refuses to abandon its message or its messenger, "waiting, pacing, watching, searching." He will not desert the task, despite coming up empty, bringing a measure of calm to those who have loved and lost or who have never loved at all. There is a period of transition and emptiness to endure before finding happiness. Here is where "Searching for a Heart" turns Zevon's normal woe-is-me template on its head. He empathetically offers well-earned advice to the lovelorn to never give up. He sings, "Keep searching," with much of the same determination he provides many of his damaged characters, all of whom he infuses with much-needed humanity. It is, again, a love song celebrating love—the elusive, penetrating, head-spinning beauty of love. It is difficult to obtain, like anything in life that's worth living for.

Back to the video, which by now, on the strength of Zevon's rising chorus, introduces scenes of characters embracing: of Mack and Claire's son Roberto coming of age and romancing a young girl (mom's emotional replacement) at camp; of Simon kissing the middle-aged confidant of the troubled Dee, Jane; of a beatific Claire warmly kissing Mack before revealing her newfound baby. There is a dream sequence in which a train pulls away from an anxious Claire as she comes to realize her destiny. Throughout are cuts of Zevon singing mostly in silhouette by his smoldering cigarette, a wonderful visual that brings home the conversational aspect of a Zevon song, his sharing of a story one-on-one as if bellying up to the bar to unburden himself. The band, including Waddy Wachtel, plays behind him, unveiling a stylistic countermelody to Zevon's syrupy phrasing. "I was really happy with the guitar I put on it," says Wachtel today. "My wife cries every time my solo comes at the end, and Warren really loved it."

All of which leads into the final verse . . .

Searching high and low for you
Trying to track you down
Certain individuals
Have finally come around

We now see a powerful slow-motion scene of Simon's embattled sister, Deborah, crawling frantically beneath a hail of bullets from a passing gang meant to assassinate her son, Otis. Zevon tellingly sings, "Searching high and low for you / Trying to track you down," as she scrambles to reach her young daughter, who walks into the carnage, dazed but miraculously unharmed. Cut to the emotionally abandoned Dee stuck in mid-morning L.A. traffic, frantic and lost, and then suddenly walking beside a handsome young cop, who comes to her aid when a vagrant tries to rob her car at gunpoint. And then Claire, who through her honesty about lost motherhood eventually reconciles with her husband, Mack, but must give up the baby when the natural mother appears.

Finally, the last of the film's main characters, Davis, is seen lying in a hospital bed bathed in morning light and staring majestically out at his uncertain future. Played with corruptible allure by Steve Martin, Davis is a late-middle-aged Hollywood producer of films filled with exploitative violence who, ironically, is taken down by it. For a fleeting moment, this shallow peddler of the kind of cookie-cutter action films that seemed to literally explode from everywhere in the 1980s begins to see the error of his ways. The victim of random gun violence, he is put back together and comes to realize that perhaps his art is contributing to the culture that eventually felled him. However, in an ultra-realist, one might say, Zevonesque maneuver, Davis eventually returns to his exploitative ways by the end of the film, rationalizing that it is the cartoonish violent movies he makes that relieves the tensions of the modern world, keeping people from wreaking more havoc on one another.

The video concludes wistfully with the characters sharing emotional moments— Mack hugs his son, Roberto, before he goes off to camp (the father, too, is losing his place as the patriarch and inviting his son into manhood, thus writing the script for his eventual incapacity and death); Simon hugs his weeping nephew, Otis, after his friend is killed in a street fight, both realizing that geography does not mean a complete escape from that lifestyle. The last shot is the final one of Kasdan's film, in which most of the main characters visit the Grand Canyon and are visibly moved by its enormity, putting into perspective both the vastness of the universe and the insignificance of their own day-to-day lives.

By 1991 and the release of *Mr. Bad Example*, Zevon had more or less become a cult figure, "the songwriter's songwriter," while beginning a flirtation with acting and gearing his musical aspirations to the screen.

It began during his early-'80s relationship with actress Kim Lankford, who garnered him an audition for a villain character on her prime-time TV serial *Knots Landing*. He did not get the part, but rehearsing with Lankford brought the ham out of a man who may have been secretly harboring a curiosity regarding the craft as far back as the early 1970s, when Zevon's then love and mother of his only son, Jordan, was a struggling actress who, despite her beauty and grace, could not crack into the business. Her agonizing flirtation with Hollywood cattle calls inspired much of his 1976 song "The French Inhaler" and Zevon's desire for more widespread fame. This is something his son Jordan told me has haunted his own striving for success in music: "It's been hard as a child of both of these people to see somebody who had looks and at least had enough talent to smile and say, 'Crest toothpaste makes my teeth turn white,' not achieve success and to see my dad have these struggling years where it just didn't seem to make sense. It was very sobering to see talented people work hard and still not kind of catch the cord of the kite while it was flying up in the sky."

Upon his finally embracing sobriety, Zevon began to use his connections in the film business to land the occasional minor role. The first of these was playing himself on the late Garry Shandling's early-'90s satire of a late-night network talk show, *The Larry Sanders Show*. Zevon spends the episode refusing to play "Werewolves of London," despite the entire staff begging him. He would eventually agree to play it reluctantly but with aplomb. A lunch meeting with one of the show's writers, Judd Apatow, now a successful Hollywood writer/director/producer, would inspire an uncompromising career. "I was going to make a movie at one point and I thought Warren Zevon would be great to score it, and I told him I was waiting for notes from the studio on the script and he looked at me and said, 'Why would you take notes from anybody? So you would change it for someone else?' And I was so embarrassed and it really blew my mind, and I thought, 'Oh, this is an artist, he writes a song and that's it, he's not checking with anyone to see if it's okay.' And it really changed my philosophy about my work and got me in a lot of trouble." Today Apatow hosts an annual tribute concert in Los Angeles in Zevon's memory.

A few years later Zevon would play himself again in a Brooke Shields situation comedy, *Suddenly Susan*, where he dryly answers Susan's friend and big fan Vicky's (Kathy Griffin) query about Neil Young playing on *Sentimental Hygiene* with "To be honest with you, I don't remember, I was a little medicated during the '80s. I'm not even sure if I'm on that album." Zevon would also appear, albeit briefly, in his friend and fellow songwriter Dwight Yoakam's 2000 western, *South of Heaven, West of Hell*. The film's star, Billy Bob Thornton, would befriend Zevon when the two were neighbors and would meet daily at the mailbox in front of their Kings Road apartments. Thornton, a man of similar self-deprecating sensibilities and dark humor, also suffered from OCD, and the two would compare maladies on a regular basis. Thornton would eventually play a significant role in Zevon's final musical statement and provide his own opening statement to the VH1 documentary that captured it.

Zevon would also contribute sound track music and songs for HBO's acclaimed series *Tales from the Crypt*, weekly vignettes in the style of the original 1950s horror comics and later feature-length films of the 1970s that ironically presaged Zevon's most compelling song villains. The twisted humor and wickedly O. Henry–meets-Poe plot twists could have been penned by him. The most notable of these episodes was "King of the Road," primarily because it features a young Brad Pitt.

Over the years, Zevon's music has been featured in television shows and films (fifty-seven as of this writing). His son Jordan tells me much of his time is taken on making sure these projects fit what his father would have wanted for his music. Perhaps the most direct use of the Zevon catalog is in the Showtime series, *Californication* (2007–14), a "dramedy" starring David Duchovny, who plays, according to IMDB, a "self-loathing, alcoholic writer [who] attempts to repair his damaged relationships with his daughter and her mother while combating sex addiction, a budding drug problem, and the seeming inability to avoid making bad decisions"—or, to be candid, Warren Zevon.

And this brings us back to "the search," or in this case "Searching for a Heart," which I would argue is Warren Zevon's great love song, or, as we have seen with the parallels to the film *Grand Canyon*, a love song about love, or finding love, and, most important, not giving up on the *search*.

Working on this book and this essay in particular I've been repeatedly reminded of Zevon's complicated relationship with his children, Jordan and Ariel, both of whom are in their forties now and still harbor many unresolved feelings about their dad that they were kind enough to share with me.

Ariel began our discussion hesitantly broaching what she would come to call her "quasi-traumatic childhood" and then beautifully navigated her way through the emotional arc between a father and daughter that would include a good deal of searching: "I assume you know that the '70s and '80s were a tumultuous time in his life, and [for me] as his daughter, early memories are not generally the peachiest. But things started changing between us when I was about eleven or twelve, which is when he got sober and stayed sober, and he was making concerted efforts to be a more consistent presence in my life."

Jordan is no less introspective. "He was a tortured man with a good heart who wasn't really ready to relate to a child, but was able to relate to an adult," he expressed to me after much thought. "So by the time I became an adult and I had my own opinions and philosophies and everything else, then we were able to connect and he was able to let me into his inner circle of thought."

Ariel agrees with this: "Our relationship really turned around in my early teens when I was finally able to have more intellectual conversations with him, but he was still a monster intellect compared to me. I remember just sort of trying to pretend like I knew what the hell he was talking about. It was around sixteen, when I got sober, because I had had my own bout with drugs and alcohol, that I went through a period where I stopped wanting his approval and got angry at him. That was when it all turned around. When we were both living in L.A. we had weekly father/daughter dates. Often we would go to the movies. That was definitely a theme for him, going to a movie."

"There was a lot of growing together," adds Jordan. "But I do feel like my growth with him was stunted, because I look back and I think there are more things that I would have wanted to address and understand a little better. At the same time, there was a part of dad that was very family-oriented, like for instance I cut this vocal track to a Sarah McLachlan song that was used on some TV show and I still have the message from him saying, 'Johnny, that was fucking amazing!'"

Ariel concludes, "By the time I got to college he would make great efforts to come out to see me. I was in theater then. He would make these grand appearances at plays. I would say it continued to grow into, for us, a good relationship."

"I wanted a dad and I loved my dad," says Jordan. "He wasn't built from the mold of Father of the Year, but I think by the end of it he really did the best he could."

"Searching for a Heart" is the finest of Warren Zevon's love songs, for it is truly an ode to not giving up on the capacity to love, no matter the boundaries, to focus the energy of your exploration on those whom you cherish, which is all part of the same journey.

Literary Inspirations: Among them *Time's Arrow* by Martin Amos and *Neuromancer* by William Gibson, from Warren Zevon's private library, 2017. *Photo by Crystal Zevon*

"The Indifference of Heaven"

All time is all time. It does not change. It does not lend itself to warnings or explanations. It simply is.

—KURT VONNEGUT, *Slaughterhouse-Five, or The Children's Crusade*

I think this is my favorite Warren Zevon song. It speaks to me, gets to the heart of me, and in many ways defines me, and it came along when I needed defining. This is true of all art, but for me it's music that hits hardest and burrows deepest. "The Indifference of Heaven" defines not only me but the time in which I was living—personal experience as well as the greater social scope of the era. The song is at once nostalgic, omnipresent, and prescient: It has eyes on the past, present, and future simultaneously. Finally, I think it possesses all the qualities that make Warren Zevon great: his unique phrasing; his evocative lyrics; his classical, Eastern European ironic stoicism. Additionally, it evokes the simplicity with which he contours difficult subject matter—literally and aurally—into a folk song.

When a song captures a moment in our societal shift, it is often imbued with or reflective of the greater culture and becomes a generational siren, as in the retrospective fondness for memories of Elvis Presley (1956) or the Beatles (1964) on the *Ed Sullivan Show*—"Heartbreak Hotel" sounding revolutionary and sexually charged in an era of buttoned-down conservatism, "I Want to Hold Your Hand" leaping from an AM radio speaker as if a reverberating monastic chant from the gods. Madonna in a crumpled wedding dress rolling around the floor moaning "Like a Virgin" at the first MTV Video Music Awards (1984), the concussive gut-punch of Nirvana's "Smells Like Teen Spirit" (1991). For me, it was Elton John performing "Pinball Wizard" in Ken Russell's *Tommy* in the spring of 1975 when he was the biggest pop star on the planet set against the eerie drugged-out spiritual imagery fucking with my preteen head; or AC/DC's Angus Young running amok in his schoolboy outfit ripping ungodly notes from his Gibson SG on *The Midnight Special* in the mid-'70s; or the feral hypnosis of the Stones' "Sympathy for the Devil," which I absorbed for the first time in a high school social studies class; or the impish glee of Green Day instigating a mud-tossing riot at the otherwise corporate snooze of 1994's Woodstock Festival.

Songs can hit the nerve of our culture and work to provide a sound track to our past; Summer of Love to the Summer of Punk. Bob Dylan's "Like a Rolling Stone" addressing the pangs of '60s liberation, CSNY's "Ohio" reviewing the fallout of the Kent State tragedy. Somewhere in the middle stands "The Indifference of Heaven," a personal lament framed in the chaotic swirl of current events. In the summer of 1993, Zevon would introduce it from the stage with little humor as "a song about the looting in Los Angeles." And we all knew what that meant before he played a single note.

The 1992 Los Angeles riots that sprang from the not-guilty verdict over the brutal beating by white police officers of a black man named Rodney King—captured on crude amateur video—in an already race-tense city began on April 29 and would last until May 4. For a solid week the anarchic violence hijacked the American psyche, as the horrifying proceedings were broadcast around the world to shocked viewers on twenty-four-hour cable news networks. It was everywhere and affected everything. And so Zevon made no bones about the subject being the inspiration of his song and thus "The Indifference of Heaven" would act as past and prologue for his city, recalling the Watts race riots of August 1965 and presaging the highly publicized and widely televised 1994 O. J. Simpson double-murder trial and its aftermath.

Once again, here is Zevon penning an ode to L.A. that recalls the sprawling and tempestuous landscape of his youth, a sequel to the ghosts of "Desperados Under the Eaves," as the '92 riots that consumed entire neighborhoods and shocked a nation would indeed be a sequel to the Watts riots. And as in "Desperados," here is the solitary man beyond redemption and powerless to intercede in his own life, much less the times. His is the recognizable voice of inertia, of the aging alcoholic coming to grips with the fuel that ignited the fires of his past abuse, just as Los Angeles remained trapped in a schizophrenic purgatory of the haves and have-nots, winners and losers, the beautiful people and the demimonde. Now, years later, in the fiery burst of angry upheaval all around him, he must accept his fate as a gentle reed being carried along a raging river.

It is important to note that this sparsely beautiful song would eventually end up on 1995's *Mutineer*, an album Zevon purposefully kept to basic guitar and piano with little accompaniment, abandoning his comfort on previous recording experiences with celebrity friends and musicians stopping by to add to the sound and revelry—with the exception of a supple harmony sung by Peter Asher, of Peter & Gordon fame, who had worked with many of Zevon's compatriots including Linda

Ronstadt, James Taylor, and J. D. Souther. Zevon pointed out in interviews at the time that his decision to simplify was based on two reasons: a desire to save money in recording and touring costs, and a wish to write, record, and present the songs in their immediate form. Zevon could—and in most cases would—play all of the material on *Mutineer* live on the ensuing tour solo.

However, it was during the previous tour of both North America and Europe that he debuted "The Indifference of Heaven." That was when it first captured me, the night I sat in the front row of New York City's legendary Town Hall and watched in rapt awe as he performed it on only a black twelve-string Ovation. Embroiled in the tumult of my personal angst, I would never forget it. Every time I hear it, like every time I hear the first side of *Excitable Boy*, I am right there again. I can see his gruffly bearded face, his long, blond ponytail, his gray tightly fitted T-shirt tucked into faded blue jeans, his muscular hands wrapped around the neck, his right arm strumming, his eyes closed as he sings the first verse assuredly. And I am again feeling the furor of my life back then: turning thirty, enduring a heart-wrenching breakup while harboring a torturous crush on a forbidden love, unsure of my professional life, wanting, *needing* to become a writer, but not yet possessing the bravery necessary to fail . . . miserably.

I had wanted to do it, flirted with it, played with it, worked on school newspapers and won amateur awards and penned comic books and screenplays and poem after lousy poem and written song lyrics and short stories, whipped off obituaries and sports blurbs for meager cash, but never had I pursued writing seriously. It was a scary time professionally, too. I had been playing music for most of the 1980s and found myself thrust back into the labor force, trying to get my grip on the written word. I did not want to lose my connection to *the edge* that I'd honed in the rock 'n' roll idiom, but I needed to grow up, needed to see the world not as a groaning beast slouching toward Bethlehem or a golden ticket owed me, but as something I must tame and grasp. It is the very precipice of aching maturity to be single, jobless, at times homeless, and pushing thirty. This is, as ever, the time when music did not abandon me. It was always there as I moved from town to town in my youth, having to battle a whole new set of neighborhood kids to prove my mettle; the strange schools and the stranger girls and the inevitable fights and the acne and the masturbation and the drugs and the parents and the death of my grandparents and the questioning of my faith and the loss of my innocence again and again and again. Music escorted me through all of it. And here I was in 1993, facing rebirth by surrendering to a dream of personal and professional discovery. Yeah, it was pretty heady stuff and a damn tough gig to lay on a song, but I did, and "The Indifference of Heaven" came through.

This is why I still prefer the live acoustic version on the 1993 live album, *Learning to Flinch*, which precedes *Mutineer* by two years, even though the studio one features only a meager drum machine, a slightly plucked bass accompaniment, and a forlornly detached harmony from veteran California vocalist Rosemary Butler. It would appear that "The Indifference of Heaven" turns out to be as peripatetic as its composer. It was almost as if Zevon needed to write it and get it out right away, before the echo of the streets faded, before his own tumult turned into regret. He had to work through it, as he'd done onstage for years with so many of his songs. It is this transparency of his creative bloodletting that endeared him to so many. We were proud to keep him with us on the periphery of fame, giving us enough breathing room to embrace a song like "The Indifference of Heaven" the way you would a J. D. Salinger short story over the garish popularity of *Catcher in the Rye* with its undertones of impudent retribution.

"In addition to being an outstanding artist, Warren was an excellent craftsman in the sense that he really became an outstanding solo performer," notes David Landau, Zevon's bandleader in the halcyon days. "Warren was always an outstanding piano player, but he was a very erratic guitar player at best during the time I knew him, especially when he was drinking and especially on electric. But when I caught his early-'90s solo show, he was just fucking brilliant. And he was playing with prerecorded tape tracks. The idea that Warren Zevon could coordinate with a prerecorded track would have been unthinkable to me, but he really delivered. Whether he had periods where he was drinking or not, he took his solo performances very seriously."

And so it opens with the guitar chords strummed as if a funeral march with a poet's defiance, laying down the bed for the simple melody and the words that capture the soul of our protagonist:

Time marches on
Time stands still
Time on my hands
Time to kill
Blood on my hands
And my hands in the till
Down at the 7-11
Gentle rain
Falls on me
All life folds back
Into the sea

We contemplate eternity
Beneath the vast indifference of heaven

When you listen to something like this, you have the feeling at first that you're not quite getting it: Who is this guy? What is he getting at? Is he killing time or is he actually searching for time to *kill*? Blood on his hands, huh? Beyond its epic brilliance, these decisively parsed sentiments and subtle character traits are almost novelistic—prose over meter, biography over glimpses—putting you inside the trapped man, not beside or in empathy with, but *inside* him. The man staring into his "empty coffee cup" in the darkness of the early 1970s, who contemplates bolting on a hotel bill, is now at the cusp of the final decade of the American century contemplating eternity. He robs a convenience store and wonders what it's all for, the lonely criminal again moving at the pace of his own desperation.

"I think one of the things that Warren was very good at is telling stories through image," remarks Pulitzer Prize–winning poet Paul Muldoon. "You see one thing and then you're seeing something else. It's very filmic. At any moment you could *see* it on your own little screen."

This, as Zevon would tell audiences, is a song about "looting." These are the words culled from the underbelly of the underbelly: not the protesters or the cops or the mob or the media, but the perpetrators who leap at the opportunity for anarchy to avail themselves. This is the single crime amidst a greater explosion of fear and rage. The chaos envelops him like a disguise. He, like the mob, only knows anonymity and must act out as if it is the last thing one could do to survive. This reminds us today of the naked, relentless fury spewed over the Internet—perhaps our last unregulated frontier. It is here where the scoundrel walks beside the hero to traverse the cyber-landscape completing their détente of unfettered freedom. For those who stalk this terrain, their hands are always "in the till."

The line "all life folds back into the sea" takes me to the ebb-and-flow of the tides at the far reaches of the Pacific lapping at the shores of the City of Angels with its golden beaches and sun-drenched illusions to the American dream juxtaposed with Salvador Dalí's arresting *Persistence of Memory*: the idea of time dragging like water torture, the slow persecution of nature eroding what we have built—fire and water, tools and enemies of civilization, the all-consuming flame and the relentless flood—and what it does to the solitary man fully comprehending morality. First it is the rain, then it is the flood, and the floods make the oceans, and the oceans mark time. Yeah, those clocks ain't melting in the desert: they're drying out.

A pleasant key change and an uplifting bridge alter the mood, as do the lyrics:

The past seems realer than the present to me now
I've got memories to last me
When the sky is gray
The way it is today
I remember the times when I was happy

I am reminded of the stream-of-consciousness of James Joyce or the fantastical imagery of Arthur Rimbaud. At their best, like Zevon, both Joyce and Rimbaud eschew the idea of time and space for the message of how we perceive these concepts, how the brain processes them and what it leaves us. The timelessness of a song about a specific news event not only puts the song into the context of a period but also speaks to our universal nature. We have the mob, the explosion of *fuck it* that seduces our baser instincts, and the man who must also face its incendiary notions.

As a side note, I recall being titillated by the first violent images from Los Angeles in 1992. Of course, people destroying everything in their path is horrifying and can never be rationally condoned, but the very thought of "losing it" courses through our blood stream. Our humanity does not allow us to separate from the mob. The mob is us. It is legion and it is singular. It is a reflection of our gene pool. It is not for us to ponder whether we would explode in uncontrollable rage if properly motivated, but when and to what extent. And what would cause us to *lose it*? That is the most enticing question. Joyce and Rimbaud were two writers—the former of prose and the latter of verse—who would assume the form of the id and work their way out. In "The Indifference of Heaven" Zevon achieves this in three and a half minutes.

The repetitiveness of thoughts trapped in time:

Same old sun
Same old moon
It's the same old story
Same old tune
They all say
Someday soon
My sins will all be forgiven

Zevon provided further insight into the theme of "trapped time" when he revealed to Steve Roeser of *Goldmine* magazine, "It's a Martin Amis song." He was referring specifically to Amis's 1991 novel *Time's Arrow or, The Nature of the Offence*, wherein the author plays with "reverse chronology" in which a life of high crimes against humanity, most pointedly the Holocaust, thrusts a Nazi doctor backward to relive the horrors he wrought through a secondary consciousness. It is sensory perception presupposed by American biologist Gerald Edelman that moves beyond the "primary consciousness" of sentient beings into an advanced self-reflective awareness, abstract thinking, volition, and metacognition. According to Edelman, "primary consciousness" is the ability to integrate observed events with memory to create an awareness of both the present and the immediate past of the world around them. In a nutshell, it is knowing about *knowing*.

In Amis's novel, all of this unhinged consciousness eventually leads the protagonist Doctor Odilo to reverse his insidious deeds and save lives rather than eradicate them. Kurt Vonnegut (a Zevon favorite) addresses a similar theme in his groundbreaking 1969 satirical novel, *Slaughterhouse-Five, or The Children's Crusade* (both books even share "or" in the title). In this case, Vonnegut's protagonist, Billy Pilgrim, held in a Nazi prison camp in Dresden, Germany, will become "unstuck in time" and transported through both the past and future by means of an intergalactic interloper. His trauma, the firebombing of Dresden by American airstrikes and the resulting fallout, remains suspended in time. In essence, there is no escape from the offense. Unlike Amis's Doctor Odilo, an institutional murderer, Pilgrim is a firsthand witness to institutional massacre. For both, as for Zevon's "looter," the crime stays fresh, as if it is continually happening or never quite concludes, reducing the experience of existence to Vonnegut's seemingly innocuous *Poo-tee-weet*—the cry of a bird innocently responding to the horrors.

There also appears to be a very real biological framework to all this consciousness stuff in *Time's Arrow*, specifically the concept of entropy—which, if you recall, Zevon toyed with on his *Transverse City* album—which British astronomer and physicist Sir Arthur Stanley Eddington termed "time's arrow." According to *Encyclopedia Britannica*, entropy is "the second law of thermodynamics that says the entropy of an isolated system can increase, but not decrease. Hence, from one perspective, 'entropy measurement' is a way of distinguishing the past from the future. However, in thermodynamic systems that are not closed, entropy can decrease with time: Many systems, including living systems, reduce local entropy at the expense of an environmental increase, resulting in a net increase in entropy. Examples of such systems and phenomena include the formation of typical crystals, the workings of a refrigerator and living organisms."

Or, more simply put: "Same old sun / Same old moon / It's the same old story / Same old tune," and who is to say that someday (whenever that day would be—the past, the future, or now) "my sins will all be forgiven"—the sins of the doctor, the sins of the Nazis, the sins of the looters, the sins of war, the sins of humankind. And it is quite obvious that sin is something Warren Zevon understood, as he groped inexorably for forgiveness in song and story throughout his art and his life. And maybe someday soon he will be forgiven—or at least the narrator will be, whose voice we take to be the more mature one of "Desperados Under the Eaves." The rent has come due. This time it is not a hotel or even a town, but the whole of the human race. It is never a question or beseeching of innocence for Zevon. No, it is a matter of forgiveness, which, by the way, is a much easier jury to convince beneath "the vast indifference."

Here the guitars pick up the pace, double-timing the static rhythm. The live acoustic version is quite disruptive: It jolts the song into another time signature, taking the sweep of a ballad and whipping it for a couple of measures into a kind of punk song. This bridge ushers in the *complaint department* commentary. Here we are back into the head of "the looter," who is disdainful of all the aphorisms and punditry and the fancy Hollywood liberal folderol driveling on and on about how "happy days are here again" or what the newly minted President Clinton co-opted in Fleetwood Mac's "Don't Stop"; all that talk about a dozen years of failed Reaganomics that promised to send all the riches trickling down to the working man that engenders "the looter." None of it has eased the suffering.

Zevon is getting down to what rock critic and essayist Greil Marcus called "the politics of the freeze-out" or the "willful avoidance of anything that one suspects might produce really deep feeling" in his brilliant *Mystery Train: Images of America in Rock 'n' Roll Music*. Marcus goes on: "Raw emotions must be avoided when one knows they will take no shape but that of chaos. In such a culture there are many choices: cynicism, which is a smug, fraudulent kind of pessimism; the sort of camp sensibility that puts all feeling at a distance; or culture that reassures counterfeit excitement and adventure, and is safe. A music as broad as rock 'n' roll will always come up with some of each, and probably that's just as well." But according to the narrator (criminal) of "The Indifference of Heaven," no one needs to hear from rock stars about our culture and togetherness and turning the page.

They say "Everything's all right"
They say "Better days are near"
They tell us "These are the good times"
But they don't live around here
Billy and Christie don't—
Bruce and Patti don't—
They don't live around here

The Billy and Bruce in question here are Billy Joel and Bruce Springsteen, two of the signature performer-songwriters of Zevon's generation, both of whom he knew well. Their acquaintanceship evidently did not deter him from noting their enormous celebrity in castigating the lofty, preachy rock star who lives such a cushy, detached life that he can barely comprehend the grim realities of the kind of inner-city strife that incites the L.A. riots. Although speaking as a character in his song, Zevon cleverly removes himself from this presumptive label. Warren Zevon is no rock star. He is the opposite. "I never got rich, and that might have been lucky," he later confessed to Jody Denberg on KGSR Radio, Austin. "There's less time you spend with the issues of being rich, like the issues of being famous—they're not real issues, so they're not real life. There's more an exchange of human ideas and feeling to be had at a bus stop than over the phone with your accountant."

Here is the folk singer making a clear demarcation between artistic expression and those who may wax poetic regarding loftier ideologies. He is the one watching his less-than-opulent neighborhood that he once described to Toronto TV personality Mike Bullard as a "half mile past squalor" go up in flames as the privileged few are safely holed up in their mansions tossing out peace-and-love axioms on demand.

Yet Zevon could have picked any rock stars, but he picked these two. Why?

Zevon often told the story of his first meeting with Billy Joel on the set of Phil Everly's variety show while acting as its musical director. The then relatively unknown singer-songwriter was fiddling on the piano during sound check when Zevon wandered over to casually observe him. After a few minutes of watching from behind as the young "Piano Man" effortlessly and flawlessly played a classical piece, Zevon turned on his heel and walked out of the building and into the street, contemplating quitting music altogether. Joel touched a rather penetrating chord in Zevon that the latter would not soon forget. Here is a man for whom the classical form meant the world, something Joel had, in Zevon's estimation, quite obviously conquered but was trading in to perform a pop song on a variety show. Perhaps Zevon saw himself selling his musical potential on the cheap.

"I guess because I played the piano when I was a kid and played it seriously and technically correct, and then got jobs playing it, I never had as much fun playing the piano as the guitar," Zevon later admitted in the Jody Denberg radio interview.

This kind of amateur psychology pales in comparison to Zevon's special, almost spiritual relationship with Bruce Springsteen, which made his biting lyrical presumptions all the more stinging.

Zevon met Springsteen in New York City during the wild and woolly *Excitable Boy* tour, when the Boss caught an invitation-only show at the tiny but hip Trax club. Powerful promoter Bill Graham and music giants like James Taylor, Linda Ronstadt, and Dickey Betts of the Allman Brothers Band were also in attendance. Rhythm guitarist David Landau, who was studying under Waddy Wachtel to take over for Wachtel when the latter left the second half of the tour, told me the original plan for two shows went awry. "We were supposed to have a break, maybe half hour, twenty minutes. And Warren disappears," he says, the panic returning as he recalls it. "When I say disappears, I mean, Warren *disappears*. So we don't know what to do. There are no cell phones. You can't track him down."

When Zevon shows up he is visibly drunk and out of control and joins an impromptu set that is his old friend J. D. Souther and other musicians in the star-studded audience engineered during his absence. Grabbing the microphone, he begins shouting the Muddy Waters staple "Mannish Boy," but instead of spelling out M-A-N, he shouts, "W-A-R-R-E-N!" which, according to Springsteen, tickled him no end. "I sat down on the edge of the stage, because he was just so fucked up and rambling and not making any sense," remembers Wachtel. "I looked at Bruce and said, 'Good pacing, huh? You like it?' It was fucking painful."

After the show, Landau, who is also the brother of Springsteen's manager, Jon, recounts a memorable few hours spent with the two songwriters wrapped in deep discussions: "Somehow I'm in a limo with Warren and Bruce, who I'd known since '74, and we ended up at a diner having breakfast at four in the morning. I don't know if Bruce had been drinking that night, but I assume he hadn't been. Warren, of course, was in his usual state, but I'll tell you, I'm a fairly smart guy and I have a pretty decent vocabulary, but for about an hour and a half I don't know if I understood more than two sentences either one of them said to each other. They were talking in some kind of artist code that I could not decipher, but they seemed to be communicating and I couldn't tell if Bruce was sort of humoring Warren or [if] he had some unbelievably intuitive way of hearing what Warren was saying through the haze of his inebriated state, but these two extraordinary talents in very different states of mind were forming a secret bond."

This secret bond would result in the composing of the Zevon classic "Jeannie Needs a Shooter." Springsteen had already written a song called "Janey Needs a Shooter" that he'd carried around since 1972 and tried to include on his first two albums, *Greetings from Asbury Park* and *The Wild, the Innocent and the E Street Shuffle*, and even demoed it for his fourth record, *Darkness at the Edge of Town*. The liner notes for Zevon's Rhino collection *I'll Sleep When I'm Dead* state that Zevon loved the title and its bare-bones plot about a young man trying to convince Janey, which he misheard as "Jeannie," that she needs "a shooter by her side," and immediately got to work writing his own opening verse and what would eventually be its dramatic string arrangement. Zevon later showed up at Springsteen's house in the middle of the night to play his version for him, prompting Springsteen to ask, *Where's the rest of it?*

"I brought it to him and we both agreed it should be a straightforward narrative," Zevon recalled to *Songwriter* magazine at the time. "We sat down and he kind of wrote the story in several verses—we spent a few hours on that and we were pretty satisfied. After the first verse, the bulk of it is his. Now, I forget what we discussed in terms of plotting, but I do have a very vivid picture of him sitting quietly with a notebook writing verses down. When I got back home, I kind of moved a few words around."

The differences in the lyrics and the tempos of both Zevon's "Jeannie" and Springsteen's "Janey" are as stark as the girls' names—Janey is doe-eyed and confused, while Jeannie possesses an impish kind of menace—and provide insight into the competing personalities of the two songwriters. Springsteen's song is slow and plodding, as the 1978 band demo attests—there is even a tamer acoustic version floating around that would have fit right in on Springsteen's somberly brilliant *Nebraska* (1981). The lyrics reflect themes Springsteen would mine throughout his career: the damsel in distress yearning for someone to rescue her from a life of mediocrity and boredom (see "Thunder Road" for the best example of this).

In a biblical motif, Springsteen's Janey is haunted by a menacing triumvirate—a doctor, a priest, and a cop (science, religion, authority)—who misconstrue her yearning to break free as some kind of "condition" that could be remedied by the protagonist's solution: "Janey needs a shooter like me on her side." The "shooter" here is the classic heroic figure of the American western, the wild but sympathetic cowboy with his trusty six-shooter. The "shooter by her side" finds its way into Zevon's "Jeannie," which is predictably a song about a woman who acts like she needs to be rescued but is instead predatory (please refer to the "Poor Poor Pitiful Me" essay in this volume for a host of examples of this). Jeannie frames the protagonist, turning tail and running away with her lawman father, who will shoot him dead.

Springsteen cannot save Janey and leaves her at the song's end: "So I held her real close she flowed like a ghost / And I told her bye, so long, I can't play that dope." Maybe she doesn't want to be saved after all, the classic sheltered Tennessee Williams heroine. Zevon's Jeannie, more reflective of a classic Philip Marlowe femme fatale, sets him up and he is a dead man as a result. And while Springsteen's lonesome cowboy rides off to save another day, Zevon's antihero, who has "the anger and the yearning, like fever in my veins," taunts her lawman father who swears "he'd shoot me dead / 'Cause he knew I wanted Jeannie and I'd have her like I said," and eventually does.

A couple of months after the haphazard New York show, Springsteen and much of his E Street Band attended the June 23 Portland, Oregon, stop on the *Excitable Boy* tour. This time Springsteen joined Zevon onstage for a rousing version of "I'll Sleep When I'm Dead," which by all accounts brought the house down. To hear Jon Landau tell it, Springsteen was forevermore obsessed with knowing what Zevon was up to musically, running out to get his latest release and listening intently to it, sharing his excitement with whomever would listen. Zevon was summarily enchanted by Springsteen, inspired to dramatically strip down his recording techniques out of reverence to the aforementioned *Nebraska*.

"Bruce had great affection for Warren and a lot of respect for his artistry, and Warren was really enamored with Bruce," concludes David Landau.

Years later, in 2003, during the taping of VH1's *(Inside) Out* documentary about the final months of Zevon's life and the recording of his last album, *The Wind*, Springsteen charted a private plane from Indianapolis during the holiday break in his tour to visit Zevon for the last time to play spirited guitar and sing background vocals on the blistering "Disorder in the House." During a break in recording, the camera catches the intimate nature of Zevon and Springsteen's relationship when Zevon blurts out something about a place he and Springsteen had visited long ago in New Jersey called "Gravity Hill," which causes Springsteen to snicker with recognition and a bit of embarrassment at the memory. Springsteen then goes on to describe to those in the control room what the two men were chuckling about: "There's this place called Gravity Hill, it's about five minutes from my house and one merry night Warren and I went over there and the thing was if you parked your car at the bottom of the hill it would roll backward up the hill. It was a classic local mystery spot. But it's gone now. They shaved it down. Too many accidents." The knowing smiles on both men's faces portray genuine affection. Later in the documentary Zevon says, "I love Bruce very much. The thing about Springsteen is he is exactly the person that everybody hopes he would be. He stuck by me through some weird stuff, real bad times."

The intimate details of the Springsteen/Zevon relationship illustrate the sheer guts or at least the compartmentalizing Zevon could summon when penning lyrics he considered impactful to his song. He thought well of Springsteen, shouting plaudits from the stage before bursting into "Jeannie Needs a Shooter," even performing a rousing cover of Springsteen's "Cadillac Ranch" on early-1980s tours, but had no qualms about using him as a metaphor for vapid celebrity-speak. When asked at the time if either Springsteen or Billy Joel had heard "The Indifference of Heaven," Zevon simply said he'd heard nothing. Knowing the depth of their friendship and the pride Springsteen has shown regarding writing songs about, and lending his name to, causes for the common man, it must have stung to be depicted by his friend as the symbol of a vacuous, out-of-touch rock star.

Having lashed out at those who could never understand the depths of depravity, Zevon's sinner must confront his own random acts of anarchy. He takes us back *inside* again, to feel the pain of the looter. It is not just anger or society or circumstance that has turned him from citizen to criminal, from clear-thinking mature man to a wild boar, but the loss of love. The woman intercedes with the city of both his dreams *and* nightmares, once again living on the edge of duplicity.

I had a girl
Now she's gone
She left town
Town burned down
Nothing left
But the sound
Of the front door closing forever
Gentle rain
Falls on me
All life folds back
Into the sea
We contemplate eternity
Beneath the vast indifference of heaven

And so I too crashed and burned in 1993. First there was the exhilaration of upheaval and the fearsome jolt of change upon a man not yet old but far from young, just about coming out of the not-in-my-twenties anymore but feeling day to day like the teenager was getting harder to tame. Life tamed him, if only for a short time, and then I railed against it and ran amok. This all led to lust and heartbreak and being lost for the sake of being lost, all of which ended up in my first published book, *Deep Tank Jersey*. I finally quit talking and started writing the moment I heard "The Indifference of Heaven," a song that put into perspective . . . *perspective*.

Paul Muldoon and Warren Zevon with the guitar upon which "My Ride's Here" was composed.
Photo and design by Suzan Alparslan

"My Ride's Here"

Literature is the ditch I'm going to die in.

—Thomas McGuane

In midsummer, 2002, I received a press kit for the new Warren Zevon album, *My Ride's Here*, which was described therein by its composer as a "meditation on death." Having been seized by his music since that oppressive summer school day in 1978, I was determined to interview the artist for the *Aquarian Weekly*, a renowned local New York/New Jersey music and pop culture paper, for which I had conducted dozens such interviews in various capacities since 1997. This was agreed to by Artemis Records, Zevon's new label. I readied my notes and tried to parse the hours of questions I would have loved to ask him but knew would not fly on a press junket, especially for the likely "phoner" that was planned.

These things usually go like this: PR person gets back to you via email and confirms the interview request and then sends you a promo copy of the CD (nowadays a temporary Internet link to the album's tracks are provided a week or so before the scheduled interview), and then usually the same person or a tour manager will call you on the agreed date and time and put the subject on the phone. I received this call a week before I would finally get my long-anticipated interview.

"We're sorry to inform you that Mr. Zevon is canceling any press for personal reasons," said the solemn-sounding woman on the other end of the line. "We'll get back to you to perhaps reschedule in the coming week."

It was the way she let the word *perhaps* slide from her throat that sounded less appeasing than resolute. It made me uneasy. At the time, I passed the feeling off as disappointment. It would not take long to burrow deeper.

Just few days later I was perusing the Internet when I saw a story in the *Los Angeles Times* reporting that Warren Zevon had been diagnosed with inoperable lung cancer.

I had to steady myself. It was weird—after all these years of everyone assuming they would find his remains splayed out in a cluttered Hollywood hotel room, the man for whom the finite had always appeared nigh was now officially on the clock, and there would be no *perhaps* rescheduling of any proposed interview.

Warren Zevon was dying.

About two months later, sometime around Halloween, I vividly recall sitting by myself in my cramped writing nook of the raised ranch my wife and I had purchased the previous year in the mountains of New Jersey, waiting for children to come banging on the door and feeling cheated. I began to furiously write about it. Eventually published as "Angry Ode to the Captain," the resulting article was a sort of eulogy before-the-fact that ran in the paper the week of November 6. This did nothing to alter a mood that shifted spastically from sadness to anger and back again.

Then I began to listen to *My Ride's Here* again, a little more intensely this time, with a fair helping of perspective. This "meditation on death" stuff started to crystallize, the same way all the songs from his previous album, *Life'll Kill Ya* did.

From "My Shit's Fucked Up":

Well, I went to the doctor
I said, "I'm feeling kind of rough"
He said, "Let me break it to you, son,
Your shit's fucked up."
I said, "My shit's fucked up?"
Well, I don't see how"
He said, "The shit that used to work—
It won't work now."

It is difficult to find a more revealing portrayal of dire medical news, especially delivered as it is above a swampy acoustic picking style reminiscent of a Bayou funeral dirge, his requisite baritone altered slightly with sharp cracks in the voicing. Despite admitting his phobia of physicians, Zevon captures the detached, almost robotic way in which doctors share the grim realities of test results, a frightening by-product of "feeling kind of rough." It must have been a dialogue he replayed in his head a million times, fueled by his crippling fear of "bad luck" with a myriad of examples of how he courted "good luck" in every form: something his old friend, collaborator, and producer Jackson Browne described to *Rolling Stone*'s David Fricke as a "fierce defiance charging that single fact of life: that it comes to a close."

"I consider that what we're essentially dealing with is an existence that we don't understand," Zevon told *Songwriter* magazine in 1981. "That's why a lot of my work is about death. I have news for everyone, including myself—don't make long-range plans, 'cause there is an inevitable *adieu* for everyone. I don't consider it a subject to be avoided."

Jorge Calderón, who had a front-row seat for most of Zevon's professional life—always lending a backup vocal, a key line to a verse, or musicianship on tour—believes the essence of *Life'll Kill Ya* lies in the Zen-like acceptance of their song "Fistful of Rain." The album's tenth track is a philosophical lullaby for those whose philosophies have failed them. Musically and lyrically, it effectively soothes the savage beast. It is only the dreamer, as Zevon sang so longingly in his masterful "Desperados Under the Eaves," who can free himself from the strains of the conscious world. And yet, there is peace in the baleful acceptance of reality.

> *You can dream the American dream*
> *But you sleep with the lights on*
> *And wake up with a scream*
> *You can hope against hope*
> *That nothing will change*
> *Grab a hold of that fistful of rain*

"We approached Warren's subject of 'fate' and what role 'luck' plays in all of our lives," explains Calderón. "We think of this and that, but all we have is that 'fistful of rain' that disappears in your hand. The fragility of existence was always behind every one of his themes."

And while the songs on *Life'll Kill Ya* forced Zevon to discuss his apparent obsession with the subject during the album's extended promotion, (the title track being a rather blatant illustration of this: "Life'll kill ya / Then you'll be dead"), there are also optimistic hymns staving off the inevitable. The best example of this is the endearing ballad "Don't Let Us Get Sick," another eerie premonition offered on the album's finale as a glimmer of hope in an otherwise dim valley of despair:

> *Don't let us get sick*
> *Don't let us get old*
> *Don't let us get stupid, all right?*
> *Just make us be brave*
> *And make us play nice*
> *And let us be together tonight*

It is a secular prayer, a wanton plea to the universe to spare us our humanity, which Zevon reminds us with achingly transparent tenderness, is both our curse and blessing: "I thought of my friends / And the troubles they've had / To keep me from thinking of mine" or the obliging "I'm lucky to be here / With someone I like / Who maketh my spirit to shine." Taking a page from his oft-adjudicated conundrum with outer forces manipulating the fortunes of our pitiable lives, this beautifully haunting and endearing song acts as his bargaining chip against the little disasters that lead to our eventual demise. With the clever, almost reverent use of the opening phrase "Don't let us"—as if left to our own devices we shall doubtless "get sick, old, and stupid"—Zevon puts the onus back on the universe, thus granting us rare forgiveness: *Yeah, don't let me get stupid, all right?* Even the use of "all right" connotes a bargain, as in "We good?"

His son Jordan expounds: "I think after all my dad did and risked it was like, 'Okay, well, I was *that* guy and maybe I should try to be *this* guy and maybe I should keep in mind that we're all going to die and that our friends get sick and that this shit is for real.' I think that by the latter half of his career that's where all those themes came in. Like, 'Hey, the '70s were fun, but holy shit some of us are getting sick and some of us are dying, and we need to grow a few more roots, so we don't just end up being a weed.'"

"It means a lot to me, because it's pretty good and I consider myself lucky for having written it, and because it has a lot of feelings for a lot of people in it," Zevon said of the song on KGSR radio upon its release. "For me to say it's got a lot of feelings for a lot of my friends in it is quite an admission. It's more than I normally say about my songs."

Jorge Calderón concurs: "When he sent me the tape of the songs I just fell on the floor at how great everything was on *Life'll Kill Ya*, specifically 'Don't Let Us Get Sick.' It is just fantastic. I told him, 'This is going to be a great record for you.' And I really think it's one of his best."

However, considering its place as the album's final track, providing solace at the conclusion of a series of songs that linger on themes of alarm and misery (the album's opener is the rollicking "I Was in the House When the House Burned Down" with its opening lines, "I had the shit till it all got smoked / I kept the promise till the vow got broke"), it can hardly ward off the demons found in the title track, which come once again in the form of a physician bearing bad news:

From the president of the United States
To the lowliest rock and roll star
The doctor is in and he'll see you now

He don't care who you are
Some get the awful, awful diseases
Some get the knife, some get the gun
Some get to die in their sleep
At the age of a hundred and one

Prevalent in the themes of aging, sickness, and death found throughout *Life'll Kill Ya* is a glimpse into Warren Zevon's state of mind, both as a man and an artist. Indeed, the years leading up to his recording *Life'll Kill Ya* were lean ones for Zevon. Ever the pragmatist about his profession, he understood its peaks and valleys better than anyone, and he was now face-to-face with the agonizing realization that his audience had dwindled below allowing him to retain even cult status. Having dabbled in serious social and political commentary with *Transverse City*, which was critiqued harshly as "too heavy" and failed to chart, Zevon scrambled back to his old pal Waddy Wachtel to put together what he believed was a classic Zevon-style album, *Mr. Bad Example*, with its tried-and-true sordid tales packed with nefarious characters and pitch-black humor. Alas, this too barely made a dent in the pop music landscape beneath the birth of hip-hop, the return of boy bands, and the sudden rise of grunge. As a result, Zevon was once again without a label, professionally homeless for the third time since the early 1970s, when it had all been in front of him. His son told me of the time: "I remember him saying to me, 'What the fuck do I have to do? What do they want from me? I gave them a Warren Zevon record and here I am.'"

"If you think about it, there weren't a lot of low-voice guys making hit records when you have Sting singing 'Roxanne' and everybody else is singing so high," reasoned Wachtel when I pressed him about Zevon's overall lack of success. "When you have a Boris Karloff kind of low baritone voice it is not a commercially acceptable tool. It is much harder to put that across, because we tried when we put out 'Searching for a Heart,' which I think is a gorgeous song, but people did not go for it. Warren's voice is even higher than he normally sang on that song, but, in the end, that low baritone is not a real selling item."

"Warren was so well-respected as a writer, and the people who knew how great he was were in awe of him, but these were mostly musicians," reasons his longtime friend and photographer Jimmy Wachtel. "I think one of his problems was he got all this respect from musicians, but he never got the acclaim from the general public. And the thing was, he always wanted to be a star. 'Werewolves of London' is one thing, but then that was it. I think there was some bitterness there, I guess. I can understand it. But you know, it was always personal for him. It was *always* about him."

"I think he was scared," says Danny Goldberg, who would soon play a major role in Zevon's final recordings. "He had been without a deal for four or five years, so he had a real clarity about the fragility of the whole process. When you first make it as an artist you just think, 'This is going to go on forever!' and he was shaken up by how hard it was to get somebody in the business to support him."

Much as he had in 1974 when Browne plucked him from obscurity, Zevon shared his new songs with his old friend, explaining to him his pragmatic stance on no longer relying on record companies to make his albums. He would do it himself and search for one to distribute it. As he was a quarter-century before, Browne was moved by what he heard.

Browne eventually introduced Zevon to record exec and music business veteran Danny Goldberg in the winter of 1999. Goldberg, who had already worked with, among others, Nirvana, Hole, Steve Earle, Sonic Youth, Beastie Boys, Bonnie Raitt, Stevie Nicks, the Allman Brothers, and Rickie Lee Jones had only recently launched Artemis Records when he received a cassette of Zevon's home recordings and immediately asked to meet with him.

"I loved what I heard," Goldberg told me over the phone from the Manhattan offices of his Gold Mountain Entertainment on a crisp late-September morning in 2016. "I think the first song on the cassette was 'I Was in the House When the House Burned Down,' and it was just so alive and brilliant and powerful and I just felt, 'There's gotta be an audience for this!' Maybe the passage of time had given him more clarity in his vision, but it's still one of my favorite records, *period*, not just one of my favorite Warren Zevon records. So it was easy to be enthusiastic about the music. In fact, it was one of the easiest decisions I ever made."

Worried about what Zevon he was meeting (yeah, he'd heard the stories), Goldberg explained to the veteran artist how much he would be expected to promote the record since he was years removed from anything resembling a hit. "It was not going to be an easy record to market," Goldberg continues. "Time had moved on from the era when there was a big rock radio infrastructure that would play a Warren Zevon record and artists just had to do so much more of the work. I didn't know him at all and he had a reputation for being difficult, but we had lunch in New York and he made a tremendous effort to reassure me of his seriousness about the work that was involved, and he couldn't have been more gracious."

Zevon waxed philosophic about his latest professional "valley" during his promotional tour of the record to Jody Denberg: "You know, I don't think it's ever been the case of being a big audience that stopped taking a ride with me, so much as a big audience that accidentally stepped on Mr. Toad's Wild Ride on the way to the fun house."

David Landau provided this take when we spoke late in 2016: "Warren had a moment in time when the door opened on the *Excitable Boy* album, and let's face it, most musicians never get that moment, and even a smaller percentage are able to sustain it for a while, and of those people a miniscule percent can sustain it over an entire career, and for those few it's extremely rare that it can continue at the highest level. Warren had that opportunity, but unfortunately when the door opened he simply wasn't prepared for it and he never got that moment back, and I think at some point he recognized that he wasn't going to be a Jackson Browne, who could tour at a certain level pretty much throughout his career. Part of the reason he didn't have bands was he couldn't afford to have bands. His records didn't sell. And to his credit he became a fantastic solo performer."

And so it may be that *Life'll Kill Ya*, perhaps Zevon's most consistently striking late-career work, is simply a more overt "meditation on death"—professionally or literally—than anything found on the entirety of *My Ride's Here*, but then Zevon didn't really do "simple" or "overt" as a rule. He was far more comfortable dabbling in witty symbolism, double entendre, and provocative proclamation, and for all of those we move on to "My Ride's Here," a fine piece of musical storytelling that will lead us to the same place, the great beyond.

Providing context to the song and the album of the same name is Zevon's gathering of all of his literary friends to contribute inspiration and titles, which afforded him welcomed creative wiggle room and a desired new perspective, as his past collaborations often did. Mostly, it was a ready excuse to facilitate a détente between the rock world and the literary one while getting to hang out with his heroes on his turf.

Zevon's respect for writers was an underlying element to his personality and provided a window into how his reverence for them stirred the depth and range of his lyrics. As the years went by, he sought the counsel and approbation of authors above even those of musical colleagues. His imagination was fired as a young boy by Norman Mailer and his affectation as a dashing figure seared into the pages of Dashiell Hammett, Raymond Chandler, and F. Scott Fitzgerald. Their world would become his world; their idiom his showcase, their characters his refuge; their smooth, effortless panoramas of words his Holy Grail.

"You have to go back to Gore Vidal's line about there's just nobody out there writing like Zevon," recounts his biographer, George Plasketes. "He's probably compared more to literary figures than his fellow songwriters. As great as Dylan is and Neil Young and Paul Simon and Randy Newman, he always had these other things going within his writing that nobody else did. He seemed to have a view that nobody else had."

The awe inspired in him by writers from novelist Ross Macdonald, whom Zevon viewed as an intellectual father figure, to the impressive list of literary figures who called him friend—Stephen King, Carl Hiaasen, Hunter S. Thompson, Thomas McGuane, Dave Barry, and many of the scribes who made up the literary band the Rock Bottom Remainders, founded in 1992 by writer Kathi Kamen Goldmark for frustrated rockers who just happened to be best-selling authors—was significant. Zevon gladly acted as its musical director from the late 1990s until his death in 2003, as it gigged for charity and even managed to open the Rock and Roll Hall of Fame in 1995. "He insisted I sing lead on his signature tune, 'Werewolves of London,'" Stephen King wrote of Zevon in the introductory dedication to his 2013 *Dr. Sleep*, a sequel to his 1977 breakthrough masterpiece about his own wrestle with alcoholism, *The Shining*. "I said I was not worthy. He insisted that I was. 'Key of G,' Warren told me, 'and howl like you mean it. Most important of all, play like Keith.'" In the same passage, King writes lovingly, "I'll never be able to play like Keith Richards, but I always did my best—and with Warren beside me, matching me note for note and laughing his fool head off, I always had a blast. Warren, this howl is for you, wherever you are. I miss you, buddy."

"For him, it was all about writing and authors," says his son Jordan. "I used to tell him, 'Dad you should write books.' He'd go, 'Johnny, I can't do that.' And I totally get it. I can make a reggae or rap song, whatever it is, but for me, comedians are like rock stars. I don't know how you get up there and put yourself on the line and just hope you're saying something funny. And he had that with authors. His inspiration was rooted in writers, and he was really thrilled to be friends with people like Stephen King and Carl Hiaasen. I can totally understand how that was the panty moistener for him."

"Warren was a *huge* fan of Ross Macdonald," remembers David Landau. "He practically recited his book *The Blue Hammer* to me on a daily basis, and of course he was also very into and became very good friends with Thomas McGuane."

"By the time I was in college we became closer," recalls his daughter Ariel. "Having not finished high school himself, but being this monster intellectual, it was exciting to him and he was *really* proud of my going to college. When I was in English lit classes he *loved* to talk about literature. That became a definite connection for us, just being able to talk about great works of literature, and music, of course."

The impressive list of cowriters on *My Ride's Here* includes the aforementioned journalist and novelist Carl Hiaasen, whose work often skews into the humorously bizarre. He had assisted Zevon on two songs for 1995's *Mutineer* album, "Rottweiler Blues" and "Seminole Bingo," having inspired both titles and added lyrical flourishes.

For *My Ride's Here*, Zevon was asked by the author to provide a song for a character in his novel about rock 'n' roll titled *Basket Case*. The song of the same name appears as the album's second track and the results are what you would expect: "Smoke on the water, water on the brain / She's pretty as a picture, and totally crazed."

Gonzo journalist and author of the seminal baby boomer socio-revolutionary freak journal *Fear & Loathing in Las Vegas* Hunter S. Thompson welcomed Zevon into his Owl Farm compound in Woody Creek, Colorado, to pen the lyrics to "You're a Whole Different Person When You're Scared," its title taken from a phrase Thompson had used in his later work, including a reference to "the kingdom of fear," which would become the title of one of his last published books. Zevon befriended the mercurially tempestuous Thompson in the early '90s, but, as with Hiaasen, the two had admired the other from afar for years and always toyed with collaborating. The experience for Zevon turned out to be both inspiring and terrifying. "It's all well and good sitting in the backyard and shooting high-powered weapons at targets with Hunter, but being trapped in his kitchen while he's drunk out of his mind waving a pistol around is another," muses Jordan Zevon.

"They ended up fighting about the song," Jorge Calderón recalls. "Warren played me these awful messages on his machine from Hunter insulting him. And he said, 'Man, I'm telling you, these people don't know what it is to write a song.' Luckily that never happened with us. If I gave him a verse and he went, 'No,' then it was 'Next!' Because I knew that the next line that we came up with would be better. But when you write with 'I'm a novelist' or 'I'm a poet,' it can get in the way."

Far less dangerous was the soft-spoken, Detroit-based sports columnist Mitch Albom, whose best-selling joint-memoir with his terminally ill college professor Morrie Schwartz, *Tuesdays with Morrie*, became a sensation in the late 1990s and spawned an Emmy Award–winning television adaptation. He would lend his expertise for "Hit Somebody! (The Hockey Song)," a classic Zevon "song-tale" filled with descriptive sports jargon, ironic humor, and deep pathos. Its signature feature is a monotonous refrain of the song's title, shouted with tongue-in-cheek delight by TV personality and Zevon fan David Letterman, which adds to the tragicomedy.

However, none of these songs reveal Zevon's claim that *My Ride's Here* is a "meditation on death" more dramatically than the title track. "My Ride's Here" is indeed spiritual, prophetic, and heroic, evoking the greatest literary travel tales of experience, escape, and transformation. It would be for Anton Fig what the esteemed session drummer and celebrated member of the *Late Show with David Letterman* band described to the *Guardian's* James Fenton as "the nicest song about being dead I've ever played on!"

I met its coauthor in the summer of 2016 on one of those steamy, mid-August, New York City early afternoons near his Upper West Side apartment. We took a stroll through his neighborhood before sitting for brunch at a corner café. Having just returned from a short sojourn in Ireland, he was as excited to talk about his friend and collaborator as any Warren Zevon fan might be. And that is exactly where the tale of "My Ride's Here" begins for Paul Muldoon.

"It was just after 9/11, and I sent Warren a fan letter saying that whenever I would get into a conversation with anyone on the subject of the great songwriters of the era, I always brought his name up, and I just wanted him to know that," recalls Muldoon, ordering a tea and some light fare. "I sent it with a copy of one of my books to his record company, and sure enough, I got a phone call one day from him saying he would be in New York for a couple of weeks subbing for Paul Shaffer on Letterman's show and we arranged to meet up at the Bryant Park Grill. We had lunch and then we went for a walk around Forty-Second Street. And in the course of our walk, he said to me, 'I'm doing this album with writers and would you like to write a song with me?' And I said, 'Of course, I would love to do that.' And that's how it started."

As ever, "My Ride's Here" is one of those titles that Zevon simply could not ignore, loaded as it was with symbolism and just the right twist of dark humor that Muldoon reminds me the songwriter first blurted out onstage at the historic Town Hall in New York's theater district—at the very show, incidentally, where I first heard him perform "The Indifference of Heaven": "During a break in the show, an ambulance siren could be heard through the walls and he said, 'Oh, my ride's here.'"

It would not take long for the two artists to form a bond. "We ended somewhere down by Grand Central when we saw this guy dragging this huge cross down the street," recalls Muldoon with a chuckle. "What was so funny about it was that we both saw it but neither of us said anything. We just went along as if it was the most natural thing in the world, and I think in a strange way, you see, in Warren's world, and perhaps even in mine, it *was*. I think we both sort of knew that we had a sort of wacky sense of the world."

Before beginning to compose the lyrics, Muldoon went on what he calls "a listening binge" of Zevon's back catalog to better capture his signature style and well-worn themes. "Anyone who's familiar with his work can see that 'My Ride's Here' is sort of written very much in a Zevonian vein," he says. "It's almost a pastiche of a Warren Zevon song. And yet I don't think it's merely a parody, but there are things about it that allude to other songs; for example the use of the word

'Jim' from 'Werewolves of London': 'He'll rip your lungs out, Jim.' There's also a 'Desperados Under the Eaves' aspect to it."

The first verse sets the mood:

I was staying at the Marriott
With Jesus and John Wayne
I was waiting for a chariot
They were waiting for a train
The sky was full of carrion
"I'll take the mazuma"
Said Jesus to Marion
"That's the 3:10 to Yuma
My ride's here. . . ."

The song's pretext of transference also doubles as an "escape route," a theme Zevon had grappled with since the aforementioned "Desperados Under the Eaves," using "ride" to denote transport as a metaphor for the freedom to flee on one's own terms while also pushing the boundaries of Zevon's death jag to the level of spiritual sublimation. "The sky is full of carrion" conjures the two men wandering through midtown Manhattan only a few months after the horrors of the 9/11 terrorist attacks on the World Trade Center. When pressed about whether the song acts as a paean to the event that would forever change the Western world, Muldoon calls it more of a "resonance" of the times.

Still, with the looming specter of terrorism and a post-traumatic national dread underscoring the very idea of safety as nothing more than illusion—a central sub-text to all of Zevon's songs—Muldoon replaces a fear of dying with a more seductive acceptance of it. In this first stanza, he saturates the imagery in dreams of a better place to be than the one presented to the narrator. For instance, Muldoon's choice of Jesus and John Wayne as central figures is a powerful lead-in: a man who would accept death with a sense of holy sacrifice is as potent a Christian symbol as the pairing of a chariot/train and its heavenly/earthly duality. Recalling Muldoon's story of him and Zevon seeing a man carrying a cross through the densely crowded city streets brings this home. John Wayne provides perspective to his reference of the high-plains "desperado" as an American hero. Both Christ and John Wayne are mythic saviors, comforting companions alongside which to travel into the great unknown. This notion is supported beautifully in the reference to the beloved 1957 western *3:10 to Yuma*.

Based on a short story by Elmore Leonard, another hard-bitten, streetwise writer Zevon admired, the film centers around two disparate personalities locked in an untenable fix. Dan Evans, a farmer played by Van Heflin, is the film's hero and moral center. He is given the unenviable task of shepherding a prisoner, the infamous gang leader Ben Wade, across the desert landscape of Arizona to a train where Wade will eventually stand trial for robbery and murder. Evans, a proud but troubled rancher with a loving family, is supposedly in charge of the situation, but instead it is Wade, played with wry glibness by Glenn Ford, who leads the narrative despite being led around in handcuffs. Evans only agrees to the job because he is confronted with crushing poverty due to lack of rain that has doomed his family. Luckless, he believes the task at hand will bring him the fortune he needs for his salvation, while Wade, a slick-talking, highly intelligent and manipulative outlaw, is a man who makes his own luck.

Both Evans and Wade are two parts of a whole in Warren Zevon and it is their conflict, between the sensitive intellectual and the howling werewolf, that fills so many of his songs. For instance, the clever and charming Wade bares his soul to an attractive barkeep about a woman he let get away, Pauline—whose name is incidentally that of the woman for whom Zevon begs forgiveness in "Bad Luck Streak in Dancing School." She rejects the outlaw to marry an authority figure, a mayor, wholly responsible for the law. Wade is only captured because he remains in town to seduce the barmaid instead of escaping to Mexico with the rest of his gang. He gambles his freedom for a remote chance at love, another of Zevon's central themes.

The film's Christian overtones, like Muldoon and Zevon's musical tale, are stark. The Evan boys' names are Matthew and Mark, after two of the four writers of the gospels, as the twelve members of the gang recall the apostles. Holed up in a hotel room with Wade, Evans is tempted by the outlaw to take money to save his farm and walk away without risking his life, much like the devil and Christ in the desert. In the end, as Evans reaches his destination and rain begins to fall upon the scene, the clock strikes three, the hour Christ would succumb to death on Good Friday.

The train, of course, stands as not only destination but salvation, for which the reference is offered by Muldoon as the song's first "ride" to be taken. The film's grand opening is awash in western vistas with a stagecoach traveling across a heavenly expanse of pristine desert, the perfect visual accompaniment to "My Ride's Here."

"I wrote the first verse pretty quickly and then I sent it to Warren by email and then he wrote the music for the rest of it," remembers Muldoon. "He then sent me back a CD with the first verse sung and then the rest of it mapped out musically. With that we started trying to finish it, which took a *long* time."

Zevon wrote the music in as stylized a fashion as Muldoon's opening canto, rich as it is in whimsical allusions. The midtempo, hymnlike quality of its opening with a wonderfully hummable countermelody played in grand Southern California style by Zevon on guitar evokes a sunnier disposition to the telling, running counter to the rest of the album's ominous tapestry. Its place as the final cut on the record speaks volumes of its underscoring of the theme and its affirmative spiritual message. This is perhaps why Zevon pushed his poet friend to make sure it measured up to his vision.

Zevon expressed his desire for lyrical perfection to *Songwriter* magazine in 1981: "Lyrics have to look good to my eye when I'm writing them—that's part of the quality check."

The two worked remotely for weeks, Zevon in L.A. and Muldoon in New York, each sending the other ideas and revisions—and all the while, the poet was getting a lesson in the fine art of songwriting. "What I didn't know is when it comes to writing songs, it's like tennis or making coffee: Some people are good at making it look very easy, and the fact is . . . it's *not* easy," says Muldoon. "I didn't understand, because this was the first song I wrote, how short a song is. There's a lot to pack in there. A lot of other songs, of course, are packed with next to nothing, but Warren's are very dense—not in a problematic way, but there's lots of interesting stuff going on."

Once again, songwriting veteran and longtime Zevon collaborator Jorge Calderón agrees: "Warren obviously had problems with people writing all the time, and I understand it, because what happens is when you're a songwriter in the rock 'n' roll idiom, you have to get the most power out of an economy of words. When you write with a novelist or a poet, they start writing a humongous thing for a three-chord, three-verse song."

Although Muldoon tells me repeatedly that it was a "wonderful experience to be apprentice to him," he experienced much of what Calderón illustrated: "We did haggle to write the rest of it. I would send him a bit and he would say, 'No! No good.' I remember having long, amorous verses about this and that, but really rubbish. So for most of the second verse, I wrote gradually":

The Houston sky was changeless
We galloped through bluebonnets
I was wrestling with an angel
You were working on a sonnet
You said, "I believe the seraphim
Will gather up my pinto
And carry us away, Jim

Across the San Jacinto
My ride's here. . . .

Muldoon continues with his Western theme, what he calls "an imagined cowboy landscape" referencing America's third-largest city, Houston, in its second-largest state, Texas, and placing his narrator in the evocative wide-open spaces of the desert plains patiently awaiting seraphim to whisk them away to the great beyond. We also get the idea that both Jesus and John Wayne have been left back at the Marriott and now, in true buddy-film idiom, Muldoon and Zevon, draped in iconicity, take the holy ride together.

It is in this verse that Muldoon's Zevonian homage resonates. One is reminded of Zevon's opening song from his first Asylum album, "Frank and Jesse James," with its mythic preamble piano and its later refrain used to presage the escapist musings of its closing number, "Desperados Under the Eaves," that concludes with an elongated western-motif coda portending the expanse of the untamed American wilderness and the outcast/outlaw abandoned by circumstance to fend for himself in a cruel and unforgiving world. Further along in their collaboration, Zevon would be equally inspired by the poet's directive to design the perfect final verse that vividly drives these images home.

Again, as in the opening stanza, there is no tension to the verse: It resounds with unwavering childlike faith, an acute sense that the ride will not be fraught with peril. Although a rarity in the Zevon oeuvre, it does strike a familiar chord in regard to the composer's obsession with the vagaries of the universe manipulating mere mortals through life as if chess pieces. Yet, where previous voices bemoaned their fate Muldoon provides Zevon with an evenly paved avenue in which to ameliorate his "blind luck" scenario. "I think ideally it's the song that inspires you; it tells you what it wants to be," says Muldoon. "And you sort of need to be ready to figure out what it wants to do. The best songs, I think, have this kind of strange inevitability about them. You know, in a sense, this song has nothing to do with me, really. I never feel that I write my own poems, never mind write songs. Obviously I had some hand in this, but at the end of the day, I think one of the reasons why it's good has got nothing to do with either of us."

The two men converge both literally and figuratively at its bridge, coalescing Muldoon's heroic, spiritual journey with Zevon's love of literary references.

Shelley and Keats were out in the street
And even Lord Byron was leaving for Greece

While back at the Hilton, last but not least
Milton was holding his sides

Saying, "You bravos had better be ready to fight
Or we'll never get out of East Texas tonight
The trail is long and the river is wide
And my ride's here"

According to Muldoon, Zevon was mostly responsible for the nods to eighteenth-century romantic poets Percy Bysshe Shelley, John Keats, and George Gordon Byron, while seventeenth-century poet John Milton was keenly absorbed. "Funny enough, I have written a bit about Byron and I've mentioned Milton 'holding his sides,'" says Muldoon. "Milton has a line as 'laughter holding his sides' and that's what that is. I had the line in an early version of the song in a different verse and so Warren took that and incorporated it into the bridge."

Muldoon's citing of "laughter holding his sides" is from Milton's 1645 pastoral poem titled "L'Allegro," which translates from Italian as "The Happy Man" and contrasts another of his poems, "Il Penseroso," translated as "The Melancholy Man"; both depicting similar days spent in the splendor of a natural tableau deep in contemplation. The resounding theme for Milton in "L'Allegro" is "mirth," or the joys of the artist being enraptured by nature. Joy and humor devoid of the haunt of death elevate its theme, as they do for Zevon in the song's bridge, lifting the mood majestically, as in the musical term, *allegro*, or "lively/cheerful."

But it is Zevon's clever use of Romantic poets, specifically Shelley and Lord Byron, contemporaries and colleagues, that is illuminating. Each inspired and challenged the other, especially on their travels together, their rapport recalling that of another traveling duo, the eponymous heroes of Zevon's rollicking "Frank and Jesse James." A joint boating tour of Geneva in 1816 inspired Shelley to write his "Hymn to Intellectual Beauty" (an ode to fantasy escapism), which prompted Byron to begin his own grand verse, which would become the following year's "Don Juan" (dubbed by Byron "an epic satire").

Here are two men (poets) experiencing their own "buddy road adventure" (Muldoon/Zevon), inspiring each other along the merry way; all of this and a delicious inner rhyme of "Hilton" and Milton" to boot.

It is the mention of Milton that brings it back to the western theme again, with Muldoon providing a monologue for the poet and placing him back into the geography of the first two verses, paying superb tribute to Zevon's flair for returning to a song's central theme within the structure of its story arc. "The trail is long and the river is wide. . . ."

I was staying at the Westin
I was playing to a draw
When in walked Charlton Heston
With the Tablets of the Law
He said, "It's still the Greatest Story"
I said, "Man, I'd like to stay
But I'm bound for glory
I'm on my way
My ride's here. . . ."

Zevon's principal contribution to the lyrics for "My Ride's Here" is found in its final verse, where all pretense of what the song is truly about is stripped bare. Muldoon smirks when recalling the first time he reviewed it, how he was pleased that Zevon had taken his transient hotel imagery, which he'd used effectively three decades earlier in "Desperados Under the Eaves," and provided it a soft, heroic landing, along with a reprise to the machismo he had presented with John Wayne, and for good measure, the spiritual primacy of Jesus Christ. Inarguably, the broad-shouldered and cavern-voiced Charlton Heston's turn as Moses from the 1956 classic *Ten Commandments* is as close to a career-defining role as Hollywood has seen in its rich history of blurring the lines between actor and character.

In the winter of 2001 into 2002, when the song was being written, Heston was the honorary president and spokesman of the controversial and influential National Rifle Association: He had held the position from 1998 and would do so until resigning in 2003. Only a year before, at the 2000 NRA convention, he'd raised a rifle over his head and declared that a potential Al Gore administration would take away his Second Amendment rights "from my cold, dead hands." This infamous quote, and the subsequent interview he granted activist director Michael Moore for Moore's anti-gun 2002 documentary *Bowling for Columbine* (which was released five months after *My Ride's Here*), would become a symbol for both the extreme gun lobby and the vociferous gun-control opposition.

The insensitive timing of Heston's call to arms, coming as it did nearly a year to the day after the anniversary of a mass shooting by two teens at Columbine High School in Jefferson County, Colorado, reverberates with Zevon touchstones: his fascination in song and story with violence, his years of gun obsession, his kinship with gun-toting gonzo journalist Hunter S. Thompson, a resident since the late 1960s of Colorado, where Zevon was once an honorary Pitkin County coroner, and the lineage between iconic characters and violence. The line in the verse preceding the Heston reference is ambiguously tasty in that "playing to a draw" denotes a microcosm of the Zevon grab bag: the looming figure of the card-playing gangster father and the western motif found in "the draw"—two dueling hombres at the center of town settling scores in a six-shooter showdown.

The final verse bursts with symbolism, which is universal, religious, iconic, and shamelessly Hollywoodesque, while also acting, as Muldoon points out, as a pastiche of the songwriter's entire catalog. The tip of the hat to American hobo/folk singer icon, Woody Guthrie's mostly fictionalized autobiography *Bound for Glory* tops the list. If, as Zevon cited again and again in interviews, Bob Dylan "invented my job" then Guthrie helped "invent" Dylan. The 1960s voice of his generation not only worshipped Guthrie but absorbed his persona, going so far as to visit the dying troubadour in a New Jersey hospital in a symbolic passing-of-the-torch-moment forever captured in the imagination of baby boomer lore. The young Robert Allen Zimmerman's Dylan persona was pure Guthrie, from its 1961 Greenwich Village roots to his own sensationalized bio that saw a middle-class, educated Jewish boy from Hibbing, Minnesota, hopping freight trains and joining carnivals to sing epic ballads of chain gangs and dust bowls with a middle-aged mid-American drawl. In his 2005 *Chronicles Volume 1*, Dylan described his transformation from Zimmerman to Dylan in the cloak of Guthrie as a way to tap into what he believed was his hero's truth of America, his songs possessing, as he wrote in his own memoir, "the infinite sweep of humanity in them."

"My Ride's Here" is Warren Zevon's ode to that "infinite sweep of humanity"— as much a song about life as it is about death, or life *after* death: a rebirth, an escape from earthly degradation to discover a new "self" invented through art. "I think at the end it does fall into kind of conventional imagining of a world beyond—the *next* world, which I don't have any time for really, and I'm not sure if Warren did," concludes Muldoon. "But as I say, it's not so much about what we thought or what we believed: it's the milieu of the song. It's not sad. I'd say, if anything, there's a kind of delighted resignation to it."

The torch passed from Guthrie to Dylan to a generation of songwriters searching for that "truth" was something of an obsession for Warren Zevon, who toiled to challenge the form with a unique voice that he needed others to hear. As it happens, that torch would symbolically and very publicly be passed to his friend Bruce Springsteen, who was discovered by John Hammond, the very executive who had signed Dylan to Columbia Records nearly a decade earlier. More than anyone who carried the mantle thrown down by Dylan, Springsteen would not only suffer comparisons but was handed the burden of the fading 1960s edict, which he would carry well into the next century. It is no coincidence that two days after Zevon passed into the great beyond, the man millions of adoring fans called the Boss would play a stripped-down and solemnly touching version of "My Ride's Here" for a Toronto audience, prefacing it with "Warren was one of the great, great American songwriters and we're going to miss him very much." Its gentle acoustic arrangement with a funereal accordion accompaniment is highlighted by Springsteen's Guthriesque underscore of Americana, his phrasing of the more western themes sounding as if he is sharing its myths as a sermon. In a master song interpreter's hands, Zevon and Muldoon's hymn becomes reverent, a weighty and passionate tribute that would eventually end up on the posthumous *Enjoy Every Sandwich*.

"I think it's one of the best songs Warren ever wrote," concludes Danny Goldberg. "And Springsteen did an extraordinary interpretation of it."

"I was thrilled when Springsteen sang it," says Muldoon a few minutes before we parted. "And I suppose one of the reasons had to do with a poignant aspect of the subject matter, but I think it comes as no surprise that Bruce Springsteen might have chosen it as the kind of archetypical Warren Zevon song, because it's full of characters and situations held in common with other songs."

On a deeper level, this version of the song would strike a lasting chord in Jorge Calderón, who was still very much grieving the loss of his dear friend when he heard it for the first time during the mastering of *Enjoy Every Sandwich*: "That did it to me. When I started hearing Bruce singing it . . . that song is *so* Warren. The words of that song are things that he loved to say, loved to read, and there's something about that song that is lyrically *very* Warren and how he liked to talk and it just killed me, man. I'm telling you, it was like somebody punched me in the chest and I went into this place that was hard for me to get out of. I remember Waddy [Wachtel] was there that day and he said, 'What's the matter?' I said, 'Dude, I don't know, man. We have to go outside. I have to come back to this,' because it really destroyed me. And what it was is that I had held all this stuff for so long, trying to be Mr. Strong to finish *The Wind* and again to do this other thing. So, yeah, it took like a year for me to really come out of this, man. I'm telling you, when you lose somebody that's close to you and [whom] you love, it's a lifelong thing."

Kindred Spirits Bring It Home: Warren Zevon and Jorge Calderón, Cherokee Studios, 2002. *Courtesy of the Jorge Calderón Collection*

The Wind

Command the last fruits: They should fully ripen,
and give them two more southern sunny days,
to reach perfection gathering
the last nectar into the heavy grapes.

—RAINER MARIA RILKE, "Autumn Day"

On August 28, 2002, Warren Zevon was diagnosed with mesothelioma, a rare, inoperable form of lung cancer. He succumbed to the disease on September 7, 2003. In the harrowing, confusing, combative, agonizingly resigned twelve months in between he wrote and recorded his final album, *The Wind*. For a little over a calendar year this was his relentless aim: finally, after years of flirting, joking, philosophizing, writing, and singing about death, he would confront it—emotionally, intellectually, artistically.

It would be, in the end, pure Zevon.

It is a deceleration. *I am dying.*

"It's not the easiest thing in the world to deal with the absolute reality of saying goodbye," he told filmmaker Nick Read in his final months for a VH1 *(Inside) Out* documentary called *Warren Zevon: Keep Me in Your Heart*, a brilliantly intimate portrait of the making of *The Wind* and the subsequent months following his fatal diagnosis.

In much of Zevon's tortured art there is his "To be or not to be" moment. The very idea of settling into the comforts of *not* challenging death to instead drift through a drama-free subsistence seemed crazy to him. Therefore he spent a lifetime studying the struggle of choosing chaos over normalcy through his music. His songs would sometimes humorously, sometimes painfully, confront the paralyzing fear of the ultimate consequence of the challenge, death, a subject others may have approached with more profundity but far less accuracy. It is as if Warren Zevon cheated death and then got cozy with it, his situation recalling Ingmar Bergman's famous black-and-white tableau of Death playing chess with a noble knight on the beach with the white stallion and the waves crashing: a friendly wager with eternity. Zevon, I think, believed he had won a few of these chess matches sitting over the board contemplating his next move against the ebony-cloaked figure gripping the scythe, its bony fingers reaching for the piece that would finally do him in.

Two years earlier Zevon discussed "dealing with death" with Marty Riemer on KMIT radio in Seattle in this exchange:

"Am I dealing with it?"

"Yeah."

"In a mature and proper way, nah, I'm just having a little fun with it."

"And that's it."

"I think so. That's the best I can do."

Zevon confessed to his friend rock journalist Paul Nelson in 1982: "I grew up with a painting of an uncle, Warren, who looked just like me. He was a military man, a golden boy, an artist. He'd been killed in action. Uncle Warren was sort of the dead figurehead of the family, and I was brought up to follow in his footsteps. My ideal was supposed to be a dead man—with my name, looks, and career intentions. A dead warrior who'd been waylaid by his heroism. I guess that kind of background gave me the idea that destroying myself was the only way to live up to expectations."

Eventually, he figured, his luck—the luck he had coveted to the point of near mental collapse—would run out. And in late summer of 2002, with the sun shining, traffic rolling along, children laughing in the streets, and banal music playing from far-off radios, he would know once and for all that the game was over. Checkmate. Death, appearing in blaring, sickening Technicolor, would ultimately, cruelly, even justifiably win. He had taken plenty of matches, but you can only lose one.

Having studied the personification of death in all its expressions through art, poetry, and prose down through the centuries, Zevon understood what he must do: create his epitaph and frame a metaphor for his plight. He would come to terms with it and describe the view for all of us, whose journey will also end one way or another. He would course his roadmap, his acceptance of existence, his final words.

As the story goes, Zevon was in the midst of a short Canadian tour of Calgary/ Edmonton in the spring of 2002 when, according to his tour manger Matt Cartsonis, he stumbled in the parking lot of a liquor store after having ironically purchased his "lucky" bottle of Diet Mountain Dew. Complaining of dizziness and shortness of breath, he finally agreed to see a doctor after continually arguing that his workout regimen, which had been the most intense of his life, might have led to random bouts of lightheadedness. "I was working out like Vin Diesel," Zevon told *Billboard* magazine that September. "I noticed that I was short of breath, and I may have dismissed it as just an old guy working out too much."

"This is what's so confusing about the whole thing: I saw him look as good as I had ever seen him look," remembered his personal manager Brigette Barr when we spoke in February of 2017. "He had been working out at the gym and he had this confidence: 'Look at me! Feel my stomach. It's so hard,' which is so tragic because he was dying at that second and you would never have known. If you knew Warren all those years and then looked at him then, you'd think, 'God, he's gotten his shit together and he's healthy!' So it was a real shock."

Due to his mother's history of heart trouble and an admission from Zevon that his issues had affected his sleep, his old pal and dentist Doctor Stan Golden suggested he see a cardiologist for a routine checkup. This turned into extended tests and, as a result, an appointment with an oncologist in late August.

The first call Zevon made was to his twenty-six-year-old daughter Ariel. "I can hear his voice on the other end of the line, even now," remembers Ariel. "In moments like that he called me Princess. He said, 'Princess, it's not good.'"

Soon after, it was confirmed that Zevon had blood in his lungs. But at that point there was still a question as to what was causing his symptoms. "He was given three months," says Ariel. "Then I had conversations with him during the early stages of being diagnosed to decide what to do, and then I remember him making the decision not to go through the chemotherapy and [to] just ride it out."

"I was lucky," Zevon said without a sliver of irony to VH1. "I got all the news, all the progression of tests, all the roller-coaster ride of hopes and shocking news in the course of one day."

His son Jordan, then thirty-three, was at work when his father called. "He always had the low voice and you know the way he speaks: 'Hello, Johnny.' And I said, 'What's going on, Pop?' He said, 'Well, I'm sick.' Then I got that feeling you get in the pit of your stomach, and I said, 'How sick?' And he said, 'Well, it's bad. It's *real* bad.'

"I use this to describe it, and it may be fruity and spiritual, but it really does describe how I felt: the way that I looked at the world changed in that instant. Colors didn't look the same. I just remember looking around the room and it was just like suddenly somebody peeled off this layer of veneer and said, 'Oh, this is what the real world looks like. Your parents are going to die.' I was floored, but I'll never forget the way that I visualized it and the way that suddenly I just felt like, 'Oh, wow. Life is different now and it's not going to go back.' I'm sure there's different ways that people learn that lesson of growing up, whether it's taking a first ass-kicking or a near-death experience, but something just snapped in that instant."

"There was a lot of silence in the call, but it wasn't an awkward silence, it was a 'being together' silence," remembers Crystal Zevon. "And then he probably called four or five times a day for the first month after he was diagnosed, because he was trying to figure out what to do. How do you deal with this? He wanted to do it right. He said, 'Do you act like a man and die with your boots on or do you give in to crying?'"

In tragically ironic Zevon fashion, the day his personal manager found out he was dying, she had hammered out a deal with the prestigious William Morris Agency to jump-start his career. "I thought I was bringing him really good news," remembers Brigette Barr. "I called him and said, 'Guess what!?' I was just so happy at that moment because I could help him achieve all he wanted in his career at that point. And he said, 'Guess what . . . ?' It was as if a knife had gone through me, because I was his friend, too. It wasn't just a business thing for me. It was just so awful."

"I did this Buddhist meditation thing and went to India a lot, so he had this idea that we would go to India and meditate by the banks of the Ganges and then when he died I would pour his ashes into the Ganges," recalls Crystal. "And he was serious . . . for about a week. He even looked up plane tickets. But I said to him, 'Well, Warren, what is it that you *really* need to do? What's not finished?' Finally he said, 'I need to do an album. That's who I am. That's what I have to do.'"

Zevon looked to perhaps his closest and most trusted friend, Jorge Calderón, to make his dying wish a reality.

Calderón: "Well, to start at the beginning, when Warren finished *My Ride's Here*, he said, 'I just made this record, and I like this one, but I spread myself too thin, cowriting with too many people, and I want just you and I to do the next one together, because we always have fun doing it.'

"A few days after we decided to work together we went to see a Clint Eastwood movie and as we were walking toward the theater he was saying, 'Walk slower, man. I'm short of breath.' At the time, I was thinking, well, maybe he had clogged arteries or something. So I told him to go see a cardiologist. And that's when I got the call. He says, 'Guess where I am? I'm at the cardiologist, but my cardiologist sent me to the oncologist. I have lung cancer.' It was like, 'Oh, fuck.' It just hit me like a ton of bricks. I literally fell down on my knees. I managed to say, 'Excuse me, Warren,' and I gave the phone to my wife to talk to him for a minute, because I couldn't. It hit me too hard. Then I came back to the phone and I said, 'Listen, Warren, whatever you need to do, we'll do.' And he said, 'I want to keep the idea of the album.' I said, 'Don't you want to get treatment or go away with your kids on vacation or something?' And I remember he just said, 'No, I want to do the album.' And that's how *The Wind* started."

Brigette Barr immediately contacted the founder and president of Artemis Records, Danny Goldberg, who would oversee the budget for the project and fund an independent publicist to promote it. "Warren immediately said to me, 'I give you permission to go showbiz on this record and use my illness so we can make the best possible record and get publicity on it," recalls Barr. "At first, I was taken back, because I didn't want to exploit him, but he kept saying, 'No. Let's do it.'" Goldberg then told Calderón, "Whatever you need," and authorized an open purchase order for any available studios. Cherokee Studios, nearly out of business, offered an exceptional rate.

Throughout sharing his memories of that time with me, Goldberg kept returning to his initial amazement at how fortunate Zevon would be to get one or two songs done, considering his prognosis. "It wasn't clear for at least about another few weeks that he actually had the vision or the strength and the ambition to do an *entire* album," says Goldberg. "That just sort of grew over time and I kept paying the bills. I had the money and I just couldn't imagine saying no to him."

Zevon confessed to the VH1 cameras, "I decided to record almost immediately, because it's one of the only things I know how to do that's engrossing and compelling and engaging that it takes your mind off whatever minor business you're conducting, with or without your agreement. The things that matter to me most are my two kids and making music."

And thus Calderón was handed the colossal mantle to usher a dying man, his dear friend for thirty years, through his final artistic statement—the singer-songwriter-guitarist whom Zevon playfully dubbed the "Puerto Rican James Joyce" or the more provocative "kill-crazy Puerto Rican intellectual in a one-eyed Karmann Ghia." Calderón explains that one with a chuckle: "Back when I first met Warren, I had a Karmann Ghia convertible that had been in an unfortunate mash-up and I didn't have money to fix it, so I was riding around with one front headlight."

According to Crystal Zevon, Calderón was Zevon's true soul mate: "Jorge is the one and only person that Warren trusted without reservation with his music. In fact, he talked to me numerous times as he was dying about if there are going to be changes made to his songs or if there are going to be things put out, Jorge needs to supervise or be involved. He and Jorge had that kind of mental agility with each other, sort of telepathic communication where they could write 'Mr. Bad Example' and just be rolling around on the floor throwing out lines together and it would just come."

They met for the first time when Crystal's then boyfriend landed in a Los Angeles drunk tank after Zevon crashed her car. "When I got the call about Warren being arrested I called his father and he bailed him out. But I had no way to pick him up, so I called Jorge."

As Calderón tells it, he received a middle-of-the-night call of desperation from Crystal, whom he had met through the Wachtel brothers. Calderón reluctantly agreed, eventually finding what would become one of the era's most respected song-writers slumped pathetically in his backseat. "He got in and she said, 'This is Warren. This is Jorge.' I said, 'Hey, how you doing?'" remembers Calderón. "We continued onto their apartment, but they couldn't get in because they were so frazzled. He didn't have the keys or she misplaced the keys, and that's when I said, 'Don't worry, I'm Puerto Rican, I can get into anybody's house.' Warren just looked at me and grinned. He was in this awful state, but yet I could see this sparkle in his eyes, like he kind of dug my deprecating humor. From that point on, he always said we traveled on the same wavelength."

Their friendship, as Calderón recalls it, evolved "organically" until he became part of Zevon's "little bag of characters" and, more important, a trusted professional confidant across a career spanning over ten studio albums, the last suddenly being the most crucial.

The clock was ticking.

"The thing we knew that we had to do was write fast, because we didn't know how long he was going to be here," says Calderón, breathlessly recalling the pressure. "It was like, 'Okay, we have *that* one now, let's start on another one. You have a title?' Or he would call me on the phone, like he did one day outside of a drugstore where he had picked up all these painkillers they were giving him, and he says to me, 'I'm numb as a statue. I may have to beg, borrow, or steal some feelings from you, so I can have some feelings too.' And we were off and running with 'Numb as a Statue.' He used to talk to me like that all the time. If he wanted to lay a line on me, he would say that in conversation and I knew him so well that I would get it. Then I would write some more. So once we had the chorus from what he told me on the phone, I started in the first verse with, 'I'm pale as a ghost. . . .' He would give me the stuff to jump-start the song."

At the beginning of the eventual recording of the song, Zevon is heard making light of how many takes the musicians had to endure to get it right, specifically his longtime friend multi-instrumentalist David Lindley, joking that he enjoys seeing the blood drain from his face. Bloodless face or not, Lindley soars on the eventual track, once again accentuating the narrator's dilemma with the sheer volume and passion of his pedal steel guitar. Before his second solo, Zevon shouts, "Now can I get a witness?" and Lindley testifies for all he is worth. The signature wail that embellished so many great Warren Zevon songs takes us back to the young and brash songwriter, solemnly profound in his observation of a man devoid of emotions who is willing to feel pain rather than nothing at all, as he did in "Ain't That Pretty at All." It would be one of Zevon's better vocals on the album, which vacillate between painfully breathless to nearly garbled, his universally respected impeccable pronunciation lost to the exhaustion of illness and extreme medication.

The bridge, which maintains Lindley's driving force, provides the album's first glimpse behind Zevon's search for his humanity faced with his mortality:

I don't care if it's superficial
You don't have to dig down deep
Just bring enough for the ritual
Get here before I fall asleep

Zevon told Nick Read at the time: "I'm writing pretty fast, and Jorge and I are writing songs pretty fast, so it seems like . . . well, I don't know . . . hopefully I'll be around to write quite a few songs for this album. The idea for a song, the inspiration for a song, it just kind of shows up in front of you, and they seem to be showing up more often, which is very exciting. One of my closest friends is a novelist. He has this superstition that once you start a novel you won't die until you're done. So it's a good reason to drag it out."

Calderón recalls that Zevon, who would tell the *New York Times* that he was suddenly thrust into "the intensest creative period of my life," had already recorded new songs in his home studio, including the album's opening track, "Dirty Life and Times," and the heart-wrenching "She's Too Good for Me." The former, which would serve as a subtitle for his ex-wife's posthumous oral history, is a classic Zevon confessional replete with woe-is-me reflections—"Some days I feel like my shadow's casting me / Some days the sun don't shine"—but its prescient nods to an uncertain future provide it with a renewed density considering his sudden crisis: "Sometimes I wonder what tomorrow's gonna bring / When I think about my dirty life and times." The second pre-diagnosis song could also be considered a confessional with a wistful theme of lost love, sung with a wounded tenderness that Zevon had perfected over the years: "I want her to be happy / I want her to be free / I want her to be everything / She couldn't be with me," sweetly accompanied by the soft Eagles-style harmonies of Don Henley and Timothy B. Schmit. But once again, as if he had envisioned his condition, Zevon must face his mortality: "I could hold my head up high / And say that I left first / Or I can hang my head and cry / Tell me which is worse."

Once the two friends began considering new material, it would become difficult to ignore Zevon's condition. "The fact of his existence and what was going on with him became the elephant in the room," remembers Calderón. "Eventually, we couldn't write about anything else but his illness, which became the underlying theme of the album without us even searching for it."

"Everything is accentuated and becomes meaningful in an oblique way," Zevon shared with journalist Jon Pareles. "There's subtext all over the place."

The first song on which Zevon requested Calderón's assistance was the achingly romantic ballad "El Amor de Mi Vida" that he had written for Annette Aguilar Ramos, whom Zevon nicknamed Pollyanna because she always saw the brighter side of life, an alien notion to him. They met in 1988 at a twelve-step meeting and Zevon was immediately smitten, so much so a character with the same name ended up in his 1989 concept album, *Transverse City*. According to Ramos's memories of their first year together in Crystal Zevon's oral biography, Zevon was driving regularly up to Fresno to care for his then sick mother and, as was his wont, refused to commit to her completely. They would fall in and out of a relationship over the ensuing years until she finally cut it off, which haunted him until the end.

Calderón recalls: "Warren said, 'Maybe you should come up with this in Spanish,' so I said, 'Okay, great, let me try,' and I came up with that whole sentiment in Spanish and then wrote a line in English—'I close my eyes, you reappear'—and then he said, 'I always carry you inside, in here.' And then I followed with 'I fall asleep, you come to me. . . .'" We started going back and forth and that was the first song we wrote for the album."

Once again, with "El Amor de Mi Vida" Zevon harkens back to his most vulnerable lyrics and vocals. This is the tender phrasing of "Hasten Down the Wind" and "Accidentally Like a Martyr," "Empty Handed Heart" and "Jesus Mentioned," "Reconsider Me" and "Mutineer." Regret weighs heavy in each line, but none is as naked as the two-line bridge that preludes the melodious chorus with razor-blade precision:

How could I have let you get away?
Why couldn't I have found a way to say?

This is the essence of the art of *The Wind* for me. The author, through his anguish, reminds you of yours, no matter how small or insurmountable it may be. It is an anguish that knows no age or gender or race or faith, an unforgotten moment that escapes our grasp. In these simple lines of lost love, and a calling out to a past that can never be rectified, he superbly realizes one of his very first compositions, "Studebaker," a song he could never capture in the way it was originally recorded, frozen in a fleeting moment of time, never to be so pure again. This is a dying man telling us that every moment that passes is itself a death. We cannot get it back, and with each instance we do not act we may alter our lives. It simply drifts away until it is too late.

Tú eres el amor de mi vida (You are the love of my life)
Si solo te pudiera encontrar (If only I could find you)
Con todo el corazon te diria (With all my heart I would tell you)
Tú eres el amor de mi vida (You are the love of my life)

As with his penetrating "Searching for a Heart," this is Zevon celebrating (in the most painful way) the infinite search for love. To him, it can only exist after it is gone. This is the majesty and tragedy of life: We realize too late what truly matters—not money or fame or even art. It is love. And here is a man face-to-face with *the end* who sees this truth more clearly than ever, the bookend of "The French Inhaler," the vicious harangue aimed at the mother of his only son, Tule Livingston, whom he hurt and who thus hurt him back and he had to put that hurt into song and then forced the both of them to live with the consequences. It is also the hidden anger in "Accidentally Like a Martyr," the young lion too prideful to stop roaring at his bride, Crystal. They twist in the wind, because he cannot fathom the depths of his own heart, wallowing in the pathos of paying so dearly for "what was already mine" and saying over and over, "Should have done . . . should have done." This is his song for a woman, *the* woman—as much as it is a song to all women that can be found in "Poor Poor Pitiful Me." And here, as well as in some of the most stirring ballads found on *The Wind*, is where Zevon processes the revelation that as much as violence and mayhem and drink and dark characters overwhelmed with the absurdity of life may have inspired dozens of his songs, these pale in comparison to the woman as muse. She brings out the best and worst in him.

"Once we really got going, Warren would call me every morning, whether he had something new or not," explains Calderón. "One time he said, 'Last night I wrote a whole bunch of stuff down, but nothing is good except for this one thing, 'Disorder in the House.' So I said, 'That's fucking great, that's our rocker!' We were looking at that point for a rock 'n' roll, up-tempo thing. He said, 'Great, why don't you jump-start it?' So I wrote the first verse. 'Disorder in the house / The tub runneth over / Plaster's falling down in pieces by the couch of pain,' all that stuff and then 'Disorder in the house / Time to duck and cover / Helicopters hover over rough terrain.' I was seeing what was going on at the time. It was 2003. Bush was gung-ho into going into Iraq and doing this thing that didn't have to be done. But I was also writing for Warren, whose personal house was in disorder. It was those two things that came out of me. And when I read him the first verse he loved the 'plaster's falling down in pieces by the couch of pain.'

"The couch of pain, at his apartment, was a couch where you had to sit when you needed to write songs. We would say, 'Are you ready to sit on the couch of pain?' And we kept coming up with different names for it: the 'divan of desperation' or 'Nauga-hyde divan' that we used in 'Mr. Bad Example,' and we ended up with 'I'm sprawled across the davenport of despair,' which he came up with and made the song.

"Then he called me and started singing it and I told him I thought he sounded like Springsteen. He said, 'Oh, yeah, well that's good, because guess who called? Bruce wants to be part of this and he's going to sing on it!' So now we've *got* to finish it, and so we got together at his house and just plowed through the rest of the song. The second verse, 'Disorder in the house . . .' We said, '*Something* wisdom. What kind of wisdom? Reptile wisdom. Okay, reptile wisdom!' And then he went into the whole 'zombies on the lawn, staggering around, disorder in the house,' the whole thing about the Lhasa Apso, you know. I went to his house and I took my notebook out, and he saw 'a fate worse than fame' and he came back with 'Even my Lhasa Apso seems to be ashamed!' Then we had Bruce Springsteen come and sing on it."

Springsteen is among an impressive list of major talents, even for the usual star-studded Zevon sessions, that came pouring into the project at the behest of Calde-rón. Once Zevon had given him the nod to fill out a roster of studio musicians to play the backing tracks, the usual contributors—Jackson Browne, David Lindley, and members of the Eagles—insisted on being included, as did legendary guitarist Ry Cooder, session drummer supreme Jim Keltner, and the inimitable Tom Petty, along with his wonderfully versatile guitarist, Mike Campbell. Emmylou Harris, the queen of country vocals; country star Dwight Yoakam; and multitalented musician/producer T Bone Burnett all delivered fantastic vocal performances.

Conspicuously absent was longtime creative igniter Waddy Wachtel, who told me in 2017 with more than a tinge of anger and regret that a classic Zevon overreaction to a misunderstanding left him uninvited: "He didn't ask me, which was very hard for me to handle that he was calling every fucking asshole in the world and not me, but that was when he was up his own ass about me, I guess. I was very offended and very hurt by it."

True to what he told Brigette Barr when they decided to go "showbiz," Zevon told Artemis president Danny Goldberg when he came to visit the studio one day, "So, how do you like your press?" Goldberg remembers: "He was completely explicit and unabashed about the fact that he wanted to use the attention he was getting from his terminal illness to draw attention to his work. He was focused like a laser and it was kind of mind-blowing to see. It was like everything he learned up to that point in his life came to the fore in the making of that record, not just in the song-writing, but [in] every nuance of the production of the record and also the way he figured out how to promote it."

"He lived for making this record until the end, and that's what kept him alive," says Calderón. "I think he would have passed away faster if he didn't have a creative ride that he had at the end, and I'm glad to have been a coconspirator with him, because the wavelength that we rode at that point just kept him going."

A stirring example of this kind of studio collaboration is found on the blues number "Rub Me Raw," which on the surface appears to be a raucous but standard tribute to the music that in one way or another inspired so many of the collected talents around him, but Zevon made sure the lament contained a painful profession of his experience, including his seeking refuge in substance abuse one last time: "Know these blues are gonna rub me raw / Every single cure seems to be against the law." The belligerently searing slide guitar played with bone-cutting passion by Joe Walsh accentuates each line:

> *Now I'm shaking all over*
> *I'm a shattering mass*
> *But I'm gonna sit up straight*
> *I'm going to take it with class*
>
> *Old man used to tell me*
> *"Son, never look back,*
> *Move on to the next case.*
> *Fold your clothes and pack."*

Incorporating the cold advice of his fast-talking gangster father, Zevon closes the final verse with an act of defiance against those who would try in vain to slap Band-Aid aphorisms on his gaping emotional wound, recalling his thieving character from

"The Indifference of Heaven" thumbing his nose at trite rock-star empathy in the face of despair.

I don't want your pity or your fifty-dollar words
I don't share your need to discuss the absurd

"Warren wrote this great song called 'Please Stay' that is to this day so touching and powerful," says Calderón, who would later bring in veteran session saxophonist Gil Bernal, whose work in the 1950s with both the Coasters and Duane Eddy lent a traditional torch song eminence to the track. "I remember him playing it for me, singing, 'Please stay / Two words I've thought I'd never learn to say / Don't go away / Please stay.' He called me and said, 'I wrote this last night. It's really simple. "Don't leave me here / When so many things so hard to see are clear / I need you near to me."' It was beautifully heartbreaking."

"I'm more interested in communicating what meager ideas I have about living and I'm interested in saying goodbye to a few people," said Zevon in the VH1 documentary, during which he admitted that just waking up every day became somewhat of a surprise to him. "I have certain things to say to people and I seemed to have been given the opportunity to get them down and get 'em recorded and get 'em out, for which I am very grateful."

Calderón confessed the obvious to me during one lengthy afternoon conversation: It would be challenging under normal circumstances to quickly and efficiently write and record songs beneath a looming deadline with his closest friend, but beneath the specter of death, it was proving immensely difficult. Still, having dealt with illness in his family, he was fully prepared to steel himself against the peaks and valleys of shifting moods during both the good and bad days to come. This included the social calisthenics involved in avoiding rankled confrontation or allowing his friend to succumb to deep bouts of depression without judgment. Calderón parsed his words to provide comfort and encouragement whenever it was called for, as well as draw on what he called "the capacity to compartmentalize," approaching any complex task as if he were a soldier in battle: "I would tell myself every day, 'He hired me to be there and get this album done.'" He told me before we began, 'I want to leave my kids something.' So that became my mission, and as a soldier, no matter what I was feeling, no matter what I was going through, *boom*, there I go."

"There is no *The Wind* without Jorge," cites Jordan Zevon. "There were times he had to prop my father up in front of the microphone just to get a verse out of him. It was like a dog trying to squeeze the sound out of a chew toy through its tiny holes."

Zevon appreciated the effort, even if the pain and anguish of his disease became too much to bear. "The beauty of songwriting and recording and playing and working with Jorge is that you're engaged in the moment," Zevon explained to VH1. "We all, more or less, know that's the lesson: to stay in the moment."

Added to the array of prescription medicines he was gobbling down, Zevon began drinking almost immediately after learning of his illness, hints of his past calling out from the core of this new tragedy. "He told me, 'What do I have to lose?' but he didn't want anyone to know about it," remembers Brigette Barr. "I hate this, but I did what he asked me to do, so I became his sneaky enabler. He would have me buy the alcohol and put it in his sodas at the studio. He decided that he was not going to be in *any* kind of pain, physically or emotionally."

Predictably, there were stretches of cantankerousness and incoherence. All the while, undaunted, Calderón kept it together, stood strong, and prodded and inspired his dying friend to keep writing. "In the beginning, when we embarked on *The Wind*, I told him, 'Two things. Let's be totally honest with each other. No bullshit, because it's better for us to do that, and also let's keep having a great time. Let's keep laughing. Let's not talk about . . . *you know what*. Let's just have fun.'"

It was in the pursuit of fun that prompted Calderón and Zevon to visit the Cave, actor/writer/director, and Zevon's old neighbor, Billy Bob Thornton's West Hollywood basement studio in October. Originally designed by Slash, the frizzy-haired, Les Paul–slinging guitarist for Guns N' Roses, and built on the site of a 1920s speakeasy—no more of a Zevonian location could there be—the Cave still exists today, and Thornton uses it as a musical hideaway for like-minded musicians. During the visit, Zevon humbly requested Thornton's band take a stab at his hero Bob Dylan's haunting 1973 ballad for the film *Pat Garrett and Billy the Kid*, another classic western-themed song that reflected his mood. "Aside from one false start, what you hear on the record is the second and only full take," remembers Calderón. "There were some great musicians there that night and the slide solo from Randy Mitchell, who was playing with Billy at the time, was *really* fantastic. Everything was live. No overdubs at all.

"I also remember there were a lot of people there hanging out, movie producers and hangers-on, but we were in our own little world cutting that song. I was in the control room and everybody else was on the floor, because since I was producing I liked to be in there playing the bass and listening to the speakers instead of earphones, and I remember there were wall-to-wall people in there. But Warren never showboated, he just did his thing. To me the entire experience and the recording was such a gospel thing."

During the final chorus Zevon sings, "Open up! Open up!" with his usual heart-felt desperation, beseeching the gates of heaven to accept this sinner, this rogue, with all his flaws and genius, his broken ego and fading light. "When he started singing that, I mean, goose bumps, man," says Calderón.

It should be pointed out that this is the first album in some time in which Zevon brings the piano back to the fore, something he fought vehemently against for most of the 1980s and '90s, so much so that he demanded to be paid as a session musician if he played the instrument on his own records. His embrace of electronic keyboards and mostly the guitar—both acoustic (twelve-string) and electric—was an explicit rejection of the creative tool that first inspired him before making him a songwriter and a star. It had now come full circle, as it was the primary instrument he would play on the record, and finally, the one on which he would perform in public for the very last time.

Smack in the middle of the album's sessions, with life slipping away, David Letterman would dedicate an entire *Late Show* to his friend. "David *loved* Warren and they treated us with the utmost kindness," remembers Brigette Barr, who took the call when the producers told her they would provide anything Zevon needed to make a final public statement, both personally and musically.

Nattily attired in a pin-striped suit—head to toe in his requisite lucky gray and moving gingerly as if he might break apart into a million pieces on national televi-sion—Zevon performed three songs that heralded a final statement in a public forum that he had called a home away from home for more than two decades. "David Letterman is the best friend my music ever had," he effused in front of the VH1 cameras before walking into the spotlight with reverent solemnity to touch on all of his most well-worn themes.

Zevon would play moving versions of "Genius," "Mutineer," and "Roland the Headless Thompson Gunner" to an audience rapt in the tense uneasiness of what transpired before them: Two men who had shared humor and mutual professional and personal respect for decades were saying goodbye. Letterman is barely able to keep it together, especially in his heartfelt opening and his interview segments with Zevon, who to his lasting credit defuses every difficult encounter with his deftly measured sense of humor. "You heard about the flu?" Zevon smiles to open the seg-ment and then explains succinctly, "I might have made a tactical error in not going to a physician for twenty years . . . it was one of those phobias that really didn't pay off." It is still to this day the most riveting television I've experienced, and, being a fan, a bittersweet trek through anger, bargaining, and acceptance.

Famously, Letterman would ask if there was something about life and death

Zevon knew that the rest of us not facing it head-on could not. "Not unless I know how much you're supposed to enjoy every sandwich," Zevon answered without a hint of sarcasm. It would be the statement left to us, the exclamation point on his memorable "I'll Sleep When I'm Dead" that would inspire a tribute album a year after his death.

But it is these final three songs, and what they depict with grandeur, that put a ribbon on the performing portion of a life in music that so many of us had grown up with and had become inspired by and felt so possessive of.

It begins with a tender reading of "Mutineer." Zevon is seated at a black grand piano and accompanied by a warmly played trumpet and a dual flute harmony, his voice ragged and torn with the paroxysmal emotions of survival: the pills, the anxiety, the pain. The microphone is turned up to allow for his straining breaths. He miraculously hits every note, stripped of the artifice unfairly attributed to him. No more "Excitable Boy" walking on the tightrope between death- wish and mania. The song becomes his personal manifesto, with lyrical insights busting at the seams:

Yo ho ho and a bottle of rum
Hoist the mainsail, here I come
Ain't no room on board for the insincere
You're my witness
I'm your mutineer

I was born to rock the boat
Some may sink but we will float
Grab your coat, let's get out of here
You're my witness
I'm your mutineer

He concludes with "Grab your coat, let's get out of here" one last time, looking up from the piano with a telling sideways glance that lets us all know we are indeed watching a finale as he brings us inside once more. We truly become his witness, as we'd always been, as he was always our fearlessly defiant mutineer.

Helping Letterman introduce the next song, "Genius," as "modestly titled" with a chuckle, Zevon ends the exhilarating rendition accompanied by a string quartet standing with his back to the audience and gently moving his hands to conduct. Not once have I watched this that the hair fails to stand up at the back of my neck.

This is Zevon showing the world his deepest love of classical arrangements and his incredible prowess to bend its purest nuances to his will.

The show ends with Letterman gushing about having begged Zevon to play the final song he will offer to the masses, "Roland the Headless Thompson Gunner." Backed by the full force of the World's Most Dangerous Band, the nickname for Paul Shaffer's world-class musical outfit that had grown in stature and legend over the years and also had the distinction of being ably led by Zevon in their leader's absence several times, the songwriter tells his sordid tale of the haunted mercenary "knee-deep in gore" whose time stands still until he "evens up the score." As he sits at the piano for one last song, we wonder, how many times has he sung it? Written during those free and easy days of the pauper troubadour as ex-patriot, playing in an Irish pub outside of Barcelona, so young and wild, he and his wife drifting along on the fumes of art, hardly sober enough to dare dream of coming back to the States at the behest of Jackson Browne to begin an epic journey that would end on a stool at the center of the Ed Sullivan Theater.

And here he sits playing the three-decade old musical short story on the same stage where Elvis and the Beatles tore through cultural boundaries to plant the flag of rock 'n' roll forever. The final lines "The eternal Thompson Gunner / Still wandering through the night / Now it's ten years later / But he still keeps up the fight" reverberate like a tolling bell through the old building, and when the song is done, he nods to the band, prompting an emotional Letterman to come up from behind, shake his hand, and tell a dying man, "Enjoy every sandwich."

"The most emotional moment for me working with Warren toward the end was certainly the David Letterman show, because it was such a physical effort for him to do it," remembers Danny Goldberg. "When he came offstage and I gave him a hug, he said to me, 'You know, I wish I really only did have the flu,' I started crying. It was just such raw emotion."

Letterman would later reflect to the *New York Times*: "Here's a guy looking right down the barrel of the gun and if he wanted to indulge himself in great hyperbole in that circumstance, who wouldn't forgive him? But that was perfect, the simplicity of that. If this guy is not a poet, who is?'"

"After the show I was in the dressing room with Warren, and David came in and he was hysterically crying," remembers Brigette Barr. "I walked out. I couldn't take it. It was breaking my heart. I saw this very stoic and funny man so broken down. It was really touching. I mean, I got it, obviously. I would go home and cry too at night, but he was just so kind and continued to offer us whatever Warren needed. He sent food for Christmas. He was really a kind friend to him and Warren really appreciated it."

Back in L.A., Calderón was finishing up "Prison Grove," a chain-gang dirge made eerily seductive by glorious slide guitar provided by Ry Cooder and the unison chants by Calderón, Billy Bob Thornton, Jackson Browne, and Jordan Zevon. The song was initially sparked by something Calderón had blurted out when he and Zevon were recording background vocals years before and the latter was tickled by how much the former was struggling to hit the high notes. Calderón remembers screaming, "What do you think I am, your fucking boy in prison that you can order me around to sing this shit?" And once again the two were off cracking each other up with prison jokes, which evolved into Zevon saying, "See you at Prison Grove!" whenever the two would break. "'Prison Grove' just stuck with me, the title was *so* good. So when he went to New York I started playing this guitar riff, writing down some lyrics, and suddenly I had the first three verses and the structure of the song, and when he got back he loved it and we decided he should write another verse and he came up with the creepy last verse, which is 'Knick Knack Paddy Wack / They say you'll hear your own bones crack / When they bend you back to bible black / Then you'll find your love.' It was also his idea for the chorus: 'Shine on all these broken lives / Shine on / Shine the light on me.' And you know what's great? He looked at me at the end when it was recorded and he said, 'Jorge, 'Prison Grove' is the cornerstone of this record.' He embraced the whole idea of comparing his fate to being in prison on death row looking out the window at Prison Grove. I mean, we were on a roll. I look back and I know now that we were on a high level. It was something that in the midst of that kind of situation it brought out the best in us, because we truly understood what we were doing and we trusted each other."

The very last song Warren Zevon would sing into a microphone for posterity was the very first song he began composing when he received his diagnosis, and it may be one of his finest. Its story from idea to composition to recording to its eventual inclusion as the final song on his final album, and thus his final statement, may be as dramatic and romantic as any tale that has filled these pages.

"When I got the diagnosis, I picked up the guitar and found myself writing this song," Zevon remembered mere days before recording it. "It might be a little of a woe-is-me song, but it made me realize what I was going to do with the rest of the time."

"He said, 'I wrote down these lines, 'Shadows are falling and I'm running out of breath / Keep me in your heart for a while,' and it just struck me, and I said to him, 'That's the song you need to write," says Calderón. "Then we got into working through everything else and as the months went by and I'd ask him, 'Are you doing anything on "Keep Me in Your Heart"?' And he would always say, 'Ahh . . .

not really.' So we kept going and wrote other things thinking that we would use. We have this other song that hasn't been recorded yet called 'I Volunteered.' It's about looking back on your life and saying, 'I don't blame you; I volunteered.' It was a really good song, but we didn't use it because 'Keep Me in Your Heart' *had* to be done and I kept telling him, 'That's your song. You have to express it.'

"He finally called me and said, 'Jorge, you're going to have to help me with this.' But I told him I couldn't write that song with him—or, more to the point, *for* him. I told him, 'You have to.' And I remember he said, 'I can't. It's just too heartbreaking and painful for me. You have to put on your songwriter hat and help me with this one. You know how to do it! We've been doing it for fucking years!' He got really mad at me. 'You got to help me with this!' And I finally said, 'Okay!' So I swallowed hard and saw what he had already written."

Shadows are falling and I'm running out of breath
Keep me in your heart for a while
If I leave you it doesn't mean I love you any less
Keep me in your heart for a while
When you get up in the morning and you see that crazy sun

Keep me in your heart for a while
The train is leaving nightly called when all is said and done
Keep me in your heart for a while

"I read that and thought, 'Oh fuck,'" remembers Calderón. "My heart was breaking with each line."

Beginning with composing a bridge that would act as a romantic release to the tenser verses, Calderón confronted a reticent Zevon: "He said to me, 'I don't know, Jorge. I don't know.' I still have the paper where I took a red pen and I put an X over those words because, remember, whenever either of us did not like the other's idea we'd trash it and go onto something else."

Calderón instead worked with Zevon to fill in the second verse, which was originally, "Sometimes when you're doing this and that around the house. . . ." In the fashion they'd perfected over the years and leaned on during the passing months of attrition, Zevon suggested, "How about 'simple things'?" Calderón quickly wrote it into the lyric sheet. Zevon then continued drawing from the emotional lyrical well that has never failed him: "Maybe you will think of me and smile." Calderón jotted it down and offered, "I know I'm tied to you like the buttons on your blouse," but

Zevon was unsure and said, "I don't know about buttons on your blouse, man. How about bangles or beads?" Nothing was decided until they would finally lay it down.

Meanwhile, time was slipping away. Zevon continued to battle deep valleys of depression, which would result in his disappearing for days and sometimes weeks, a mystery even to his son. "At the time both of us were not in a great place, so we conveniently avoided each other," recalls Jordan. "Even though we should have been embracing each other. But we did have these intimate moments. I remember lying in bed with him and watching *Jeopardy* and trying impress him with how many answers I would get. One time he turned to me and said, 'I'm afraid' and I said, 'Me too.'"

The job of shielding Zevon from anyone during these periods and throughout his illness fell to his personal manager, who'd taken on much more than was expected of one. "I was the only one for months, except for Jorge and Noah [Scot Snyder, coproducer and engineer], who had any contact with him," says Brigette Barr. "I was the person that went to the doctor with him. I was the person that talked to the kids and his business managers. Every relative, every friend would call my office. I was the one that set up his home health care. It was a hard relationship, because I was still having to work my other artists but needed to give him so much of my personal time. I had to go through everything with him. He wouldn't go anywhere that I didn't go with him. We had to film the VH1 special. I was in the background of every scene. It was all-consuming."

"When I found out how sick he was I said to Jorge, 'Well now's the time to get a bottle of vodka, some coke, weed, and cigarettes and go over there and just fucking sit down and have a ball, because let's face it, the wick is burning down, so why not chase it?'" remembers Zevon's longtime combative friend and hearty collaborator Waddy Wachtel. "We wanted to, but we never did it."

Crystal Zevon remembers: "I went to see him at his apartment and he said, 'Crystal, I started drinking. I'm sorry. I wish I'd done it differently.' I said, 'You don't need to regret it, but the people who supported you when you got sober are still there.' He never did follow through with that, and it got bad for a while until he got so sick he couldn't drink. But you know, he said to me all along, 'They'll give me all them Elvis drugs.' I said, 'Is that what you want?' It was a difficult situation, because we'd been divorced for a long time. He was looking for answers, but I knew very well that I couldn't give him any. Those were his to find."

"He checked out," concludes Barr. "I think it was right after Christmas where for a couple of months he didn't want to deal with anything and he was drinking and drugging, the *legal* drugs, and I think emotionally and physically closing himself off. We went so fast into this record for a while it kept him occupied enough that he didn't deal with it, and I think after our little Christmas together with the kids it started to really hit him."

"We had these four songs that Warren had to sing, including 'Keep Me in Your Heart,' and we were waiting on him to be able to do it because he was so down and depressed," says Calderón. "He'd say, 'I can't do that. You do it, Jorge.' And I would tell him, 'I can't do it. It's your fucking record'. He was so insecure about it."

Calderón, Noah Scot Snyder, and Barr cajoled Zevon with pep talks, appealing to his sense of closure. "We would tell him, 'We're almost there. You've got so much more to say!'" says Barr. "When we started out we all said we'd do what we can and if we can't finish it, we can't finish it. I kept telling him, 'It's no big deal. Just do what you can,' without any pressure, but he was so close at that point that it was like, 'You've got to finish this! There's just a little bit more to say and you know it.' And those last couple of songs were the most emotional and honest."

It was during these final, lost months when Zevon would be invited backstage at Bob Dylan's show in Los Angeles. Since hearing of his illness, Dylan had been playing "Mutineer," "Lawyers, Guns and Money," and "Accidentally Like a Martyr" every night. Zevon describes to Jon Pareles of the *New York Times* the two men standing silent before Dylan mumbled condolences and said, "I hope you like what you hear." Flooded with memories of a career trying to follow the pathways of the man he said time and again "invented my job," Zevon concluded that listening to Dylan play his songs in tribute was "beyond an honor."

Of course, the ever-present Barr was there and recounted to me, "Honest to God, I think it was one of, not compared to having children, but one of the happiest times of his life. To hear somebody he respected so much and shouting like an excited little kid, 'He's singing my song! He's singing my song!' He couldn't believe it. It was so beautiful. It meant so much to him. I don't think Dylan realized what it meant to him."

"Finally, he got the strength to finish the record," says Calderón. "He called me and said, 'Okay, I'm ready. Let's do it.'"

April 12, 2003: The final vocal sessions for *The Wind*. Zevon on "the couch of pain" flanked by Calderón and his daughter Ariel, within days of giving birth to his grandsons, Maximus Patrick and Augustus Warren, whom he had vowed to live long enough to meet. "That day I told him we had chosen the names for the boys and that Gus's middle name was to be Warren and . . . what can you say about it? The funny thing about those kinds of scenes with my dad is they were profound and incredible and amazing, but they were also always sort of awkward and surreal. You've got that kind of vibe anyway in that apartment and then it's crowded for a recording session. Everyone sitting awkwardly perched on a couch next to him as he's singing. But even so, it was incredible. The song is obviously heavy and moving, but also beautiful."

Visibly weaker, as depicted in the VH1 documentary, his hands shaking involuntarily, eerily reflecting his lyrical confession of "Desperados Under the Eaves," and his eyes struggling to focus on the lyric sheet, Zevon gingerly worked his voice through the song.

In what may be one of the most arresting vocals in popular music history—sung by a man hanging onto his final breaths and expressing its magnitude with penetratingly vulnerable poignancy—it becomes a final, concussive measure of Warren Zevon's tortured art.

Engine driver's headed north up to Pleasant Stream
Keep me in your heart for a while
These wheels keep turnin' but they're runnin' out of steam
Keep me in your heart for a while

Sha-lalala-lala-li-lalala-lo
Keep me in your heart for a while
Sha-lalala-lala-li-lalala-lo
Keep me in your heart for a while

Keep me in your heart for a while

"Before we sat down to do it, we realized we hadn't decided on those final lines in the bridge that I'd written but Warren rejected," remembers Calderón. "Then he said, 'You know what, Jorge, it's all good. The line about the "buttons on your blouse" and the "hold me in your thoughts" bridge is great'. So I took back the paper that I had crossed out the bridge with an X and put all the lyrics together and he sang it beautifully."

Hold me in your thoughts
Take me to your dreams
Touch me as I fall into view
When the winter comes
Keep the fires lit
And I will be right next to you

"The day he recorded 'Keep Me in Your Heart' his vocal was *perfect*," recalls Barr. "I don't know where it came from, but it was so beautiful. There were other times it was so hard for Jorge to drag a vocal out of him, but that day, for that song, I couldn't believe it. We all looked at each other: 'Where did that come from?' It was flawless. They say sometimes when people are dying, they get a last burst, but *that* was scary. It was like divine intervention. Everyone had chills. It was incredible."

"To this day that song is very moving to a lot of people," Calderón concludes. "Whenever I perform it everyone tells me how beautiful it is. I am heartbreakingly happy to have been part of a song that almost *didn't* get written, but it *did*, and I owe this to him and our perseverance. Under all that heartbreaking pressure, we did it. But that's how hard it was to finish, because it was 'It's too painful.' And I have to say the women in his life that were around him at the time had a lot to do with convincing him that what we had was good. They loved the 'button on your blouse' bridge. They said, 'Warren, don't you see how great this is?' Now it proves itself."

Crystal Zevon made sure I understood something key to the completion of *The Wind* that was crucial to comprehending the artist as the man: "The thing that stands out for me and that I think people should know, and in many ways I always sort of knew and considered, is that Warren was the artist *first*. That was who he was. So in the end when he finished his album, he was *done*, and he became the *man*. I believe, after he completed the music, he stayed alive to see his grandsons born. He stayed alive to be a grandfather, to be a father, to be a husband—to be the man and not the macho man."

Four months later on August 23, 2003, Artemis Records released *The Wind* to a deluge of rave reviews and unprecedented publicity for a Warren Zevon release that did not include a song about werewolves. Just a few days before his death, Zevon would learn that *The Wind* had entered the *Billboard* charts at no. 16, his highest charting album since 1980's *Bad Luck Streak in Dancing School*, selling 147,000. Dying, it turned out for Zevon, was truly "showbiz," and his best career move to date. "Heaven knows I've been pounding this subject into the ground for decades," he told *Rolling Stone*'s Robert Fricke. "You get in front of people and say, 'Here's the deal we all dread. But here's some laughs. I don't see what harm it could do.'"

When I pressed Danny Goldberg about his label providing Zevon a forum to express his final musical wishes and its eventual success, the pride in his voice was evident. "I don't sing or write songs, but I love music," he said. "I've spent most of my adult life around musicians and trying to make myself useful and trying to get paid for it, and there are a handful of highlights, and working with Warren is absolutely one. I really got to know him and I miss him. I go back and listen to his work a lot and I think as a songwriter, particularly as a lyricist, he's one of the greats. He's absolutely in the heavyweight division. It's one of the real honors of my life that I got to work with him."

The Wind would go on to be nominated for five Grammys and would win two, both honors firsts for Warren Zevon, who would not live to see it.

"I think my dad would have seen the tribute as very poetic," says Ariel today. "It was very true to his experience as a musician in the business: 'Yeah, sure, recognize me when I'm dying or after I'm gone.' I think that he absolutely had a sense of macabre sarcasm around that, but I think that after he had worked relentlessly for a lifetime, to be finally recognized in that kind of a spotlight would have meant a tremendous deal to him. And in the same vein, all the people that came into the studio for that last album meant a huge deal to him too. He really respected and admired his peers: All those incredible artists that came to the studio in his last days absolutely meant the world to him."

"He got to see the record come out, which I was so grateful for, and the VH1 special, but he didn't get to hear the Grammy nominations, which I wish he would have been able to see, because we talked about that quite a bit," says Brigette Barr. "He'd ask me, 'Do you think I'll get a Grammy? They'll at least give me a folk Grammy, won't they?' And I'd tell him, 'Absolutely!' But when they announced those five nominations that morning, I would have been happy if they said one. Then they kept going. It was like, 'He's up there doing this! He's making this happen! He's driving this show!'"

Ariel, Jordan, and Jorge would be there to accept the awards and join in with Jackson Browne, Emmylou Harris, Timothy B. Schmit, Billy Bob Thornton, and Dwight Yoakam for a combined video and live tribute version of "Keep Me in Your Heart."

"When I was on the stage to accept his award, I held the Grammy up to the sky, and I imagined him saying, 'Oh, yeah, Johnny.'"

A Portrait of the Artist as a Young Man. *Courtesy of the Crystal Zevon Collection*

BACKS TURNED LOOKING DOWN THE PATH

Some writers are only appreciated for what they do at the beginning and what they do at the end of their career.

—Warren Zevon

Count this as an epilogue. Every great epic has one and Warren Zevon's music deserves it. Turns out he may have already given us one. He insisted for years that "Back Turned Looking Down the Path," the third track and perhaps the least-known song off his outstanding debut Asylum record, may have been his best work, or at least underrated. "He wrote it when we left for Spain and he used to say that it's the best love song he ever wrote,'" says Crystal Zevon. "Well, it's *not* his greatest song, but I love the sentiment of it."

If nothing else, it is a beautifully structured song, sonically pleasing from the rock-steady backbeat and grooved bass line to the warmly strummed acoustic guitar and engaging acoustic lead. And then there is Zevon, confidently singing without trepidation about nagging trepidation.

I was caught between the years
Cost me nearly all my tears
With my back turned looking down the path

Hit me like a ton of bricks
Had to have my outlook fixed
With my back turned looking down the path

There is an unpredictably melodious half-time bridge, sweetly sung and lyrically compelling, which works against some of the grappling with regret: such a bold statement from a man who is not quite *too* young, but young enough to not apologize for it.

People always ask me why
What's the matter with me?
Nothing matters when I'm with my ba-a-by
With my back turned looking down the path

And so Warren Zevon died on September 7, 2003.

I found out about it somehow: a friend, an Internet notice, a phone call or email. Not sure. Didn't matter. Doesn't matter now.

"I think I probably heard that Warren had passed from Danny Goldberg," recalls his old traveling buddy Burt Stein. "Maybe it was J. D. Souther, who is a dear and close friend. Or Jackson even. I can't remember exactly when I heard it, but the thought of him suddenly not being here was just heartbreaking."

Many waxed poetic about his passing, including celebrated authors and journalists. He received tributary asides on network news broadcasts, classic rock radio accolades, and blurbs in magazines, wherein several respected contemporaries and students of his art lent their voices to the multitudes that still miss him today.

His friend then Tennessee senator Steve Cohen would eulogize Zevon: "When I first learned of Warren's illness, whenever we talked, I guess I got a little maudlin, we talked about how good our friendship was and how much he meant to me. And I guess he could tell I was about to lose it. Warren cautioned me, 'Don't get bluesy.' Well, I remembered that and tried not to get bluesy again. His last message to me was about a week ago and he told me, 'It's really not quite so harrowing as it sounds. Don't worry.' Warren was concerned about us while we were concerned about him."

Pulitzer Prize–winning Irish poet and collaborator on two of Zevon's songs Paul Muldoon took a year to compose a dramatically metered poem titled "Sillyhow Stride," done in the style of Dante, which he stressed to me was a form most associated with the rawest poetic expression of death. The lengthy, stream-of-consciousness elegy contains references to many of Zevon's most tormenting and beloved themes, as well as endearing snapshots from their time working together: "It was inspired partly by one of my favorite poets, John Donne. Toward the end, Warren wrote me and asked, 'What should I be reading?' So I sent him much of Donne's poetry, including 'Death Be Not Proud.'"

"I couldn't go to Warren's funeral, because it would be like going to my own," said Waddy Wachtel before we parted ways. "Even though we were miles apart sometimes, we were still inside each other deeply. What can I say? He was an obnoxious asshole *and* a great guy. What a musical pal I had in my life."

"He wanted to be an outlaw and he *was* an outlaw," concluded his dear friend

George Gruel. "He was a mutineer, a pirate. I went to Frank and Jesse James's home a couple of years ago in Kansas and there was a gift shop with little old ladies running it and I played them 'Frank and Jesse James' and one of them says, 'I've never heard that!' It really blew them away."

"He was a tortured soul, which is why he wrote those great songs," reasoned guitarist Zeke Zirngiebel when I shared with him the subtitle to this book. "Of course it was all brought on by him, by his demons. But you know, I remember talking to a friend who was good friends with Bill Szymczyk, the guy who produced all the Eagles stuff, when there was talk of him possibly producing an album for Zevon in the later years, and Szymczyk asked my friend, 'Well, is he drinking?' and he told him no, so Szymczyk says, 'Ah, then I don't want to do it. The songs are all going to be "I'm clean and I'm sober and my life is groovy." I don't want that. I want the *rubbing a pot roast all over his chest* guy.'"

"Beyond the classical structure and elegance that his material had, the one piece of advice that any young writer would infer from listening to Warren's songs is 'Don't be afraid of language,'" J. D. Souther told me from his Tennessee ranch one chilly December day in 2017. "This guy was not afraid to say anything, and I think that kind of boldness is what makes a career singular and what makes it unique."

"It's a tough thing to even think about him being gone, because Warren had such a powerful influence over my life in so many ways," says Andy Slater, who would go on from his early days of pulling Zevon from the abyss to producing and managing the Beastie Boys, Fiona Apple, and Macy Gray, among others, and running Capitol Records. "I miss him, you know? I miss him. He was at my brother's wedding. I was at a loss for words to speak, and I will never forget this, Warren wrote my speech. Right there. One paragraph, and it was as good as any verse."

"The Warren Zevon I knew was a real role model of how to be a man," Artemis Records founder Danny Goldberg said when we wrapped up our discussion. "He stuck to his guns. He stuck to his artistic vision. He was extremely loyal to his friends. He was polite. He had a real sense of what it was to be Warren Zevon. He took his vocation seriously. He took being a family member seriously. Now, like all artists, he could be a little irrational sometimes and a little self-centered, a little paranoid, but he kept those qualities in check and was really just the greatest. I loved him."

Brigette Barr, his last personal manager, who received the phone call from Zevon's girlfriend Ryan Rayston when the paramedics failed to revive him, wanted me to know this: "There was such a sensitive side to him and how much he wanted adulation and needed it and how much he appreciated it when he got it. I think he tried to play it cool a lot in his life. I think his sarcasm and his attitudes left people believing that he was a lot tougher than he was."

"I hope that his whole body of work will be re-celebrated, by a whole new generation of writers and listeners," Jackson Browne told *Rolling Stone* mere weeks after his long-time friend's death. "His songs are like short stories—the best songs always are. They tell much more about life than books; they communicate so much more than a longer volume would. But it's funny. Here we are, talking at great lengths, to describe something that was the very opposite of that—a guy who could say something in a few words that was immediately understood."

Taylor Goldsmith, who has kept Zevon's music alive for a new generation by covering many of his songs with his band, Dawes, concludes that the songwriter's outlook is more suited for the contemporary world we're living in now more than ever: "I feel like it's a more cynical time, where the more serious and sensitive someone gets the more we're likely to wince. I think the younger generation, who look for songwriters that speak for them in the way that they see the world, the way that they're willing to laugh at everything, the way they're willing to take an ironic perspective, even to our own detriment, that Zevon might actually be the greatest ambassador of it we could find. Not that nothing is sacred, but that *everything* is sacred; we can talk about a Hawaiian vacation and really probe the depths through that just as easily as we can talk about your broken heart. That's something I always try to communicate when I'm trying to turn people on to it. He was the perfect blend of all of it in a way that I feel should bring us further in rather than push us further away."

Zevon's former bandleader David Landau was exiting his favorite movie theater in Hollywood when he saw a man wearing a Charlie Brown T-shirt, showing the famously forlorn Charles Schulz character standing with his head down and looking sad, with a caption that read, I STILL MISS WARREN ZEVON. "It blew my mind," he told me. "I was going to stop the guy and ask him about it, but it was just one of those things that happened in a second and he was gone. It was the perfect, unexpected thing . . . and so true."

His son Jordan insisted to me one day, "From what I've observed he had a hard time telling the people that he loved how he truly felt. I think the difference between us is that I've learned to make sure that I express those feelings in the here and now. Of course, I didn't shoot Magnums out the window, so I'm a little more approachable. But I do hope for the people who may wonder if my dad truly and deeply loved them, if there is any hesitation, they should be rest assured. You're not alone; it's hard to hug a hand grenade."

"I really feel in some ways like the fans who listen to his music know him the most intimately," Zevon's daughter Ariel told me when I asked her to share something about her dad that maybe all of us didn't know. "I feel like what Jordan said of him not knowing how to show love in person, in his intimate relationships, well, I think that's what he did in his music. I think his most intimate message is in his lyrics and his melodies and in his compositions, truly. He was a musician through and through and that was his means of expressing his innermost, truest insights and feelings. In some ways I feel like the people who are intimate with his songs and music know him more deeply than those of us who were closest to him in person."

We'll go walkin' hand in hand
Laughin' fit to beat the band
With our backs turned looking down the path

"I remember him holding the twins at the end," says his cousin, Paul Zevon, who had his own bouts with addiction that he told me his cousin helped him through. "His face was all bloated and you could hardly recognize him from all the drugs, but he made it. He got to hold his grandsons. And the look on his face was pure joy."

Crystal Zevon left me with this moment she shared with her ex-husband a few weeks before he was gone. "When the boys were born Warren got a room at the hotel across the street from the hospital and he came over and saw Ariel and them. Then he took my arm and led me out into the hallway and said, 'I know where the chapel is in this joint. Let's go up there.' The door was locked but there was a bench out in the hallway in a little foyer in front of the chapel and he said, 'Let's sit down.' So we sat there holding hands, both of us kind of teary in our joy over the babies and being grandparents. Years before he had written a song called 'Old Girl' about us growing old together that he would never perform or record because we had split up. But I remember sitting there and he said, 'We made it to the front porch didn't we old girl?'"

Some may have and some may not
God, I'm thankful for what I got
With my back turned looking down the path
With my back turned looking down the path
With my back turned looking down the path

ACKNOWLEDGMENTS

This book would not be without the contributions of these incredibly gifted people, many of whom provided the greatest perk in writing it; getting closer to one of my favorite songwriters and a continued inspiration to this day; the late, great, Warren Zevon.

To my loving wife, Erin D. Moore, who was by my side against the front of the stage for my very last Warren Zevon show on a snowy night in Rochester, New York, at the Water Street Music Hall on the eleventh day of March 2000. For your support and your inspiring art and for being the best mom ever, I love you. I will forever remember you reading my "Angry Ode to the Captain" so beautifully on my forty-fourth birthday on the spot of the old Pageant bookstore on Astor Place in New York City.

Also thanx to my daughter, Scarlet, who will be nine when I finish this book and ten when it hits the shelves, and who is getting better and better every day on the piano, an instrument I have yet to fathom. You could have been named Zevon, if you were a boy, but instead you are my girl and my best buddy and one of the only reasons I come up for air when working on a book.

To my hearty and beautiful assistant, Danielle Sariyan, who transcribed every interview in this volume and kept me off several ledges during its final weeks, I offer my sincerest gratitude and I hope the baby you carry as I finish this loves life as much as you do.

To the Zevon family—ex-wife, Crystal; Warren and Crystal's daughter, Ariel; and his son, Jordan—I thank you for your blessing right from the beginning and your invaluable insights into the man and the artist. And to the extended family: Uncle Sanford "Sandy" Zevon, his wife, Madeline, and their son, Paul, for their time and memories. It was Jordan's call when I was on the road that gave me the kick in the ass I needed to bring this home. I am in his debt not only for our impromptu talks, on and off the record, but for his sending me audio clips of outtakes and demos from his private stash, and his generous inclusion of all of his dad's lyrics that are a cherished part of this work. Oh, and to his sweet and highly motivated girlfriend,

Suzan Alparslan, for her incredible dedication to taking and compiling some of the intimate photos herein. And further appreciation in obtaining of the Zevon lyrical catalogue for this volume goes out to the yeoman's work done by Cody Schnieders of Universal Publishing Group and the Zevon Estate.

Jorge Calderón's commentary, insights, and memories provide a gravitas to this endeavor that could not have been achieved without him. He is a wonderful soul and one talented bastard, and his love for Warren pours out of him with such rare honesty that I can only hope it resonates in these pages. I am a better person for having known him.

To all the principals who shared their memories and lent intimate commentary to this work, especially the ultra-talented Waddy Wachtel, whose stories were both hilarious and moving, and the inimitable J. D. Souther for his intimate portraits of his dear friend.

Thanks to George Gruel (my first interview) for his infectious laughter and for putting the word out to many of the people above and below.

To Burt Stein, Danny Goldberg, Andy Slater, David Landau, Zeke Zirngiebel, J. D. Souther, Jimmy Wachtel (for bugging your brother to call me), Paul Muldoon (I owe you a brunch, so let's book it), and the dear Brigette Barr: Thanks to you all for your tales and passion.

I must thank my pal and songwriting hero Adam Duritz for his thoughts on the man with whom he once had a healthy obsession and for continuously plugging my efforts to any and all we meet as we work together on a joint literary venture, and for introducing me to Taylor Goldsmith—and thanks to you, Taylor, for giving me your time and thoughts. I love your band and your enthusiasm for reading this book.

A special thanks to my fellow Zevon author, Professor George Plasketes, for your fine book, for your quotes in this one, and for your words and notes of encouragement on this journey: Only you know what I went through.

I truly appreciate the efforts of Ms. Nicole Schmit from Burt Stein Entertainment for enduring my incessant requests to get Mr. Stein on the record. The same goes for Alexandra Pettus for assisting me greatly in nailing down Andy Slater, and Jill Hoffman for getting me together with J. D. Souther.

Also many thanks to Mark (Lauren) Gleed, the man who tried so hard to connect me with the late LeRoy Marinell, who unfortunately was very ill when I was working on this book and passed before we could speak. And gratitude to Beryl Foreman for your kind words of encouragement.

To my dear friend Peter Blasevick, thank you, as always, for sitting with me at the piano to help me better understand the musical depth of Warren Zevon's songwriting.

This is getting to be a habit I do not want to break. I expect your expertise for every book.

And thanks to my creative partner Roberto Tatis for touching up some of the photos in this volume.

Thanks to WarrenZevonAddict on YouTube for providing such incredible content that helped me review much of his past. I implore all fans and the interested to check out his channel. It is chock full of great Zevoniana.

Props to Relisten.net for the Zevon shows I listened to whilst enduring the long hours of working on the notations for this volume.

Thanks to filmmaker Connor Reid and his DP Gregg De Domenico for their support, mutual contacts, and invite to appear in their Zevon documentary. I wish them all the best.

Also, thanks to Carol Meyer for giving me insights into Warren's times with Tule in Beachwood Canyon when Jordan was "running around in dirty diapers."

Thanks to photographers Suzan Alparslan (www.suzanlparslan.com), Joel Bernstein (www.joelbernstein.com), and Andrew L. Seymour (www.aseymour.com) for allowing their wonderful images to appear in this work.

Special thanks to the woman who not only believes in my work but is my favorite editor ever, Bernadette Malavarca. This is my second book with you, and I hope we have a few more in us. You make this fun.

As always, last but certainly not least, to my mom and dad, Phyllis and James, for enduring the rock 'n' roll that blasted from my room.

To my brother P. J. and his wonderful family, and my sisters-in-law, Lauren and Shannon; their husbands, Donald and Tom; and all my nieces and nephews, Alex, Matthew, Ty, Claire, Sydney, Claudia, and Ava; my cousin (sis) Michelle and her husband, Gene, and their girls, Nicole and Gianna. I thank you for your support, but mostly for calling me family.

SOURCES

AUTHOR INTERVIEWS

Brigette Barr, February 20, 2017.

Jackson Browne, January 27 and March 18, 2017.

Jorge Calderón, September 11 and December 28, 2016.

Adam Duritz, February 17, 2017.

Danny Goldberg, September 28, 2016.

Taylor Goldsmith, February 15, 2017.

George Gruel, May 15, 2015.

David Landau, November 7, 2016.

Paul Muldoon, August 16, 2016.

George Plasketes, September 30, 2016.

Andy Slater, September 28, 2017.

J. D. Souther, December 1, 2017.

Burt Stein, August 10, 2016.

Jimmy Wachtel, November 10, 2016.

Waddy Wachtel, February 27, 2017.

Ariel Zevon, February 5, 2017.

Crystal Zevon, February 5, 2017.

Jordan Zevon, August 12, July 16, and September 20, 2016.

Sanford Zevon, December 16, 2017.

Madeline Zevon, December 16, 2017.

Paul Zevon, December 16, 2017.

Zeke Zirngiebel, December 11, 2016.

BOOKS

Avery, Ken. *Everything Is an Afterthought: The Life and Writings of Paul Nelson.* Seattle: Fantagraphics Books, 2011.

Christgau, Robert. *Record Guide: Rock Albums of the '70s.* Boston: Ticknor & Fields, 1981.

Courrier, Kevin. *Randy Newman's American Dreams.* Toronto: ECW Press, 2005.

Dylan, Bob. *Chronicles Volume 1.* New York, New York: Simon & Schuster, 2005.

Gavinson, Anita, and Jonathan Valania. *You Turn Me On, I'm a Radio: My Wild Rock 'n' Roll Life.* Philadelphia, 2012.

Goldberg, Danny. *Bumping into Geniuses: My Life Inside the Rock and Roll Business.* New York: Avery, 2009.

Hiney, Tom. *Raymond Chandler: A Biography.* New York: Grove Press, 1999.

Hoskyns, Barney. *Hotel California: Singer-Songwriters and Cocaine Cowboys in the LA Canyons, 1967–1968.* Hoboken: John Wiley & Sons, 2006.

Kerouac, Jack. *On the Road.* London: Penguin Classics, 2003.

King, Stephen. *Dr. Sleep.* New York: Scribner, 2013.

Marcus, Greil. *Mystery Train: Images of America in Rock 'n' Roll Music.* 6th ed. New York: Plume, 2015.

Nolan, Tom. *Ross Macdonald: A Biography.* New York: Scribner, 1999.

Plasketes, George. *Warren Zevon: Desperado of Los Angeles.* New York: Rowman & Littlefield, 2016.

Poe, Edgar Allan. "The Raven." In *The Yale Book of American Verse*, edited by Thomas R. Lounsbury. New Haven, CT: Yale University Press, 1912.

Preludes: Rare and Unreleased Recordings CD booklet.

Rilke, Rainer Maria. "Autumn Day." In *Ahead of All Parting: The Selected Poetry and Prose of Rainer Maria Rilke.* New York: Everyman's Library, Knopf, 1996.

Shelley, Mary. *Frankenstein.* New York: Bantam, 1981.

Shroder, Maurice Z. *Icarus: The Image of the Artist in French Romanticism.* Cambridge, MA: Harvard University Press, 1961.

Vonnegut Jr., Kurt. *Slaughterhouse-Five, or The Children's Crusade.* New York: Dell Publishing, 1969.

Zevon, Crystal. *I'll Sleep When I'm Dead.* New York: HarperCollins, 2007.

INTERNET

"Judd Apatow's Thoughts on Warren Zevon." Published on YouTube March 20, 2016, by DrSotosOctopus. https://www.youtube.com/watch?v=JhX2bPMYj10.

Allan Handelman Show, Rock Talk, IFITRocks.com. Published on YouTube September 18, 2012, by Allan Handelman. https://www.youtube.com/watch?v=pAbbSZ2us3o.

BBC.com, 2006.

"Browne Remembers Zevon." Rolling Stone.com. September 19, 2003.

Cohen, Steve. "The Genius." *KnoxViews* (Tennessee), October 14, 2006.

Skanse, Richard. "Warren Zevon." *Rolling Stone*, January 28, 2000.

MAGAZINES AND NEWSPAPERS

Alfonso, Barry. "Rock's Stout-Hearted Man: Warren Zevon." *Songwriter*, April 1981.

Barackman, Michael. "Warren Zevon: Jackson Browne as Producer." *Phonograph Record*, May 1976.

Berlins, Marcel. "Why Boxing Makes for Top-Class Writing." *Guardian*, January 2, 2007.

Branton, Michael. "Warren Zevon's Mystery Dance." *BAM*, March 7, 1980.

Campion, James. "Recalling the Eternal Wave: A Brief Conversation with the Legendary Brian Wilson." *Aquarian Weekly*, July 2, 2015.

DeCurtis, Anthony. "Warren Zevon's New LP: A Star-Studded Comeback." *Rolling Stone*, June 18, 1987.

Diliberto, Gioia. "Breaking the Cycle." *People*, August 6, 1984.

Duka, John. "Elizabeth Taylor: Journal of Recovery." *New York Times*, February 4, 1985.

Fenton, James. "Between Rock and a Hard Place." *Guardian*, September 19, 2003.

Fretts, Bruce. "Rocker Turned Scorer: Warren Zevon." *Entertainment Weekly*, June 4, 1993.

Fricke, David. "Warren Zevon: He Faced Death the Way He Faced Life—with Unflinching Rock & Roll." *Rolling Stone*, October 16, 2003.

Fusilli, Jim. "Warren Zevon, Song Noir Storyteller of Wit and Irony." *Wall Street Journal*, September 9, 2003.

Gilmore, Mikal. "Warren Zevon Takes Control of His Life and His Art." *Rolling Stone*, September 16, 1982.

Goldberg, Joe. "Hyperactive Ho-Hum?" *Creem*, May 1978.

Hards, Trevor. "Buried Treasure." *Mojo Filter*, August 1971.

Hilburn, Robert. "Warren Zevon: Cynicism Cum Concern." *Los Angeles Times*, August 8, 1976.

Lim, Gerrie. "Warren Zevon: The Mutineer and His Bounty." *The Big O*, Spring 1993.

Marcus, Greil. "Excitable Boy." *Rolling Stone*, March 6, 1978.

Marsh, Dave. "Warren Zevon on the Loose in Los Angeles." *Rolling Stone*, March 9, 1978.

Maslin, Janet. "Salty Margaritas." *Newsweek*, August 2, 1976.

McGrath, Charles. "An Author Still Writing His Way Through Big Sky Country." *New York Times*, October 20, 2010.

Morris, Chris. "Declarations of Independents." *Billboard*, September 21, 2002.

Nelson, Paul. "The Crack-Up and Resurrection of Warren Zevon: How He Saved Himself from a Coward's Death." *Rolling Stone*, March 19, 1981.

Nelson, Paul. "We Are All On Tour: Are You Prepared for the Pretender—Jackson Browne?" *Rolling Stone*, December 16, 1976.

Nolan, Tom. "The Rock Commando Warren Zevon Un-Leashed." *Phonograph Record*, March 1978.

Palmer, Robert. "Warren Zevon's Checkered Career Takes a Happy Turn." *New York Times*, July 18, 1982.

Pareles, Jon. "Warren Zevon's Last Waltz." *New York Times*, January 26, 2003.

Patterson, Rob. "Warren Zevon: Baying at the Moon?" *Creem*, July 1978.

Putnam, Pat. "It Was Boom! Boom! Boom!" *Sports Illustrated*, January 23, 1984.

Roeser, Steve. "Warren Zevon: Left Jabs and Roundhouse Rights." *Goldmine*, August 18, 1995.

Schruers, Fred. "The Charming Cynic's Excitable Boy." *Circus*, March 30, 1978.

Soeder, John. "The Return of the Hindu Love God." *Scene*, November 29, 1990.

Torn, Luke. "The Life and Times (and Music) of Warren Zevon." *Wall Street Journal*, March 25, 2003.

Virgin Records Press Release, 1987.

Wheeler, Steve P. "The Many Faces of Warren Zevon." *Music Connection*, March 18, 1990.

RADIO AND CONCERTS

Zevon, Warren. Interview by Matt the Cat. *The Coffee Break Concert*, WMMS Studios, Cleveland, October 13, 1976. CD.

Browne, Jackson. "Mama Couldn't Be Persuaded," Birmingham, AL, October 14, 2015. Published on YouTube September 16, 2005, by glenn1075. https://www.youtube.com/watch?v=p4XzOhiwECQ.

Denberg, Jody. KGSR Radio, Los Angeles, January 22, 2000.

TELEVISION

George Carlin, *Jammin in New York*, HBO, 1992. DVD.

Late Show with David Letterman, 1987. Published on YouTube June 21, 2013, by Redrumrock1093. https://www.youtube.com/watch?v=ihKcmvcLcJI.

Howard Cosell, ABC TV "Larry Holmes Vs. Randall 'Tex' Cobb Championship Bout," November 26, 1982. Published on YouTube November 26, 2013, by Boxing Hall of Fame Las Vegas. https://www.youtube.com/watch?v=5e_vS1rmgA8.

Inside/Out: Warren Zevon, VH1 Documentary DVD and Supplement Material, 2004

Mike Bullard Show, CTV, Toronto, 2000. Published on YouTube July 27, 2012, by Warren Zevon Addict. https://www.youtube.com/watch?v=WA88P_gNm-M.

INDEX

PERMISSIONS

"Nobody's in Love This Year" (Zevon) Copyright © 1989 Warren Zevon, Universal Music Publishing Group

"Numb As a Statue" (Zevon/Calderón) Copyright © 2003 Warren Zevon/Jorge Calderón, Universal Music Publishing Group/Jorge Calderón

"Play It All Night Long" (Zevon) Copyright © 1980 Warren Zevon, Universal Music Publishing Group

"Please Stay" (Zevon) Copyright © 2003 Warren Zevon, Universal Music Publishing Group

"Poor Poor Pitiful Me." Words and Music by WARREN ZEVON. Copyright © 1973 (Renewed) WARNER-TAMERLANE PUBLISHING CORP. & DARKROOM MUSIC. All Rights Administered by WARNER-TAMERLANE PUBLISHING CORP. All Rights Reserved. Used By Permission of Alfred Music.

"Prison Grove" (Zevon/Calderón) Copyright © 2003 Warren Zevon/Jorge Calderón, Universal Music Publishing Group/Jorge Calderón

"Reconsider Me" (Zevon) Copyright © 1987 Warren Zevon, Universal Music Publishing Group

"Roland the Headless Thompson Gunner" (Zevon/Lindell) Copyright © 1978 Warren Zevon/David Lindell, Universal Music Publishing Group

"Rub Me Raw" (Zevon/Calderón) Copyright © 2003 Warren Zevon/Jorge Calderón, Universal Music Publishing Group/Jorge Calderón

"Run Straight Down" (Zevon) Copyright © 1989 Warren Zevon, Universal Music Publishing Group

"Searching for a Heart" (Zevon) Copyright © 1991 Warren Zevon, Universal Music Publishing Group

"Sentimental Hygiene" (Zevon) Copyright © 1987 Warren Zevon, Universal Music Publishing Group

"She's Too Good for Me" (Zevon) Copyright © 2003 Warren Zevon, Universal Music Publishing Group

"Splendid Isolation" (Zevon) Copyright © 1989 Warren Zevon, Universal Music Publishing Group

"Studebaker" (Zevon) Copyright © 1972 Warren Zevon, Universal Music Publishing Group

"The Factory" (Zevon) Copyright © 1987 Warren Zevon, Universal Music Publishing Group

"The French Inhaler." Words and Music by WARREN ZEVON. Copyright © 1973 (Renewed) WARNER-TAMERLANE PUBLISHING CORP. & DARKROOM MUSIC. All Rights Administered by WARNER-TAMERLANE PUBLISHING CORP. All Rights Reserved. Used By Permission of Alfred Music.

"The Indifference of Heaven" (Zevon) Copyright © 1993 Warren Zevon, Universal Music Publishing Group

"The Long Arm of the Law" (Zevon) Copyright © 1989 Warren Zevon, Universal Music Publishing Group

"The Sin" (Zevon) Copyright © 1980 Warren Zevon, Universal Music Publishing Group

"Trouble Waiting to Happen" (Zevon/Souther) Copyright © 1987 Warren Zevon/J. D. Souther, Universal Music Publishing Group/J. D. Souther

"Turbulence" (Zevon) Copyright © 1989 Warren Zevon, Universal Music Publishing Group

"Veracruz" (Zevon/Calderón) Copyright © 1978 Warren Zevon/Jorge Calderón, Universal Music Publishing Group/Jorge Calderón